WELFARE POLICY IN BRITAIN
THE ROAD FROM 1945

CONTEMPORARY HISTORY IN CONTEXT
Published in association with the Institute of Contemporary British History

General Editor: Peter Catterall, Director, Institute of Contemporary British History

Titles include:

Oliver Bange
THE EEC CRISIS OF 1963: Kennedy, Macmillan, de Gaulle and Adenauer in Conflict

Christopher Brady
UNITED STATES FOREIGN POLICY TOWARDS CAMBODIA, 1977–92

Peter Catterall and Sean McDougall (*editors*)
THE NORTHERN IRELAND QUESTION IN BRITISH POLITICS

Helen Fawcett and Rodney Lowe (*editors*)
WELFARE POLICY IN BRITAIN: The Road from 1945

Harriet Jones and Michael Kandiah (*editors*)
THE MYTH OF CONSENSUS: New Views on British History, 1945–64

Wolfram Kaiser
USING EUROPE, ABUSING THE EUROPEANS: Britain and European Integration, 1945–63

Spencer Mawby
CONTAINING GERMANY: Britain and the Arming of the Federal Republic

Jeffrey Pickering
BRITAIN'S WITHDRAWAL FROM EAST OF SUEZ: The Politics of Retrenchment

L.V. Scott
MACMILLAN, KENNEDY AND THE CUBAN MISSILE CRISIS: Political, Military and Intelligence Aspects

Paul Sharp
THATCHER'S DIPLOMACY: The Revival of British Foreign Policy

Contemporary History in Context
Series Standing Order ISBN 0–333–71470–9
(*outside North America only*)

You can receive future titles in this series as they are published by placing a standing order. Please contact your bookseller or, in case of difficulty, write to us at the address below with your name and address, the title of the series and the ISBN quoted above.

Customer Services Department, Macmillan Distribution Ltd
Houndmills, Basingstoke, Hampshire RG21 6XS, England

Welfare Policy in Britain

The Road from 1945

Edited by

Helen Fawcett
Jean Monnet Fellow and Lecturer in European Public Policy
University of Strathclyde

and

Rodney Lowe
Professor of Contemporary History
University of Bristol

Published by PALGRAVE MACMILLAN
Houndmills, Basingstoke, Hampshire RG21 6XS and
175 Fifth Avenue, New York, N.Y. 10010
Companies and representatives throughout the world

PALGRAVE MACMILLAN is the global academic imprint of the Palgrave
Macmillan division of St. Martin's Press, LLC and of Palgrave Macmillan Ltd.
Macmillan® is a registered trademark in the United States, United Kingdom
and other countries. Palgrave is a registered trademark in the European
Union and other countries.

Outside North America
ISBN 0–333–67513–4

In North America
ISBN 0–312–21954–7

This book is printed on paper suitable for recycling and
made from fully managed and sustained forest sources.

A catalogue record for this book is available from the British Library.

Library of Congress Catalog Card Number: 98–47548

Transferred to digital printing 2002

Printed and bound in Great Britain by
Antony Rowe Ltd, Chippenham and Eastbourne

Contents

Notes on the Contributors

Helen Fawcett is Jean Monnet Fellow and Lecturer in European Public Policy at the University of Strathclyde. She was previously University Lecturer in European Studies at the University of Oxford and Visiting Scholar at the Center for European Studies at the University of Harvard. She has published on the theory of welfare state regimes, the impact of social democracy on welfare provision, state pension policy and unemployment arrangements in the European Union, and the development of the 'social dimension' in Europe.

David Gladstone previously worked in the Scottish Office and at the University of Exeter before moving to the University of Bristol where he is currently director of undergraduate programmes in Social Policy. His research and teaching interests are in nineteenth and twentieth century social policy. He is editor of *British Social Welfare: Past, Present and Future* (1995) and of *Pioneers in Social Welfare*, a major reprint from primary sources (1995–9). In addition, he has published a considerable number of articles, chapters in edited collections and reports on welfare past and present, and has held several visiting appointments especially in the USA.

Jane Lewis is Professor of Social Policy at the University of Nottingham, having held similar posts at the London School of Economics and the University of Oxford. She has written extensively on the history of welfare policy as well as current practice in Britain and Europe, with a particular emphasis on gender issues. Amongst her latest publications are *The Voluntary Sector, the State and Social Work in Britain* (1995); with H. Glennerster, *Implementing Community Care* (1996); and, with K. Kiernan and H. Land, *Lone Motherhood in Twentieth Century Britain* (1998)

Rodney Lowe is Professor of Contemporary History at the University of Bristol. He is the author of *The Welfare State in Britain since 1945* (1998) and has published widely on twentieth-century welfare history.

Paul Johnson is Reader in Economic History at the London School of Economics and Political Science. He has written widely on the history of the welfare state, retirement and living standards, and is editor of *Twentieth Century Britain: Economic, Social and Cultural Change* (1994).

John Macnicol is Reader in Social Policy at Royal Holloway, University of London. He has published widely in the history of social policy, and is currently researching the history of the 'underclass' idea, and of old age, retirement and state pensions. His latest book is *The Politics of Retirement, 1878–1948* (1998).

Lord Plant is Master of St Catherine's College, Oxford, and was previously Professor of Politics at Southampton University. He is a Labour peer and has published eight books on political theory.

Chris Pierson is Professor of Politics at the University of Nottingham. His work focuses upon the reform of welfare states and more general problems of social democratic governance. His most recent publications include *Socialism After Commission: The New Market Socialism* (1995) and *The Modern State* (1996).

Shamit Saggar is Senior Lecturer in Government at Queen Mary and Westfield College, London. His books include *Race and Public Policy* (1991) and *Race and Politics in Britain* (1992).

John Veit-Wilson is Emeritus Professor of Social Policy at the University of Northumbria and Visiting Professor in the Department of Social Policy at the University of Newcastle-upon-Tyne. A member of the Abel-Smith and Townsend poverty research team in the 1960s, his principal research interests since then have focused on concepts of poverty and minimum human needs. He is currently working on a ten-country study of Government Minimum Income Standards.

General Editor's Preface

In 1910, in a lecture to the Royal Statistical Society, Lord George Hamilton complained: 'We, the richest nation in Europe, have the heaviest pauperism, yet the more we spend the worse the position seems to be.'[1] Britain is certainly no longer the richest nation in Europe. But it is ending the century with all parties uncomfortably aware of the rising cost of welfare. This in itself is not a new aspect of the post-war years; concern about the cost of the welfare state has been a recurring theme throughout its history. To this, however, has been added growing doubts about the efficacy of that spending. This problem has proved a major factor in the increasing willingness shown in recent years to question aspects of the state welfarism which emerged in the aftermath of the Second World War, and to shift its focus.

The 1940s in contrast marked the culmination of a long-term trend towards growing faith in the state as the key provider of solutions to social problems. Unemployment, cyclical in the late nineteenth century and mass during the inter-war years, was one key factor in this process. The labour market policy of the Poor Law, the deterrent effect of less eligibility, was, as Hamilton recognised, a failure in addressing this. And the particular problem to which he drew attention was the consequent ineffectiveness of Poor Law expenditure. Instead, the operation of the Poor Law was largely remedial. Alongside it, however, the state was in contrast from the 1880s increasingly portrayed as ameliorative, able to intervene to promote social welfare and important corollaries such as national efficiency.

The perceived fiscal constraints upon the state nevertheless acted to slow its advance into social policy before 1945. Nor was there much agreement, at this time, even within the parties, over exactly what form that intervention should take. For instance, at various times elements within the labour movement favoured action through industrial restructuring or through municipalisation, rather than through the central government route essentially adopted by the Attlee Government. There was nothing preordained about the character of the Welfare State that then emerged.

If, nevertheless, the Attlee Government decided the form of the Welfare State, what was the Welfare State then set up actually for?

viii

Some New Liberals had been tutored by the idealism of T. H. Green to see state action as a means of advancing liberty for those constrained by the limitations of *laissez-faire* capitalism. Many early socialists similarly saw state action as necessary for the advancement of liberty and personal fulfillment. As one recollected in 1956:

> We would be wise to remind ourselves that the pioneers of the Movement sought what is now called the Welfare State not as an end in itself but as a means of providing people with opportunities for greater happiness.[2]

The question was how: through the eradication of hardship and poverty, the promotion of social equality, the encouragement of active citizenship, the use of social policy as a supply side measure? There were elements of all these objectives in the 1940s, even if some, not least citizenship, were less conspicuous in the thinking behind the eventual Attlee legislation. But not all of them featured in all the legislation; indeed some, such as social equality, were clearly felt to be neglected by the left in, for instance, the implementation of the 1944 Education Act. There was thus no one theme to the Welfare State, and certainly not as it developed in ensuing years.

The complexity of the post-war British welfare state is reflected in the various contributions to this volume in the **Contemporary History in Context** series. The work of the Institute of Contemporary British History, the progenitor of this series, is to promote awareness of the nature of the recent past. This it does through its various educational publications and activities, through its support for archival deposition and its involvement in the collection of oral archives and, as in this book, through the encouragement of new research. All of the essays that follow present new findings and several draw heavily on previously untrawled material from the Public Record Office or elsewhere. In the process they all also highlight the way in which thinking about social policy in post-war Britain has addressed one or other of the range of objectives mentioned above. Different chapters examine the debates taking place in particular policy areas within Whitehall, the political parties, the trade union movement or the voluntary sector. Their interest lies not only in the stages of development in thinking about social policy which they examine, and their clarification of the policy process within these various bodies. They also cast light upon the criteria on which that thinking was based. And without such criteria it is correspondingly difficult to establish the basis on which the efficacy of welfare can be measured. It is only through the establishment of such criteria and assessments that Hamilton's concern about the efficacy of welfare can be answered.

London

PETER CATTERALL

Notes

1. *Journal of the Royal Society of Arts*, 59, 1910–11, p. 128.
2. W. Emrys Davies, 'The Late R. J. Davies', in *Ince and Westhoughton Constituencies and Parts of Wigan Souvenir Booklet 1906–1956* (Wigan, 1956), pp. 16–18.

Acknowledgements

The publisher and editors would like to thank Random House for permission to include an updated version of 'Democratic Socialism and Equality', which first appeared in Lipsey, D. and Leonard, D. (eds) (1981) *The Socialist Agenda: Crosland's Legacy*; and Cambridge University Press for permission to reproduce Figure 1.1 from Hills, J. (ed.) (1996) *New Inequalities: the changing distribution of income and wealth in the United Kingdom*, in Chapter 2 of this volume.

1 Introduction: The Road from 1945

Rodney Lowe

The essays in this volume originated as papers in the 1995 conference of the Institute of Contemporary British History on *British History, 1945–1995: the state of the art*. The dual purpose of the conference was both to take stock of the existing literature and to identify ways in which the writing of contemporary history could be made more rigorous and challenging. Welfare policy attracted a disproportionate number of papers at the conference, actively reflecting the variety and vitality of research in this area. At an international level, for instance, the work of Peter Flora and the current initiatives of both the Swedish Institute for Social Research and the French Ministère des Affaires Sociales, de la Santé et de la Ville, have provided a focus for comparative work.[1] At an interdisciplinary level, experts in social policy, sociology, political science and economics have examined in depth the fundamental causes, mechanics and rationality of policy change. The richness of the resulting research is reflected in the succeeding essays. Methodologically, they vary from broad surveys to detailed case studies. Analytically, they range from past policies to current concerns and extend the conventional boundaries of welfare to cover issues such as industrial relations and race.

There has, however, been one notable set of absentees from the feast: historians in specialist history departments. Only one other contributor to this volume indeed fits such a description. This reticence is not another British peculiarity but a world-wide phenomenon. It was noted by Peter Baldwin in 1992; and despite the boldness of his later claim that the creation of Britain's welfare state was 'an historic event equivalent in importance and stature to the French and Russian revolutions', few have responded to his rallying cry of 'aux stylos, aux stilos, les historiens!'[2] A principal reason for this reticence is the sheer complexity of analysis. To succeed, welfare historians must be ever alert to the full range of ways in which government, intentionally and unintentionally, can influence individual welfare and be informed by

the conflicting general theories of government growth. Yet simultaneously they must provide convincing explanations for the passage (or
non-passage) of individual pieces of legislation and demonstrate a
mastery of legislative small print (which often reveals the full
significance of government action). 'The nuts and bolts of social
policy', as Baldwin has again written, 'testify to the heated struggles of
classes and interests. The battles behind the welfare state lay bare the
structure and conflicts of modern society'.[3] Similarly, they must enrich
their analysis with comparisons of other contemporary societies and
the present-day. Yet they must eschew too easy parallels with the past,
which minimize differences between national cultures and institutions,
and with the present, which gloss over the very different contexts of
policy-making. Finally, historians must remain faithful to the full
range of evidence at their disposal whilst synthesising the insights of
other disciplines. The writing of contemporary welfare history, in
short, presents a formidable challenge, but that should be its major
attraction.

The essays in this volume do not aspire to be comprehensive. Since
the fiftieth anniversary of the Beveridge Report in 1992 at least six
general surveys of Britain's postwar welfare state have been published,
so that there is no longer the need – as there certainly was before 1992
– to provide a synoptic survey or sustained analyses of each area of
policy.[4] Rather they highlight the new directions and the new perspectives welfare history should take, particularly in relation to the analysis
of services for the underprivileged. The purpose of this introduction is
to provide a common focus for these essays by placing them in the
context of conventional wisdom about the definition, evolution and
analysis of the postwar British welfare state.

DEFINING THE WELFARE STATE

There is no generally accepted definition of the welfare state. After a
lifetime of study, the pre-eminent commentator on postwar welfare
policy, Richard Titmuss, concluded rather lamely: 'I am no more
enamoured of the indefinable abstraction the "welfare state" than I
was some twenty years ago ... Generalized slogans rarely induce con-
centration of thought: more often they prevent us from asking
significant questions about reality.'[5] However, if analysts in different
disciplines and countries are to talk to rather than past each other on
these 'significant questions', a working definition is required.

The origin of the term 'welfare state' is significant although not entirely helpful. In both Germany and the USA it started as, and to a considerable degree remains, a term of disparagement. The Weimar Republic was retrospectively attacked in the 1930s for being a 'wohlfahrstaat', because the excessive social 'rights' and expenditure it had endorsed ultimately undermined its legitimacy. The preferred description in Germany of a positive, yet realistic, commitment by government to advance individual welfare is 'sozialstaat'. Likewise, the term was used in the USA by opponents of attempts to expand the provisions of the New Deal in the 1940s; and 'welfare' still carries with it the stigma associated with means-tested benefits for those incapable of providing for themselves. In Britain, the phrase was initially used simply as an antonym for the totalitarian 'warfare' state; but it was rejected by Beveridge as implying an amoral 'Santa Claus' state in which government was required to guarantee certain rights to all its citizens, but was owed no duties in return.[6] It was only when analysts such as T. H. Marshall and Labour Party campaign managers in the late 1940s were seeking a collective term for the social legislation of the postwar Attlee government that the phrase was given a less pejorative meaning. It was then that, in its positive sense, it entered popular usage both in Britain and abroad.

What precisely does it include? Clearly cash benefits (social security) and care for those in need (the personal social services) are at the heart of any welfare state. So too is the National Health Service which, in Britain, is frequently taken as its synonym. Education and housing also are conventionally classified as part of the welfare state although their economic effects (the raising, for instance, of productivity and the facilitating of labour mobility) have on occasion taken political precedence over their social objectives (such as the achievement of greater equality of opportunity and the provision of a secure base for family life).

The definition of the welfare state should be extended from these five core services to three further policy areas into which welfare historians and analysts have traditionally been more reluctant to penetrate. The first is employment policy. 'Full' employment was one of the three assumptions upon which Beveridge based his plan for social security in 1942, which is often taken as the blueprint for the British welfare state. He did so for technical, financial and moral reasons. Were there not full employment, how could a claimant's willingness to work be tested? Without maximizing government revenue and minimizing the number of claimants through full employment how – as governments in the 1930s and 1980s found – could adequate welfare services be funded? Beveridge's main argument, however, was moral. If government genuinely sought to maximize individual welfare, it had to do all in its power to guarantee everyone a rewarding, well-paid job. Despite later (and frequently sterile) controversies, therefore, the postwar British welfare state as originally conceived was concerned as much with economic as with social policy and with the encouragement, not discouragement, of individual initiative.[7]

The other two areas, overlooked by Beveridge but later highlighted by Titmuss, are fiscal and occupational welfare.[8] The way in which welfare expenditure is financed by government is as important to the distribution of resources as the way in which it is targeted, and so the incidence of taxation should be of the greatest importance to the welfare historian. Indeed the secret history of the British postwar welfare state is the decreasing progressiveness of the tax system as a switch was made from company to personal, and from direct to indirect, taxation. Successive governments have also used fiscal policy to encourage employers to provide a wide range of benefits for their employees, such as company cars and occupational pensions, usually to the advantage of the better-off. Such a policy was the professed objective of the Conservative Party after the publication of its *Industrial Charter* in 1947. Comparative analysis, however, does underline the fact that Britain has had a far less active labour market policy (covering issues such as working conditions, minimum wages and worker participation) than continental Europe. Just as British governments have traditionally been more reluctant than their continental counterparts to impose on employers the burden of financing and administrating statutory welfare benefits, so they have also been reluctant to intervene in the 'management's right to manage'.

The definition of the welfare state has been taken further by some analysts to include legislation concerned with private morality including divorce, homosexuality and abortion. Glennerster, for example, has recently argued that such legislation has 'directly affected very large numbers of people probably more deeply and personally than the changes to the structure of pension schemes or the National Health Service' with which welfare historians are traditionally concerned.[9] This further widening of the definition, however, does concern many. Unquestionably welfare policy should be analysed in its widest economic and social context, but if detailed comparisons are to be made over time and between countries, what should be at the heart and what on the periphery of analysis? The eight policy areas identified already, after all, have been drawn essentially from the British experience. American historians traditionally concentrate more closely on cash benefits whilst continental European historians place greater focus on labour market policy. Where is the necessary common ground to be found? The continuing debate, however, does at least underline the crucial fact that there is not, and never has been, an agreed definition of the welfare state. Each person who uses, or has used, the phrase is using their own personal construct – and such constructs can impede as well as advance understanding.[10]

THE EVOLUTION OF THE BRITISH WELFARE STATE

The broad outline of the evolution of the postwar British welfare state is less controversial. There have been three main turning points. The first was the publication of the Beveridge Report and its corollary, the implementation of a wide range of social legislation by the Attlee government on 5 July 1948 – the so-called 'appointed day' and, for many, the official birthday of the welfare state. As historians have increasingly demonstrated, the Report was essentially an ineffective and conservative document. It was ineffective as a blueprint for a comprehensive welfare policy because it confronted only want, and not the other four 'giants' (disease, ignorance, squalor and idleness) which such a policy, on Beveridge's own admission, needed to confront; and even here each of its six guiding principles to social insurance had been breached by the 1960s.[11] It was conservative in four major respects. It advocated a system of contributory insurance which guaranteed only minimal benefits and a very restricted concept of citizenship. Flat-rate contributory insurance, as opposed to the inter-war Labour Party's tax-financed proposals, limited the redistribution of income between classes. Benefits failed not only to ensure claimants their accustomed standard of living, as on the continent, but even – on Veit-Wilson's evidence – the opportunity to enable them actively to participate in society.[12] Finally, since the automatic right to social security (as opposed to education and health care) was dependent on contributions made at work, those who did not or could not work – such as full-time housewives and the civil disabled – were effectively denied 'citizenship'.

Has the importance of the Beveridge Report, therefore, been exaggerated? The answer is clearly no, because of its immense historical impact at both a popular and political level. In Britain it created high, if ill-informed, popular expectation which forced Churchill, the Conservative Party and the Treasury – very much against their wills – to change their public, if not their private, views on state welfare. It also remains the reference point for governments and social reformers to this day (although, to a certain extent, this reflects an unresolved tension within the Report about the relative responsibility of the individual and government for personal welfare).[13] Outside Britain, as Baldwin has shown, its rhetoric and broad vision had a huge impact not only on occupied Europe but on peacetime welfare policy. When confronted with mass unemployment in the inter-war years, liberal democracies had appeared feeble in relation to totalitarian regimes. After the war, they appeared highly efficient as, through the adoption of contributory insurance, they seemed to have resolved the age-old dilemma of how to combine the communal security traditionally provided by feudal or totalitarian states with the individual freedom theoretically offered by liberal, market-oriented regimes. This achievement was dependent on the adoption of two basic principles. The first was universalism, or the equal inclusion of everyone in a given country in the same insurance scheme or 'risk pool'. This ensured a feeling of 'social solidarity'. The second was comprehensiveness, or the insurance of everyone against every possible risk by which, through no fault of their own, their income might be lost. This guaranteed 'social security' or the freedom from the fear of poverty. It was this freedom which immediately raised the quality of everyone's life in a way which no retrospective analysis or cold quantification can deny.

The second turning point was the abandonment of the commitment to full employment by the Labour Government in 1976. The importance that Beveridge placed on this commitment has already been noted. Its abandonment represented the collapse of the optimism with which the welfare state had been created – that, given the political will, all problems were soluble – and a return to the fatalism of the inter-war period. It also meant the re-creation of the two nations of the employed and the unemployed, with the danger that the latter might be turned into a permanent underclass dependent on state handouts. In addition, it meant a constant search by government for economies and the consequent impression, despite rising real expenditure, of meanness as sub-optimum revenue was insufficient to meet the needs not just of the unemployed but also of an ageing population. More surreptitiously, the distinction between economic and social policy reopened with welfare policy again damned as an impediment to, rather than a precondition of, economic growth. Taxpayers too became more selective in their views, supporting those benefits (such as pensions) which would directly benefit themselves but attacking those targeted on minorities, such as the unemployed and single parents.[14]

The removal of one of the major props to the 'classic welfare state', therefore, signalled a fundamental change in policy even before the election in 1979 of a Conservative government headed by Mrs Thatcher. Although in real terms welfare expenditure only fell between 1977 and 1978, its period of continuous expansion was over. Never again was it to consume so high a percentage of GDP. The nature of the public expenditure also changed, as increased emphasis was placed on economic services such as industrial investment and vocational training. So too did the nature of taxation. Indirect taxation (conventionally assumed to be regressive) rose whilst, ironically, the value of benefits for those in need declined. Simultaneously direct taxation (conventionally accepted as progressive) fell whilst the value of tax allowances for the better-off rose. The inevitable consequence was an increase in inequality.

The third turning point was in 1988, the year 'when the dog finally barked'.[15] Despite the rhetoric of the first two Thatcher administrations, few structural changes had been made to the welfare state. Those changes that had been made were more marginal, such as the freezing of child benefit and the ending of earnings-related unemployment and sickness pay. 1988, however, was the focus for a series of complementary, if improvised, reforms. The 1986 Social Security Act was implemented. This replaced the discretionary payments which supplementary benefit claimants had been able to request for exceptional needs with loans from the Social Fund (which had to be repaid) and the cash-limiting of local social security offices (to restrict officials' powers of discretion). The Housing and Education Reform Acts were also passed. They sought to empower the consumers of welfare and foster competition amongst its producers. Council tenants, for instance, were given the right to choose an alternative landlord and housing associations were encouraged as an alternative source of new housing. Likewise the powers of parent-governors were strengthened and schools given the right to opt out of local government control. These reforms were completed by the 1990 National Health Service and Community Care Act which introduced the principle of the 'purchaser–provider divide'. Services were to continue to be funded by government, but they were to be delivered under contract by a range of competing agencies such as hospital trusts, private residential homes and charities.

These reforms also represented a return to the 1930s and its decentralised traditions of a 'mixed economy' of welfare. Individuals and, in particular, families, were expected to be more independent. Where services were provided by government, the power of consumers was strengthened in relation to the producers of welfare – be they local authorities or members of a profession. Where services were contracted out, greater efficiency was to be achieved by competition, whether through genuine or 'quasi' markets.[16] In short, the centralised bureaucratic nature of the classic welfare state was condemned as an aberration caused by the peculiar circumstances of its birth. The Second World War had temporarily bestowed an aura of efficiency on centralised planning. However, as has been recently argued, 'the aspect of the welfare state that was most in tune with its time, the centrally planned, national monopoly element, was least perfect and ... aged the most'.[17] It needed to be replaced.

The three major turning points in postwar welfare policy saw, therefore, the successive promotion of a grand vision, the kicking away of one of its major props and a fundamental restructuring of service delivery. Within each historical phase, however, there were other significant developments which have aroused historical controversy. There has been an extended debate, for example, on the extent to which the period between 1942 and 1976 was one of consensus. The debate stems from Paul Addison's seminal work on the wartime planning of reconstruction, *The Road to 1945*, and has been unnecessarily complicated by the ignoring of his major qualifications and a reluctance to define terms.[18] Did the consensus, if it existed, flourish at an elite or a popular level? Was it ideological or pragmatic? Was it essentially a negative consensus (the acceptance that certain options, such as the abandonment of 'full' employment, were politically impractical) or positive (the acknowledgement that, in an advanced industrial democracy, state welfare must make good proven market failures)? Clearly there was no ideological consensus. At root, the Labour Party – especially by the 1960s – was committed to the use of state action to increase equality and thereby individual freedom. In contrast, the Conservative Party sought to increase individual freedom through greater reliance on the market even if that meant greater inequality. For it, equity meant exceptional returns for exceptional talent and effort, not a broadly equal distribution of resources overseen by the state. Electoral and economic reality, however, forced both parties increasingly to adopt convergent policies to resolve the economic and social problems associated with Britain's relative decline. As Timmins has recently concluded of the available evidence:

> None of this amounts to a true consensus – absolute agreement on what should be done about every area at every time. What it does demonstrate is a large degree of consensus in action ... Up to the 1980s, the differences between the parties produced for the welfare state services an oscillation around a mean, rather than any great swing in one direction.[19]

In the creation of these convergent solutions, three incursions of welfare policy into high politics were of importance. The first was the resignation of Bevan in 1951 over the Labour Government's introduction of dental and opthalmic charges. The second was the resignation of Thorneycroft as Chancellor of the Exchequer, with his two junior Treasury ministers, in 1958 over the Conservative Cabinet's refusal to cap public expenditure and in particular to withdraw family allowances from the second child. Both resignations have been taken as evidence of a lack of consensus even within the two major parties; but in fact they demonstrate the exact opposite. The defeat of these two 'extremist' figures (the one seeking a faster advance to socialism, the latter a faster return to a market economy) cleared the way for moderates within both parties to address Britain's needs more positively. This is the importance of the third event, or rather non-event: the failure of Selwyn Lloyd as Chancellor of the Exchequer in 1962 to honour his pledge to the IMF to restrict the annual growth of public expenditure to $2\frac{1}{2}$ per cent. Within Cabinet and Whitehall, the battle was fought and largely won on the issue of 'national efficiency'. The market was acknowledged to be imperfect: government alone had the potential to remove the institutional impediments to its effective working and to supply those necessary welfare measures which it either under-supplied or provided inefficiently. Hence the drafting and partial implementation under the Conservatives of a wide range of reforms – including earnings-related welfare benefits, community care, the replanning of the NHS, the expansion of higher education, regional policy, redundancy payments and industrial welfare – which the later Labour Government either continued or fully implemented.[20]

Under the thirty year rule, the archival evidence for this period of apparent consensus is increasingly available to historians. It needs to be examined so that a full appreciation can be gained of the extent to which, and the reasons why, in the heyday of the 'classic welfare state' the perceived potential of government intervention went unrealised. This research is important in its own right. It is also a necessary pre-condition for a better understanding of the later backlash against welfare expenditure.

ANALYSING THE WELFARE STATE

Until the late 1960s, the analysis of the growth of welfare states was relatively unproblematic. The centralised provision of welfare services was seen to be a natural feature of all modern societies, in which urbanisation and industrialisation had both destroyed traditional support systems and created new social problems. There were two principal agents of change. Those already in power acted either out of humanitarianism or in response to the revelations of experts about the causes of social problems. Alternatively, 'dispossessed' manual workers – congregated in towns and enfranchised – used their increased industrial and political strength to demand a more equitable distribution of resources.

Intellectual developments in the 1960s, bolstered by the 'crisis' of the welfare state in the mid-1970s, revolutionised the analysis of con-temporary welfare policy and, in due course, welfare history. Marxist analysis questioned the motivation behind legislation. Rather than being for the benefit of the 'dispossessed', it maintained, such legisla-tion represented the commandeering by the ruling elite of public resources either to advantage private industry ('social capital') or to bribe people to accept the legitimacy of government, thereby ensuring law and order ('social expenses').[21] The New Right also questioned the benevolence of government growth, asserting that it was designed ultimately for the benefit of the producers rather than the consumers of welfare. In the most colourful application of these beliefs to postwar British history, Corelli Barnett has indeed identified profligate welfare expenditure as a principal cause of Britain's rela-tive decline – an assertion which, as has been pointed out, sits rather awkwardly with the fact that welfare expenditure as a percentage of GDP has been considerably higher in the most successful of Britain's economic competitors.[22] Equally powerfully, feminists have rediscov-ered the active role played by women in the development of welfare policy and the complex ways in which it has both advantaged and disadvantaged them. After an initial polemic as colourful as Barnett's, however, attention has been largely concentrated on the period before 1945.[23]

The greater choice of theoretical explanations has encouraged more subtle analysis. Instead of the one centralised model of welfare provision being assumed to be the ideal for all modernising societies, three competing 'worlds of welfare' have been identified by Esping-Andersen.[24] In the ideal social democratic model, as aspired to in Sweden, the state relieves individuals of traditional market and family constraints by providing both benefits which enable claimants to enjoy their accustomed living standards and a full range of caring services for dependants. In the corporatist model of Central Europe the state provides equally high benefits but fewer services. In the residual liberal model, as adhered to in the USA and increasingly in Britain, the state is responsible for only a minimum of services. If citizens wish to maintain their accustomed living standards when not working, or to be relieved of family responsibilities, they have to rely on the market (albeit with frequent subsidies). To these three worlds Castles has added a fourth, the Australian 'wage-earners' welfare state'. With its restricted range of services, it appears to conform to Esping-Andersen's liberal model. In reality, however, state intervention is at its most invasive since it is designed to anticipate rather than to react to need. Through compulsory arbitration, wages are fixed on the basis of workers' social needs rather than, as is more conventional, their economic value to employers. Everyone therefore, in theory at least, has the financial independence to resolve their own problems.

This variety of ideal types has freed historians from the tyranny of one over-arching theory and encouraged them to examine, as should be their first instinct, the peculiar circumstances of particular countries at particular times. This has served to emphasise divergences as well as convergences and the frequent dysfunctional decisions that have been taken as the result of temporary and fragile coalition governments. In the analysis of welfare policy, therefore, it has been re-established that long-term cultural traditions and constitutional conventions as well as short-term political expediency must be given equal weight to underlying social forces for change and the functional 'needs' of a modernising society. This in turn has focused attention on previously neglected topics such as the role of farmers (rather than industrial workers) and the need for social security of the middle class (rather than the poor) in the shaping of policy.[25]

THE STATE OF THE ART

The contested definition and variety of approaches to welfare policy make it a rich area for research and debate, as the succeeding essays demonstrate. Paul Johnson builds on the historical perspective and quantitative precision with which he has previously challenged New Right assertions about the adverse impact of welfare expenditure on individual initiative and economic growth.[26] His subject is at the heart of the postwar ideological divide, income equality, and his analysis confirms the importance of the three postwar watersheds. The wartime reduction in inequality was sustained for three decades. Then just before the 1979 Conservative victory it was reversed, and since the late 1980s inequality has rapidly accelerated. His analysis also highlights the full range of variables which welfare historians should ideally address. Attention has to be concentrated not just on the 'output' of a specific policy but on the overall 'outcome' – the combined impact of policy and other autonomous forces in society. In the case of equality, changes to taxation and welfare benefits (which are rightly analysed together) are shown simply to have neutralised the automatic mechanisms by which increases in inequality were previously checked. The positive engines for increased inequality have principally been changes in the structure of earnings and households.

The next two essays provide an overview of the service focused on the most vulnerable: the personal social services. It has for long been a 'Cinderella' service, not only starved of money by government but also neglected by academics. This neglect needs now to end because by being amenable to a 'bottom-up' approach to social welfare – and the consequent insights into the evolving relationship between family, neighbourhood, voluntary associations, the market and the state – this is the service best able to correct oversimplified comparisons by highlighting the significant cultural differences between countries and over time. In providing a broad organisational structure for future research, David Gladstone identifies the continuing transfer of responsibility between and within the four sectors of welfare; in so doing he reveals how, for example, the resilience of the Poor Law concept of the 'liable relative' discouraged any move within Britain from a liberal to a social democratic model of welfare. He also shows how the potential for state action, so optimistically assumed at the time of the 1968 Seebohm Report, went unrealised in the 1970s, with the result that the service became a principal focus for the 'purchaser–provider' divide in the 1990s.

Complementing Gladstone's analysis, Jane Lewis places in a clear theoretical framework the development of the non-profit-making voluntary sector. Her analysis demonstrates just how dangerous comparison over time can be. The partnership between the state and voluntary provision, reactivated by quasi-markets, has been frequently depicted as a return to Victorian values. The reality, however, is very different. Voluntary associations in Victorian times were seen ideally, even if they were not always in practice, the true expression of corporate life. The relationship between the giver and the recipient was also seen, as much as the simple casting of a vote, as a fundamental ingredient of democracy. In the 1990s voluntary agencies may well have become an alternative to government in the provision of services, but government as the paymaster controls the terms of the contract and thus determines the ultimate nature of both the service and the agency. The nature of the partnership and thus the balance of power has radically changed.

Two case studies follow. John Macnicol analyses the social construction of the postwar 'problem family' and above all the increasingly feverish search for its defining characteristics once 'unemployability' (the hallmark of the prewar residuum) and 'lack of family affection' (an alleged characteristic of the present-day underclass) were found to be invalid. The answer was promiscuously to conflate a wide range of problems facing families in need, thereby reducing a 'complex variety of human conditions ... to one unitary category'. There is a lesson here for present-day constructions of an underclass. The essay also underlines the essential optimism of the immediate postwar years in terms of both social conditions (full employment and stable households) and analysis. In contrast to earlier and later assertions that the underclass is genetically determined and hence irredeemable, many of those working in the field in the 1940s and 1950s believed that by intensive rehabilitation – as practised by Victorian voluntary associations – 'problem families' could be successfully socialised.

Whilst Macnicol based his research on the private archives of the Eugenics Society, John Veit-Wilson has based his on a judicious mixture of public records (yet to be fully released) and interviews. He is thereby able to make a major contribution to the growing awareness of the vitality of policy-making in the early 1960s and then the continuity of policy under Conservative and Labour governments. Just as officials in prestigious departments such as the Treasury were reconsidering fundamental issues such as the nature of taxation and its redistributory impact, so officials in one of the least fashionable (the National Assistance Board) were reconsidering means-tested benefit from first principles. In anticipation of, and later both in tandem and in conflict with, the 'rediscovery of poverty' by social scientists centred on the London School of Economics, officials became convinced that both the amount and administration of benefit were defective. Poverty was recognised to be a relative rather than an absolute concept with claimants thereby entitled to a 'minimum participatory' rather than a 'minimum subsistence' level of benefit. The exercise of discretion by officials was also discovered to be highly idiosyncratic rather than scientific. It was therefore indefensible. The remedy lay in the conflation of 'exceptional grants' with the basic rate of benefit even if this necessitated, in defiance of Beveridge, different rates for long-term and short-term claimants. This case study is one of a pioneering set of studies, itemised in chapter six, which demonstrates how – with a clear theoretical framework – public records can be used to document fundamental changes in both the official and public perception of poverty.

The final essays extend the traditional boundaries of welfare history. Helen Fawcett tackles a core area of welfare policy: pensions. Their transformation from a flat-rate to a fully earnings-related basis between 1957 and 1975 was long and complex. They therefore provide an ideal example of how, as Baldwin maintained, seemingly arcane legislative detail can be used to lay bare the 'heated struggles of classes and interests'. Her essay demonstrates why conventional analysis should be both deepened and widened. Political struggles within the Labour Party alone reveal how 'rationality' in policy-making can be disrupted, while the inclusion of pensions in the 'social contract' of the early 1970s highlights the interrelationship between welfare policy and industrial relations. On the continent the trade-off between the 'social' and the 'industrial wage' has long been recognised. Why are British policy-makers and analysts so reluctant to acknowledge it? Shamit Saggar's subject is race. He is concerned less by the extent to which welfare policy has been adapted, or proved adaptable, to the special needs of ethnic minorities than by the general assumptions underlying immigration policy. This policy has been an example of continuing cross-party consensus despite the 1976 'divide'; but since the late 1950s, it has been based on an essentially negative consensus designed to ensure tolerance, and a measure of cultural diversity, for a strictly limited number of immigrants. The welfare of both racial minorities and the country as a whole, it is argued, would be better served by a return to the policies of the early 1950s, which stressed the economic benefits of immigration. This would not only counter social prejudice but also facilitate the economic growth on which the welfare of all depends.

The desirability of a return to the 1950s, in some measure at least, is implicit also in the two final essays. In 1956 Crosland transformed postwar politics by publishing *The Future of Socialism*. It identified equality not just as the core principle dividing the major parties but also as the key to reduced resentment and hence better industrial relations and sustained economic growth. Lord Plant re-examines, and seeks to make more explicit than Crosland himself, the moral basis on which a popular consensus can be constructed for so important a goal. The essential amorality of the distribution of resources by the market, predominant in the 1980s, is rejected as are the concepts of equality of opportunity and result. In their place 'democratic equality', with its presumption of equality tempered by the acknowledged need for 'justified inequalities', is advanced as the means to minimise resentment (and hence retain communal solidarity) whilst preserving personal rewards (and thus individual incentive). In the real world of politics, similar considerations of social justice together with the conviction (reminiscent of Beveridge) that full employment is essential to any concept of welfare policy permeated the Labour Party's Borrie Report of 1994. However, Chris Pierson's critique of the Report suggests that, despite the promptings of analysts such as Lord Plant, little substantial progress had been achieved since the 1950s. What choice in practice is the Party to make between the different definitions of social justice and the conflicting means of maintaining full employment?

This relative barrenness of thought in the present-day debate merely serves to underline the pressing need to deepen and widen the history of postwar welfare policy. The road from 1945 was characterised initially by over-optimism about the potential of state welfare. Later it was scarred by unjustified pessimism. A better and fuller historical appreciation of the past fifty years can provide the context for greater realism amongst both analysts and policy-makers in the future.

Notes

1. Flora's work is summarised in the multi-volumed *State, Economy and Society in Western Europe, 1815–1975* (London: Macmillan, 1983–87) and *Growth to Limits* (Berlin: DeGruyter, 1986). The French Ministry of Social Affairs has sponsored three international conferences since 1994 and in the proceedings of the first there is a summary of the Swedish programme by Walter Korpi. See A.–M. Gillemard et al.,

Comparing Social Welfare Systems in Europe (Paris: MIRE, Ministry of Social Affairs, 1995).

2. P. Baldwin, 'The Welfare State for Historians', *Comparative Studies in Society and History*, 34 (1992), 695–707; 'Beveridge in the *Longue Durée*' in J. Hills et al., *Beveridge and Social Security* (Oxford: Oxford University Press, 1994), p. 40.

3. P. Baldwin, *The Politics of Social Solidarity* (Cambridge: Cambridge University Press, 1990), p. 1.

4. R. Lowe, *The Welfare State in Britain since 1945* (Basingstoke: Macmillan, 1998) identifies the broad range of concepts required for analysis and concentrates on 'classic welfare state' up to 1975; M. Hill, *The Welfare State in Britain* (Aldershot: Edward Elgar, 1993) offers a government-by-government approach; N. Timmins, *The Five Giants* (London: HarperCollins, 1995) is an example of 'high journalism' which is particularly enlightening on the NHS and the Thatcher years; D. Gladstone, *British Social Welfare* (London: UCL Press, 1995) is a collection of interdisciplinary essays covering the whole period; finally H. Glennerster, *British Social Policy since 1945* (Oxford: Blackwell, 1995) and M. Sullivan, *The Development of the Welfare State* (London: Harvester Wheatsheaf, 1996) also cover the whole postwar period and use an historical perspective to raise important questions about future policy.

5. In B. Abel-Smith and K. Titmuss, *The Philosophy of Welfare* (London: Allen & Unwin, 1987), p. 141.

6. R. Lowe, 'The Second World War, Consensus and the Foundation of the Welfare State', *Twentieth Century British History*, 1 (1990), p. 154; J. Harris, *William Beveridge* (Oxford: Oxford University Press, 1977), p. 448.

7. Cmd 6404, *Social Insurance and Allied Services* (the Beveridge Report: London, 1942), paras. 9, 440.

8. R. Titmuss, *Essays on 'the Welfare State'* (London: Allen & Unwin, 1958), ch. 2. The incidence of subsidies, such as food subsidies, is as important as that of taxes.

9. Glennerster, *British Social Policy*, op. cit., p. 153.

10. N. Whiteside, 'Creating the Welfare State in Britain, 1945–1960', *Journal of Social Policy*, 25 (1996), 83–103.

11. R. Lowe, 'A Prophet Dishonoured in his own Country' in Hills, *Beveridge*, ch. 8.

12. J. Veit-Wilson, 'Condemned to Deprivation?' in Hills, *Beveridge*, ch. 7.

13. See, in particular, J. Harris ' Political Ideas and the Debate on State Welfare' in H. L. Smith, *War and Social Change* (Manchester: Manchester University Press, 1986) and Baldwin, 'Beveridge', pp. 53–4.

14. P. Taylor-Gooby, *Public Opinion, Ideology and State Welfare* (London: Routledge & Kegan Paul, 1985), ch. 2. The slowing down in the rate of economic growth would, in itself, have posed problems for the expansion of welfare expenditure; but the under-employment of the country's productive capacity accentuated the problem.

15. J. Le Grand in Hills, *States of Welfare*, p. 351.

16. For an overview, see J. Le Grand and W. Bartlett, *Quasi-Markets and Social Policy* (Basingstoke: Macmillan, 1993). For the concept of a

'mixed economy', see G. Finlayson, 'A Moving Frontier', *Twentieth Century British History*, 1 (1990), 183–206.

17. Glennerster, *British Social Policy*, p. 8. Institutional reform reflected a fundamental tension in the Conservative cabinet. Was it an ideologically driven attack on state welfare or a rational response to increasing consumer demand and the need to allocate scarce resources more efficiently? See Glennerster, ch. 9 and the debate inspired by his views in ch. 3 of Guillemard, *Comparing Welfare Systems*.

18. For an overview, see D. Kavanagh and P. Morris, *Consensus Politics* (Oxford: Blackwell, 1989) and Lowe 'Second World War', For a recent reappraisal, see H. Jones and M. Kandiah, *The Myth of Consensus?* (Basingstoke: Macmillan, 1996).

19. Timmins, *Five Giants*, p. 170.

20. R. Lowe, 'The Replanning of the Welfare State, 1957–64' in M. Francis and I. Zweiniger–Bargielowska, *The Conservatives and British Society, 1880–1900* (Cardiff: University of Wales Press, 1996), p. 255–73. For a guide to official records in this period, see P. Bridgen and R. Lowe, *Welfare Policy under the Conservatives, 1951–64* (London: PRO Publications, 1998).

21. See I. Gough, *The Political Economy of the Welfare State* (London: Macmillan, 1979).

22. C. Barnett, *The Audit of War* (London: Macmillan, 1986) and *The Lost Victory* (London: Macmillan, 1995) which ignores the strictures of J. Harris in 'Enterprise and Welfare States' published in T. Gourvish and A. O'Day, *Britain since 1945* (Basingstoke: Macmillan, 1991).

23. E. Wilson, *Women and the Welfare State*, (London: Tavistock, 1977). See also J. Lewis, *Women in Britain since 1945* (Oxford: Blackwell, 1992) with its particularly full bibliography.

24. G. Esping-Andersen, *The Three Worlds of Welfare Capitalism* (Cambridge: Polity, 1990); F. Castles and D. Mitchell, 'Identifying Welfare State Regimes', *Governance* 5 (1992), 1–26.

25. See especially Esping-Andersen, *Three Worlds of Welfare Capitalism*, ch. 1 and Baldwin, *Politics of Social Solidarity*, ch. 1. A determinedly political analysis is D. E. Ashford, *The Emergence of Welfare States* (Oxford: Blackwell, 1986).

26. P. Johnson, 'The Welfare State' in R. Floud and D. McCloskey, *The Economic History of Britain since 1700* (Cambridge: Cambridge University Press, 1994), vol. 3, p. 284–317.

2 Inequality, Redistribution and Living Standards in Britain since 1945

Paul Johnson

INTRODUCTION

In the fifty years since the end of the Second World War, the British people have enjoyed the fruits of an unprecedented period of sustained economic growth. Real personal disposable income per capita (i.e. income after direct tax) has grown at an average annual rate of 2.4 per cent over the period 1949–95.[1] This means that people today are about three times as well-off as in the late 1940s, and now, in real terms, earn and spend £2.95 for every £1 they earned and spent in 1949. Yet despite the palpable economic achievements of the postwar period, there has been intermittent, and over the last decade rather more continuous, concern about the failure to distribute the benefits of economic growth to all sections of the population. There has, moreover, been a growing belief in the 1980s that measured economic growth has been achieved at the expense of unmeasured costs – the costs of occupational stress, congestion and pollution, environmental degradation and familial and societal disintegration. If the idea of the 'standard of living' is to involve more than simply the summation of market activity, then it should, in some way, take into account those qualitative changes in British society over the last five decades that do not figure in estimates of real income per capita.

This chapter addresses the subject of inequality, redistribution and living standards in Britain since 1945 in three distinct ways. First, looking at earnings and incomes, it presents an outline of *what* has changed over time. Then it considers the more complex and contentious issue of *why* incomes and earnings have changed, separating the causes into those that result from individual choice, those brought about by structural change, and those that are directly attributable to public policy. Finally, it turns to analyse some non-economic indicators of well-being and considers whether or to what extent they corroborate the more familiar economic data.

EARNINGS AND INCOMES: WHAT HAS CHANGED?

For economists, earnings and incomes are not unambiguous concepts, and many different definitions have been used in the literature on inequality and living standards. Income can be reported either inclusive (gross) or exclusive (net) of income tax, mortgage interest expenditure, housing costs and social security benefits, it can be counted on a household, individual, tax-unit or equivalent-individual basis; it can be measured weekly or monthly or annually. Although these differences can matter for the evaluation of short-run changes in inequality, Jenkins, in a review of the literature, notes that 'the same general trends are apparent from all the inequality indices'.[2] This is fortunate because the amount of detailed data is relatively sparse before the 1970s, and fragmentary for the 1940s and 1950s. In the following account dissimilar data are drawn from separate sources to patch together a picture of change over time – only where different sources reveal divergent trends will attention be drawn to the definitional problems.

The indicator that is easiest to measure over time in an unambiguous way is the earnings of clearly defined groups of workers. This procedure has a long historical pedigree going back to the nineteenth-century work of Bowley and Wood, and most famously expressed in the estimation by Phelps Brown and Hopkins that over the five centuries up to 1914, skilled workers in the building trades consistently earned 50 per cent more than building labourers.[3] Phelps Brown has suggested that this wage premium for skill diminished over the first half of the twentieth century, with changes particularly noticeable in the immediate aftermath of each of the two world wars.[4] On the other hand, a more representative measure of wage dispersion across the manual workforce shows remarkable stability in the dispersion of male manual wages over the period of 1886–1976.[5] Although there is this disagreement in the literature about whether the spread of manual wages was stable or became more compressed in the period up to the mid-1970s, over the past two decades there has been an unambiguous movement towards greater inequality of pay, with the earnings of the top 10 per cent of male manual workers rising relative to the mean, and the earnings of the bottom 10 per cent falling.[6]

Although these findings about male manual earnings are unambiguous, they do not necessarily tell us much about general living standards because over time the earnings of male manual workers have become less representative of the overall population, for four separate reasons. First, manual work has declined relative to non-manual since 1945, with the key factor being a relative contraction of the manufacturing sector in which manual work was concentrated. In 1950 manufacturing accounted for 35 per cent of all employment, a figure which had fallen to under 22 per cent by the beginning of 1995.[7] Secondly, male earnings have declined as a proportion of total household earnings because the proportion of married women aged 15–59 in employment rose from 26 per cent in 1951 to 62 per cent in 1981.[8] Thirdly, wages and salaries have declined as a proportion of total household income as the relative shares of income from self-employment, social security benefits, pensions and investments have risen.[9] Finally, average household circumstances have altered with an ageing of the population and an increase in lone parenthood. The proportion of the population over pension age has risen from under 13 to over 18 per cent since 1948, while single parent families increased from 8 to 14 per cent of all families with dependent children between the early 1970s and the late 1980s.[10] These changes to occupational income and household structures can have complementary or countervailing influences on the living standards of the population, and in order to see their combined effect it is necessary to examine changes in the overall distribution of income over time. We know that *average* real disposable income has risen almost threefold since 1949 – but does this mean all groups in the population have benefited to the same extent?

This is, technically, a difficult question to address, because the available data change in definition and coverage over time, and it is only since the early 1970s that detailed income survey data have allowed researchers to select standardised categories. Figure 2.1 shows different, but overlapping, estimates of what has happened to overall income inequality between 1950 and 1993. The graph represents an index of inequality called the Gini coefficient, which ranges between 0 and 100. The closer the coefficient is to 0, the more equitably income is distributed across the population; conversely, as it tends toward 100, the distribution of income becomes more and more unequal with a small group of rich people taking an ever growing share.

The top lines (the 'Blue Book' series) are based on Inland Revenue data relating to the disposable income of 'tax units' with no adjustment

Figure 2.1   Trends in income inequality in Britain, 1949–93

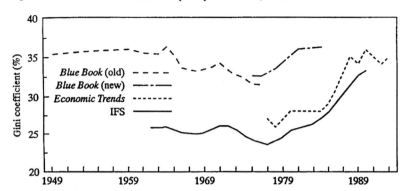

Source: J. Hills (ed.), *New Inequalities* (Cambridge: Cambridge University Press, 1996), p. 3.

for household size. A 'tax unit' can relate to a single adult, a married couple, or a family with several dependent children. The middle line ('Economic Trends') shows disposable income adjusted for family size, and the bottom line shows long-run estimates on a slightly different basis created by the Institute for Fiscal Studies for the Joseph Rowntree Foundation inquiry into Income and Wealth.[11] There is significant variance in the *level* of income inequality identified by these different methods, but the *trend* is common to all three series.

Income inequality appears to have been more or less constant through the 1950s – people had never been having it so good in equal measure. It should be noted that this plateau represents a considerable change since the pre-war period. Comparing 1938 and 1949 (there are no Inland Revenue data for the intermediate years), the Gini coefficient on income after tax fell from around 43 to 35. This was due to a decline in the disposable income of the richest tenth of the population (their share fell from 35 to 26 per cent of total after-direct-tax income), and this was itself primarily due to a fall in the earnings and increase in the tax liability of the richest one per cent of the population, who saw their share of disposable income fall from 12 to 6 per cent of the total over this period.[12] It is worth noting that this wartime curtailment of the income privileges of the very highest of earners was sustained through two decades of postwar economic and fiscal management, by both Labour and Conservative governments. In this respect, at least, a postwar political consensus is very apparent in the data.[13]

From 1964 to 1969, however, there is a clear reduction of inequality in disposable income, and this was due overwhelmingly to the tax policies of the Labour government, since income inequality before tax fell only marginally in this period. Inequality rose slightly in 1971–2, then fell to the mid-1970s. It appears to have been increasing *before* the electoral victory of Margaret Thatcher in 1979, but it is clear that inequality has increased very rapidly since that date. By 1985, according to the 'Blue Book' series, income inequality was greater than at any time since 1949, and the income share of the richest fifth of the population – at 43.1 per cent of the total – was higher than at any time since the Second World War. Since the mid-1980s income inequality has grown more rapidly than at any period since the war, and more rapidly than in any other OECD country, with the possible exception of New Zealand. These developments over the last decade still leave Britain with a more equitable income distribution than the USA or Canada, where inequality has also been rising since the early 1980s – though only slowly. Yet within the European Union, British income inequality now appears to exceed that of France, which had long led the European inequality league. Moreover, many European countries – Italy, Denmark, Spain, Portugal and Ireland, for instance – experienced declining inequality in the 1980s.[14] This is significant because it shows that generic and international explanations for rising inequality, such as the globalisation of the international economy, the rise of new technologies, changes in relative prices, and the impact of European economic integration, are insufficient. If we are to look for causes, the search must begin at home.

EARNINGS AND INCOMES: WHY HAVE THEY CHANGED?

Overall income inequality can change because of movements at the top (high pay) or bottom (low pay) of the income distribution. If the overall income distribution is divided into deciles, and each separate income group is examined over time, then we find that over the period 1961–79 each income group enjoyed a growth of real net income very close to the mean for the entire population, with the exception of the poorest decile which experienced an increase in real income 50 per cent above the mean (54 percentage points, compared with a mean growth over this period of 36 per cent).[15] The general decline in measured inequality over this period came through a considerable reduction in the relative poverty of the poorest tenth of the population, within a context of significant income increases for *everyone*. In the period 1979–92, however, the picture is very different. Although the average income of the entire population again rose by 36 per cent in this period, it was the richest fifth who enjoyed real income growth higher than the average, whereas the poorest one-tenth of the population enjoyed no real income growth at all over this 13 year period. How can this remarkable transformation over time in the relative fortunes of the rich and poor be explained?

Potential explanations can be grouped under three headings: those that result from individual choice, from structural change, and from public policy. Individual choice reflects decisions made by adults about what type of household to live in, by women about whether or how much to work, by juveniles about whether to enter the labour market or stay in full-time education to gain additional qualifications. Structural change, both economic and demographic, has altered the age structure of the population, the types of job people do, and their sensitivity to macroeconomic fluctuations. Public policy has influenced income distribution indirectly through systems of wage control, and directly through changes in the tax and benefit system. Clearly there are linkages between these explanatory factors. Public policy may dampen or exacerbate the business cycle, it may even influence the decision of single unemployed women about whether to have children, but uncertainty about the scale or direction of these interaction effects means that they cannot easily be given any quantitative evaluation, and attention must therefore be confined to the separate impact of choice, structural and policy variables.

Individual Choice

Women's work

Rising rates of labour force participation for women since 1945 have had a major impact on the level of household incomes, but we cannot *a priori* know whether this has increased or reduced the equality of incomes across the population. The number of working-age couples with two earners has risen by over 50 per cent between 1975 and 1993. At the same time female earnings have risen relative to men's, with the result that male earnings as a proportion of gross family income have declined from 75 to 60 per cent.[16] All this might suggest that the expansion of the female workforce will have reduced income inequality. However, married women's employment tends to be highest among the wives of relatively well-paid men, and wives' earnings tend to be positively correlated with those of their husbands. The net result of a careful decomposition of household earnings by subgroup carried out by Jenkins shows that the expansion of female employment *increased* earnings inequality for households in the period 1971–6.[17] A factor here was the Equal Pay Act (passed in 1970 and having statutory effect from 1975) which initially had greatest impact on the relative earnings of women in white collar jobs. In the 1980s, however, as female participation rates continued to rise, the effect was to reduce overall income inequality.

Household type
Changes in the distribution of the population across different types of household – more pensioners, more single adults, more double-earner households, fewer 'traditional' married couples with dependent children – appear to explain almost none of the fall or rise in income inequality since the 1970s. There have been important changes for subgroups, for instance pensioner inequality fell sharply 1971–6, and single adult household inequality rose sharply 1981–6, but overall the effects cancel out.

Education
Recent research by Schmitt shows that between one-third and one-half of the growing wage dispersion in 1980s is explained by the higher wage premia commanded by workers with greater experience and/or educational qualifications. This trend is the opposite of that experienced in the later 1970s when the wage premium paid to better educated workers was narrowing. In 1975, men with university education earned double the wage of a male with no qualifications, whilst those with five or more 'O' levels earned 60 per cent more. By 1970, these wage premia had fallen to 78 per cent and 35 per cent respectively, but by 1988 the graduate's wage premium over a man with no qualifications had risen sharply to 90 per cent, while for someone with five 'O' levels the premium had edged up to 42 per cent.[18] This increase in the financial return to education since the late 1970s has occurred despite a rise in the numbers reaching each qualification level, which suggests that employer demand for educated workers has risen faster than supply. The rising relative wages of graduates since 1979 can, therefore, help to explain some of the general increase in earnings inequality in the 1980s, but this cannot explain why inequality has risen to a level so much higher than in the early 1970s.

Structural Change

Population structure
Older workers tend to earn more than young workers, with the typical 21–24 year old receiving only 60 per cent of the typical 40–49 year old.[19] Nevertheless, pensioners tend to have below average earnings. The ageing of the population has increased both the ratio of older to younger workers within the workforce and the ratio of pensioners to workers. These changes have tended to cancel each other out so that over the period since 1965 they have had little impact on trends in inequality.

Industrial structure
Important sectoral shifts in the structure of employment since 1945, often summarised by the term 'deindustrialisation', have altered the balance of traditionally high wage and low wage employment. For instance, between 1951 and 1991 male employment in high wage mining declined from 5.6 to 1.1 per cent of the total. On the other hand, employment in low wage agriculture fell by a similar amount, from 6.9 to 2.7 per cent. Meanwhile the service sector has expanded, but this has happened both in high wage financial services and in low wage retail distribution. Again the net effects of changes in the relative size of sectors appear to be minimal.[20] However, an analysis of the dispersion of earnings *within* rather than *between* sectors does highlight some significant changes. In the period 1971–6 there was a substantial reduction of earnings inequality among male employees, which was followed by a clear increase in inequality in both 1976–81 and 1981–6.[21] This widening from the mid-1970s of pay inequality within sectors is indicative of a general market response to low wage differentials and possibly to skill shortages which pre-dates the Conservative election success of 1979.

Employment structure
Of even greater importance in the 1980s has been the expansion of self-employment. The proportion of household income derived from self-employment rose from 8 to 11 per cent over the decade from 1980, before falling back slightly in the 1990s. The labour incomes of the self-employed are much more dispersed than are those of employees. This is particularly true for women, some of whom receive exceptionally low incomes in what might be described as a late twentieth-century version of Victorian 'sweated trades'.[22] Jenkins has found this growth of self-employment to be the largest single contributor to growing income inequality since 1981,[23] but how far this

rise in self-employment should be considered a *choice* or a *structural* factor is unclear. This depends on whether people have volunteered for or been pushed into self-employment. The self-employed are over-represented in both the upper and the lower tails of the income distribution, symbolising respectively both winners and losers from the shift to an 'enterprise culture' in the 1980s.

Earnings structure
The last two decades have witnessed a considerable growth of households with no reported earnings, and this has had a substantial impact on income inequality. Despite many rhetorical political assertions to the contrary, most people experience a substantial fall in income when they become unemployed and start to draw social security benefits. In 1990 the number of *individuals* of working age not in work was the same as in 1975, but the number of *households* receiving no income from employment had doubled. By 1993 over 40 per cent of single-adult households had no earnings (22 per cent in 1975), and the same was true for 11 per cent of two-adult households (3 per cent in 1975).[24] This change was largely a consequence of longer spells of unemployment. Comparing 1979 and 1993, the length of time a two-adult no-earner household could expect to spend before one of the adults re-entered employment increased from 18 to 54 months.

One possible explanation for this change is the nature of the social security means test. Once a person moves onto benefit, the marginal tax rates become very high, especially as a widening of the earnings distribution has driven down entry-level wages. Another factor is the attitude of employers who appear increasingly to discriminate against the long-term unemployed in their hiring policy.

Public Policy

The final suspect in this hunt for the reason for changes in income inequality over time is public policy. Here there are two quite different possible effects, the first being the way governments can consciously affect the distribution of earnings through various sorts of incomes policy, the second being the way they can use the tax and benefit structure to alter final household income.

Incomes policy
Governments have been directly interfering in the determination of wage rates in Britain since the Trade Boards Act of 1909. The range

of occupations covered has never been large, but the knock-on effect on wages throughout the rest of the manual workforce could be significant. Machin and Manning have shown that through the 1980s the declining 'toughness' of wage council regulation has been directly related to increased wage dispersion in the industries covered (still affecting 2.5 million workers in 1990, but now restricted to agricultural workers).[25] This was good news for some workers in those industries who saw their relative earnings rise, but bad news for the majority who saw real income fall.

This is just the opposite of what occurred during the Labour Government of 1974–9. Labour's 'social contract' with the unions significantly squeezed wage differentials in all sectors. It is not clear that this was the intention of the social contract, but it was the inevitable outcome of the flat-rate (or flat rate plus a fixed percentage) wage increases. In so far as Conservative arguments since 1979 about restoring wage incentives in the economy have validity, they do so primarily in relation to a widening of the wage dispersion around its central point, rather than at the top end (where, for a very small minority, income incentives have always been strong).

A further way in which governments have affected the earnings distribution is in their relationship with the trade unions. The Wilson and Callaghan governments were consciously corporatist, the Thatcher governments deliberately antagonistic towards organised labour. These attitudes have had an effect on earnings distribution, because up to the late 1970s unions were generally effective at preserving skills distinctions and formal skill premia. A study by the Institute for Fiscal Studies has shown that pay dispersion for semi-skilled workers rose rapidly in the 1980s, but much more so for the semi-skilled in non-unionised firms.[26] The Conservative attack on union status and bargaining power has allowed employers to reduce pay rates for some semi-skilled workers, but to increase them above union guidelines for those with highly marketable skills. Conservative anti-union and anti-wage council policy has therefore more than undone the 1970s 'squeeze' on earnings dispersion. In this respect the labour market in the 1980s has become more responsive to supply and demand forces than it was in the 1960s or 1970s.

Taxes and benefits

Governments can have a more direct influence on income inequality through tax and benefit policy, and this is the set of policies that is most frequently mentioned in discussions of inequality and living standards.

Details of the structure and performance of the postwar welfare state are presented in other chapters, and here the analysis will be confined to the distributional impact. The cash benefit system works unambiguously to reduce inequality – this is necessarily the case with means-tested benefits, and also true of the main universal cash benefits – the old age pension and child benefit – because pensioners and families with dependent children tend to be in the lower part of the overall income distribution. On the other hand, as Goodin and Le Grand have shown, some benefits in kind are 'captured' by the middle class – most notably university education – and so serve to increase overall inequality.[27] In aggregate, however, the equalising effects dominate. On the taxation side, direct taxation serves to reduce inequality, and indirect tax increases it, since it bears relatively more heavily on low-income households.

What impact have changes in taxes and benefits had on the overall income distribution over time, and in particular what changes have occurred with a shift from a Labour Government in the 1970s committed to welfarism to a Conservative Government in the 1980s committed to low taxation? According to a study of inequality trends 1971–86 carried out by Jenkins, 'Changes in the direction of cash social security benefits, income tax payments and employee national insurance contributions' can be acquitted of blame for the trends through the 15 year period.[28] On the other hand, a study by the Institute for Fiscal Studies [IFS] looking at 1979–88 concluded that half the rise in inequality could be attributed to the tax and benefit system.[29] The first of these conclusions seems surprising, given what we know of reductions in higher rates of income tax, a shift towards indirect taxation, and a curtailment of the growth of cash benefits under the Conservative governments since 1979. In fact, looking at the impact of just these discretionary (i.e. policy) changes, then the IFS conclusion is correct – inequality has been enormously increased by tax/benefit changes. Comparing the 1978/9 tax/benefit system with the 1994/5 system, it can be seen that the poorest one-tenth would have been 40 per cent better off in 1994/5 if the 1978/9 tax/benefit system had still been in place; only the richest tenth of the population gained unambiguously from the intervening tax and benefit changes. However, Jenkins' conclusion that there was no net effect from tax/benefit changes is also correct, because he takes into account not only discretionary changes, but also automatic changes. As real incomes rise over time, as they did in the 1980s, a progressive income tax system will automatically become more redistributive (and therefore more equalising) as more people move into higher tax bands. According to Jenkins' estimates, this automatic effect almost exactly balanced the impact of discretionary change, so that the combined tax/benefit system maintained its redistributionary effects despite an increase in real income.

NON-ECONOMIC INDICATORS OF WELL-BEING

We are, as a nation, considerably richer today than we were 50 years ago, but are we better off in a broader sense? Have there been other social and economic trends that might run counter to the picture shown by the data on income? And if so, has the increase in income been bought at the cost of broader social dysfunctionality? In the more extreme versions of environmentalism it is sometimes suggested that economic growth is a zero-sum game: higher incomes necessarily involve equal but opposite societal costs, but ones which are seldom taken account of because social evils – pollution, stress, family disintegration – are not elements of the market economy and so are not readily measured and aggregated. A more moderate position rejects the idea of a zero-sum game, but insists that there are important non-economic consequences of economic growth of which we should be aware.

The highly restricted nature of income measures as proxies for well-being has been fully recognised by economists since the beginning of economics. Adam Smith noted that the divisions of labour could have deleterious mental or moral effects on the labourer; for at least 25 years economists have recognised that Gross National Product is a far from ideal measure of welfare, and have suggested how a range of non-economic factors might be incorporated into an index of well-being. The United Nations now advocates the use of a Human Development Index in which income measures are combined with measures of life expectancy and literacy.[30] Dasgupta has extended this approach to include measures of political and civil liberty.[31]

None of these alternative accounting procedures has any major impact on assessment of British well-being since 1945. It is hard to argue that there has been any significant change in civil or political liberties, literacy was already practically universal in 1945 and has remained so, and life-expectancy has risen for all age groups, thereby confirming the income trends (though to some extent this involves an element of double counting, since higher life-expectancy has to some extent been achieved as a *result* of rising real incomes).

Other qualitative indicators produce ambiguous results. Certainly there is more congestion on the roads, but then higher incomes have produced more roads, more cars and more leisure opportunities to use them. The average working week for male manual workers has fallen from 47.5 to 39 hours between 1946 and 1994. Car exhaust fumes are thought by some to be responsible for record levels of child-hood asthma, but overall air quality in London and other major cities is better today than it was in the early 1950s before Clean Air legislation was introduced.

There is one respect, however, in which it may be quite true to argue that income growth has been bought at a social cost – the cost of declining fertility. In a stimulating analysis of the New Zealand welfare system, Thomson has argued that since the 1970s young married adults have deliberately restricted fertility and increased female labour force participation in order to maintain the level of income growth that had been experienced by single-earner households in the 1950s and 1960s.[32] In the UK fertility has declined and married female employment has risen since the 1950s, although this approximate correlation does not necessarily imply causation. It is clear, however, that rising female employment has contributed to overall income growth. A simple coun-terfactual exercise shows that if female labour force participation rates in 1991 had been at the 1951 level, but allowing for the increase over time in female wages relevant to male, then total household income would have been 5.4 per cent lower than it actually was (this figure is relatively small because so much female employment is part-time and low-paid). It is possible to argue, therefore, that some (small) part of the overall income growth since 1945 has been purchased at the cost of less free time (and less family time) for women, and therefore that the monetary measures of rising real income in the postwar period over-state the gains for women relative to men. To address this issue directly would, of course, require much more information about the distribu-tion of work and income within the household unit.

CONCLUSION

Looking at the 50 year period since 1945 it is clear that real incomes grew at more or less the same rate for people at all points in the income distribution until 1976 (with a slight inequality blip during the 'Barber boom' of 1971–2), but that over the last two decades real income gains, which have been substantial, have been captured by people in the top three deciles of the income distribution who have enjoyed above average income increases, while people in the bottom four deciles have experienced real income increases less than half the average. Those changes have been driven primarily by a widening earnings distribution for people in work, together with a growing number of non-earner households. Government policy since 1979 has exacerbated the inequality trend by means of a series of discretionary tax and benefit changes which have negated the automatic redistributive effect of direct taxation during a period of earnings growth.

It is not necessarily the case, however, that the experience of individuals matches that of broad analytical groups investigated by the various researchers. Income distribution studies decompose the population into various categories – for instance by employment status or household type – and then see to what extent the fortune of these categories changes over time. This method involves a categorical determinism which is not reflected in real life. Over their life-course individuals will live in a variety of different household types, will experience a number of different employment statuses, and so on. Furthermore, movement between categories has probably increased over time; this is certainly true of household type and employment as both family forms and the labour market have fragmented over the past two decades.

A detailed study by Noble and Smith of low income households in Oldham and Oxford has shown that relative stability in total numbers in receipt of income support conceals considerable inflow and outflow among this group, with, for instance, almost 30 per cent of single non-pensioner claimants leaving income support between July 1993 and January 1994.[33] Likewise, many of today's impoverished pensioners aged over 80 had been in receipt of average or above average incomes when in full-time employment during the boom years of the 1950s. Because no representative data on people's lifetime income profiles has been collected for Britain, we cannot know how many people move up and down the income distribution over their life-course, nor how far they move. However, a simulation study by Falkingham and Hills, based on 1986 data, indicates that lifetime income is considerably more equally distributed than cross-sectional studies at one point of time would suggest.[34]

What we do not yet know is whether the increasing income inequality of the 1980s and 1990s has been accompanied by greater mobility across the income distribution over the average life course, or whether those at the top have enjoyed substantial real income growth without any greater risk of falling to a lower decile of the distribution. Are the financial costs and benefits of more cut-throat enterprise and competition accompanied by greater insecurity for everyone, or only for the lower skilled and lower paid? Are these trends towards growing income inequality a harbinger of the 'classless society' dreamed of by John Major, or a manifestation of a new network of prestige and privilege that is recreating historic divisions of wealth and class in British society? We will need another fifty years of British history to know.

Notes

1. Calculated from successive issues of the *Annual Abstract of Statistics*.
2. S. P. Jenkins, 'Accounting for inequality trends; decomposition analysis for the UK, 1971–86', *Economica* 62 (1995), pp. 29–63.
3. E. H. Phelps Brown and S. V. Hopkins, 'Seven centuries of building wages', *Economica*, 22 (1955), pp. 195–206.
4. H. Phelps Brown, *A Century of Pay* (Oxford: Oxford University Press, 1977), p. 73.
5. A. R. Thatcher, 'The New Earnings Survey and the distribution of earnings' in A. B. Atkinson (ed.), *The Personal Distribution of Income* (London: George Allen & Unwin, 1976).
6. A. Gosling, S. Machin and C. Meghir, 'What has happened to the wages of men since 1966?' in J. Hills (ed.), *New Inequalities* (Cambridge: Cambridge University Press, 1996), pp. 135–57.
7. C. H. Feinstein, *Statistical Tables of National Income, Expenditure and Output of the UK, 1855–1965* (Cambridge: Cambridge University Press, 1972), Table 59; *Employment Gazette*, June 1995, tables 1.3 and 7.1.
8. J. Lewis, *Women in Britain since 1945* (Oxford: Basil Blackwell, 1992), p. 65.
9. J. Hills, *Income and Wealth, Volume 2* (York: Joseph Rowntree Foundation, 1995), p. 53.
10. Central Statistical Office, *Social Trends 1991* (London: HMSO, 1991), p. 38.
11. Results of the inquiry were published as *Inquiry into Income and Wealth, Volume 1* (York: Joseph Rowntree Foundation, 1995).
12. *Royal Commission on the Distribution of Income and Wealth*, Report no. 1 (Cmnd 6171, July 1975), p. 36.
13. For a discussion of the nature of consensus in postwar economic policy see N. Rollings, '"Poor Mr Butskell: A short life, wrecked by schizophrenia"', *20th Century British History* 5 (1992), pp. 183–205.
14. A. B. Atkinson, *Incomes and the Welfare State* (Cambridge: Cambridge University Press, 1996), chapter 2.
15. J. Hills, 'Introduction after the turning point' in J. Hills (ed.), *New Inequalities* (Cambridge: Cambridge University Press, 1996), p. 4.
16. S. Harkness, S. Machin and J. Waldfogel, 'Women's pay and family incomes in Britain, 1979–91' in Hills, *New Inequalities*, pp. 158–80.
17. Jenkins, 'Accounting for inequality trends', p. 50.

18. J. Schmitt, 'The changing structure of male earnings in Britain, 1974–88' in R. Freeman and L. Katz (eds), *Changes and Differences in Wage Structures* (Chicago: University of Chicago Press, 1994).

19. Central Statistical Office, *New Earnings Survey, 1995; Part E* (London: HMSO, 1995), table 124.

20. A. B. Atkinson, *Incomes and the Welfare State*, p. 38.

21. Gosling et al., 'What has happened', p. 135.

22. N. Meager, G. Court and J. Moralee, 'Self-employment and the distribution of income' in Hills, *New Inequalities*, pp. 208–35.

23. Jenkins, 'Accounting', p. 56.

24. P. Gregg and J. Wadsworth, 'More workers in fewer households?', in Hills, *New Inequalities*, pp. 181–207.

25. S. Machin and A. Manning, 'Minimum wages, wage dispersion and employment: Evidence from UK wages councils', *Industrial and Labor Relations Review* 47 (1994), pp. 319–29.

26. A. Goodman and S. Webb, *For Richer, for Poorer: the changing distribution of income in the United Kingdom 1961–1991* (London: Institute for Fiscal Studies, 1994).

27. R. C. Goodin and J. Le Grand, *Not only the Poor: the middle classes and the welfare state* (London: Allen & Unwin, 1987).

28. Jenkins, 'Accounting', pp. 55–6.

29. P. Johnson and S. Webb, 'Explaining the growth in UK income inequality', *Economic Journal* (103) 1993, pp. 429–43.

30. United Nations, *Human Development Report, 1994* (New York: United Nations, 1994).

31. P. Dasgupta, *An Enquiry into Well-Being and Destitution* (Oxford: Clarendon Press, 1993).

32. D. Thomson, *Selfish Generations?: The ageing of New Zealand's welfare state* (Wellington, NZ: Williams Books, 1991).

33. M. Noble and G. Smith, 'Two nations? Changing patterns of income and wealth in two contrasting areas' in Hills, *New Inequalities*, pp. 292–318.

34. J. Falkingham and J. Hills, 'Lifetime incomes and the welfare state' in J. Falkingham and J. Hills (eds), *The Dynamic of Welfare* (Hemel Hempstead: Prentice Hall Harvester Wheatsheaf, 1995), pp. 108–136.

3 Renegotiating the Boundaries: Risk and Responsibility in Personal Welfare since 1945
David Gladstone

'One of the most ill-defined, neglected and yet vital parts of the Welfare State'.[1] This recent assessment indicates something of the paradox of the services for individual welfare, most usually known as the personal social services. On the one hand, they are concerned with the vital individual experiences of dependency, risk and need: conditions that potentially threaten everyone. On the other hand, they represent one of the more marginal and residual sectors of the postwar welfare state. The purpose of this chapter is to assist future analysis by providing a broad survey of its changing organisation, nature and scope over time. First however, a working definition is required.

The precise boundaries of the personal social services are hard to define because over the past half century no central government department has had sole responsibility for this sector. Even at the time of their most rapid expansion in the late 1960s and early 1970s, they have never had the resources of other services such as health, education or income maintenance. And they have seldom attracted much public attention, except when scandals have generated usually short-lived headlines pointing an accusing finger at professional, managerial or policy failure. They have, furthermore, been one of the less conflictual arenas of social policy. The 1940s, according to Hill, were a period when individual welfare was 'largely unpoliticised'.[2] Later decades witnessed considerable cross-party support for the objectives of the personal social services even when, as in the 1980s, 'the means employed to achieve them changed considerably'.[3] Such a political consensus, however, should not obscure the occasionally bitter conflicts between government departments for control of the sector, such as occurred in the 1940s and the 1960s, nor the consequences of the compromises that resulted.

Such organisational matters are only one of the boundary issues that have characterised the personal social services over the past 50 years. Perhaps more than any other part of the welfare state, they have also been the arena for a fundamental ideological debate over the responsibility for the *supply* of welfare. As a result, any discussion of the personal social services has to be concerned not only with the changing boundaries within the statutory sector of central and local government services but also on the broader canvas of the mixed economy of welfare. This latter term suggests that, in addition to statutory provision, a variety of actual and potential suppliers may be involved in personal welfare. These may include family members, informal networks, formal voluntary organisations and the private market. Any historical review, therefore, has to be concerned with the notion of responsibility negotiated over time between the varied suppliers, and involves a mapping exercise of what Finlayson has termed 'the moving frontier' between voluntarism and the state.[4]

The boundaries between cash and care must also be recognised. In the statutory sector, the cash/care divide was established by the organisational separation of services for personal welfare from those of income maintenance. But the issue is broader for, as Thomson argues in relation to older people: 'We appear to agree now that families bear little duty to supplement the monetary incomes of the aged ... But when those same elderly persons need care ... we require families to give time and money to save the community from this type of expense.'[5] Care, however, is not the only objective of the personal social services. Alongside social protection (as, for example, in child care) and the social integration of those who would otherwise be marginalised in a competitive environment (such as disabled people), Evandrou et al list social control, reminding us that 'the whole debate about the creation of the personal social services began with concern about juvenile delinquency'.[6] Intervention by the statutory sector in particular is thus balanced between supporting vulnerable individuals (a care function) and protecting society from deviant, distressing and difficult situations (a controlling function). It also involves discussion around the nature of risk – in the sense of threats to individual welfare and how and by whom they are defined over time – and responsibility – in the sense of who could and should respond to those perceived and defined threats.

Where that responsibility should be exercised represents yet another boundary issue. Should services be supplied at home (that is through domiciliary care services), in a home (that is in a residential care setting) or by some more flexible combination of the two? One of the major transformations over the past 50 years in the delivery of personal welfare has been the closure of the long-stay institutions (especially for the mentally ill and those with a learning disability) and their replacement by community-based services.

Against that background, subsequent sections of this chapter will examine the changing fortunes of the statutory sector of personal welfare over the past 50 years as well as the shifting boundaries of responsibility between the state and other suppliers in the mixed economy of care.

ORGANISATION AND MANAGEMENT

The term personal social services is itself a product of the 1960s, being first used in the remit given to Seebohm Committee in 1965.[7] In demarcating its area of interest, the Committee focused on the responsibilities for individual welfare given to local authorities by three Acts of Parliament passed between 1946 and 1948. By the National Assistance Act 1948 local authorities were given responsibility for providing services for elderly and handicapped people. The Children Act of the same year gave them considerably increased responsibilities for child care. Finally, in the tripartite structure created by the National Health Service Act 1946, local authorities were given charge of community health services. The services thus created inherited three different traditions. First, there was the Poor Law tradition inherited from the treatment of destitute children and the public provision of residential care. Secondly, there was the voluntarist tradition in relation especially to the care of those who were blind, disabled or elderly infirm. In some instances the work of such organisations had already led to increased state responsibility. Finally, there was a tradition best exemplified in the care of maltreated or neglected children, where state action had increasingly developed since the passage of the first prevention of cruelty act in 1889.

The legislation of the 1940s firmly embedded the statutory sector of individual welfare within local government, thereby continuing into the welfare state the Poor Law tradition of localism. In some cases the legislation of the 1940s confirmed the responsibilities which local authorities had assumed on the demise of Boards of Guardians in 1929. In others, it significantly extended them. The effect, however, was the same: individual welfare was an integral part of the locally delivered welfare state. In that process, local authorities worked within the broad parameters of policy laid down by central government (by the Home Office in the case of children and by the Ministry of Health in relation to other services) and were dependent on a mixture of central and local government finance.

By the 1960s research had begun to highlight one consequence of local autonomy: the territorial injustice, in a needs-based service, of wide variations in both the number of those receiving services and in the amount being spent by different local authorities.[8] More recent analysis of the spending patterns of Social Services Departments (SSDs) has confirmed that considerable variation persists and it has been attributed to 'a wide variety of factors, some of which are the product of local politics, others the result of central government rules about rate and charge capping'.[9]

The 1980s were a period of increasingly conflictual relations between central and local government in which the balance of power shifted in the direction of the former. In common with other elements of the local welfare state, the personal social services experienced the impact both financially and in terms of the challenge by central government to traditional methods of service delivery. Controls on local government spending introduced in the early 1980s were superseded by rate capping, a tactic designed to penalise those authorities which exceeded levels of spending prescribed by Whitehall. At the same time, there was also a search for new methods of delivery that would reduce both the direct service role of local authorities, and their monopoly supply of services. Norman Fowler's speech at Buxton in 1984, when Secretary of State for the Social Services, was an early indication of this change of direction. In it he argued in favour of an enabling role for local authority SSDs, stimulating the widest possible contribution to care from all the resources of local communities. It was not long, however, before the language of enabling which was somewhat redolent of the rhetoric of the Seebohm and Barclay Reports,[10] was joined by that of competition. The Griffiths Report of 1988 envisaged SSDs as purchasers of care within a market of competing providers – although it was, more precisely, a quasi-market in which central government would retain considerable power and be increasingly able to use its funding arrangements to ensure local authority compliance.[11]

The trend of the past 50 years has, therefore, been away from local autonomy towards increasingly centralised control and a decidedly more pluralistic and competitive environment for the delivery of individual welfare. It is thus possible to identify three phases that characterise the changing balance of power over the past half century. First, there was a phase in which the parliamentary legislation of the 1940s gave local authorities increased responsibilities, but where there was also discretionary power to permit the continuing supply of personal welfare services by voluntary organisations. Secondly, there was a period characterised by the expansion of direct statutory responsibility, symbolised by the Health and Welfare White Paper of 1963, the notion of Ten Year forward plans and legislation such as the 1970 Chronically Sick and Disabled Persons Act. Finally, there was the introduction of quasi-markets in the NHS and Community Care Act 1990. These were implemented in the care sector in 1993 and embody a contracting of care between local authorities and what is now termed the 'independent sector' incorporating private care providers along with other suppliers.

The re-negotiation of boundaries between central and local government has not been the only area of change. Just three years after the Local Authority Social Services Act, local government reorganisation in 1974 altered the level of local government at which responsibility for supplying individual welfare operated. The early 1990s local government review presages further change, especially in favour of the unitary authorities which were created in April 1996.

Superimposed on these changes, there have also been organisational changes within the local authority departments concerned with individual welfare. Over the past 50 years the change has been from two or three separate departments via one generic SSD introduced after the Seebohm Report to a more recent bifurcation consequent on the new and different responsibilities imposed by the Children Act 1989 and the community care legislation of the following year.

The legislation of the 1940s produced one local authority department concerned with children's services, and either separate or combined health and welfare departments. In practice this represented a distinction between services for children and adults. Means and Smith have pointed to the inevitability of this division after the appointment of the Curtis Committee in 1944. Thereafter, they suggest: 'It became certain that the final break up of the poor law legislation would contain two elements, a children's bill and a bill dealing with other remaining issues, including state welfare provision for elderly people.'[12] But the situation was by no means uncontroversial. Parker has described the complexities from which emerged the new administrative arrangements. They involved both civil servants and ministers, spanned the Coalition and postwar

Labour governments, and concerned the future responsibilities of both central and local government departments.[13]

Once the local authority arrangements were in place, some interesting differences emerged. Health departments possessed a variety of professionally qualified social work staff-almoners, psychiatric social workers and mental welfare workers – but overall direction remained with the Medical Officer of Health. Welfare departments inherited staff from the Public Assistance Committees and continued to rely on largely untrained staff.[14] The situation in the children's departments was different again. Though their budgets tended to be smaller than the other departments, they 'provided a setting where trained social workers began to be employed for the first time in significant numbers'.[15] Since they were also in control of their departments, child care workers 'could claim considerable occupational status and expertise'.[16] That would be to their advantage in the later development of the social work profession. Furthermore, most of the staff in children's departments were female. As a result, as Glennerster notes 'women had for the first time been given a route to the top in local government and in the Home Office'.[17]

Hall[18] and Cooper[19] have explored in considerable detail the process by which this administrative fragmentation became part of an agenda for greater rationalisation and change, especially in the 1960s. The Seebohm Committee Report, *Local Authority and Allied Personal Social Services*, published in 1968, played a major part in that process. But the appointment of the Committee in 1965 was itself the result of changes and debates that were already in progress. One of these was the emergence of an increasingly common identity among the varied social work professionals which was symbolised by the creation in 1963 of the Standing Conference of Organisations of Social Workers. Another concerned the emergent debates about the development of a family service, not least in the context of juvenile crime.

One of the origins of the notion of a family service was the Ingleby Committee Report (1960) which expressed itself critical of the diversity of existing statutory provision: 'As long as these services are organised in something like their present form, their effective co-ordination is clearly essential.'[20] A related strand is in the Labour Party study group chaired by Lord Longford whose report *Crime – a challenge to us all* (1964) emphasised the role of a family service as a preventive measure, and in particular as a way of forestalling juvenile delinquency. Reporting only months before Labour was returned to power at the 1964 general election, seven members of Longford's committee went on to take influential posts in the Labour administration. They 'would ensure that the proposals were not forgotten'.[21]

As Crossman's account makes clear, the issues became more complex in government.[22] While Longford, as Lord Privy Seal, sought the early introduction of a Family Services Bill, there was countervailing academic and political pressure (including from Crossman himself) in favour of consultation with local authorities and an independent inquiry. And once the Seebohm Committee had reported, discussion of its proposals in government became enmeshed in the contemporaneous discussion of plans for local government reorganisation and NHS reform.

Central to the Seebohm Committee's proposals was amalgamation of the existing departments into new, all purpose, generic SSDs –a relatively uncontroversial measure, given the 1960s fashion for larger units of government and the professional unification already taking place. But in recommending 'one central government department responsible... for the relationship between central government and SSDs'[23] the Report generated considerable animosity between James Callaghan at the Home Office and Richard Crossman, Secretary of State-designate for the newly created Department of Health and Social Security. Neither of them was prepared to give up any of the services for which they were responsible:

> Crossman saw the new, enlarged DHSS as the obvious location for the personal social services. Callaghan, on the other hand, was anxious to protect the children's services, since the Home Office had a good reputation for administration in this field and without these services the department was reduced ... to functions of a primarily social control nature.[24]

In the light of that assessment it is especially interesting to remember that the 1945 Machinery of Government Committee had decided that the Home Office rather than the Ministry of Health should be responsible for children's services. Since it had just lost responsibility for the Factory Acts, it was felt 'contrary to the public interest for the Home Office to be shorn of too many functions not purely repressive in character'.[25]

The royal assent for the Local Authority Social Services Bill in 1970, the formation of the Central Council for Education and Training in Social Work and the creation of the British Association of Social Workers, all contributed to 'a mood of optimism, a feeling that great things were going to happen and that SSDs were going to transform the plight of the disadvantaged'.[26] That confidence, however, was short-lived. The oil price shock of 1973 and its attendant consequences for public spending, resulting in the Labour government's *Priorities* document of 1976, was part of the story. Another, occurring in 1973 was the first of the child death tragedies that have embroiled SSDs, that of Maria Colwell. Organisations, especially those representing blind and deaf people, were also becoming increasingly critical of the genericism of SSDs. Finally, the local government reorganisation of 1974 presented yet another challenge, while the contemporaneous reorganisation of the NHS 'raised boundary problems between the two services in areas such as the community care of mentally ill or handicapped people'.[27]

Together with a growing commitment to decentralisation, which was symbolised by locality offices and 'patch' principles in social work, many of these issues remained part of the SSDs agenda in the 1980s, at the same time as they also had to face the other changes in local government finance and methods of service delivery that have already been discussed. It was, however, the 1989 Children Act and the community care arrangements of the following year that 'signalled the break-up of the last of the local state's "bureau professional" welfare empires and threatened the professional base of social work itself'.[28] The organisational division between services for children and adults, that was already reappearing, was reinforced and – according to Wistow and his colleagues – it was a division of unequals. Directors and chairs of SSDs showed a 'relative ignorance and lack of interest in community care' compared to their 'far greater level and breadth of interest in the Children Act'.[29] This situation was hardly new, as the foregoing discussion has shown it merely represented a reversion to the situation in the 1940s and 1950s.

THE LOCATION OF CARE

The distinction between services for children and adults is not only a matter of management and organisation. There are also important policy differences between them which centre on the location of care. Over the past 50 years the pattern in all sectors of individual welfare has been a shift from residential care to what is perceived to be the less costly alternative of community-based provision. Such broad trends, however, conceal considerable differences. For almost the whole of the period, there has been a reduction in the number of children in residential care. For example, though the trend was not consistently downward, the number of those in local authority children's homes declined from 17,500 to 10,535 between 1954 and 1984.[30] Residential care, by contrast, has remained of continuing importance for adults, especially for the elderly. Despite the developing emphasis on community care, for instance, only nine per cent of those aged over 65 were reported as receiving a home help in the early 1980s;[31] and the number of those accommodated in residential homes increased by 51 per cent between 1976 and 1986.[32] Community care for the mentally ill and the mentally handicapped has also been a policy objective, at least since the 1959 Mental Health Act. It was only after the mid-1970s, however, that programmes of deinstitutionalisation began to develop and a decade later a government report concluded starkly that 'progress towards community care has been slow'.[33]

The fundamental difference between residential and community care was established immediately after the war. In the National Assistance Act, residential provision for elderly people was accepted without question. By contrast, the Children Act of the same year envisaged it as a final resort. The much more favoured option for children was boarding out or fostering – an option with much support, not only among professionals and child care experts but also in the Treasury, since the costs of foster care were considerably less than residential provision. Accordingly, between 1949 and 1963 the national boarding out rate rose from 35 per cent to 52 per cent, although there was considerable variation between local authorities.

Why was residential care regarded as an appropriate form of care for some – such as older people – but not for children? The answer lies with both the wartime debates and the different traditions inherited by the separate local authority departments. During the war, the Ministry of Health was under pressure to improve rather than replace public assistance institutions for older people. This explains the much vaunted 'hotel' concept of residential care at the time of the National Assistance Act, in which residents would pay their rent out of their old age pension. In child welfare, by contrast, there had been a concerted campaign against residential care, largely orchestrated by Lady Allen of Hurtwood. Though the 1946 Curtis Committee Report was not so critical of residential establishments as she had been, it expressed considerable support for the already well-established practice of boarding out. 'There was, we thought, much greater happiness for the child integrated by boarding out into a family of normal size in a normal home.'[34]

Meanwhile, there were also significant differences between the local authority departments concerned with individual welfare. Child care, freed from any poor law inheritance, developed as a specialist service staffed by qualified professionals. Their departments, according to one assessment, 'gained prestige as their boarding out rates climbed and their homes closed'. Furthermore, 'as the morale and status of fieldworkers was enhanced, so that of the residential worker declined'.[35] The welfare departments, by contrast, inherited staff and buildings from the poor law tradition and the Public Assistance Committees. That inheritance helps to explain both the continuing reliance on residential care and Townsend's finding at the end of the 1950s that old workhouse buildings were still the mainstay of local authority residential services for the handicapped and aged.[36]

If the search for substitute care was one of the activities which enhanced the 'bureau-professional' status of the Children's Departments, another was the development of preventive work. During the 1950s and 1960s that mainly meant work with those perceived as vulnerable or 'problem' families, designed either to prevent the entry of children into care or to allay the alarm created by the rising rate of juvenile delinquency. In the 1980s, however, prevention took on a new meaning. Mainly as a result of the publicity surrounding cases of child abuse, a principal aspect of statutory intervention became the prevention of further abuse both 'by keeping children away from their abusing families' and by 'finding them permanent adoptive and foster homes'.[37] Thus as part of the developing awareness that the welfare of the child was not necessarily co-terminous with that of their natural family, the child abuse scandals raised contentious issues about the respective responsibilities of parents and the state which led to the establishment of a 'new set of political and professional balances'[38] by the 1989 Children Act.

Despite the rhetoric, reports and legislation of the past thirty years, community alternatives to residential care, for groups other than able-bodied children, had a slower and more uneven development. There were three main pressures for change. First a consensus of enlightened opinion was ranged against the depersonalisation and batch living symbolised by the institution. The 'alarm mindedness' created by the scandals of the long-stay hospitals, Goffman's characterisation of the 'total institution', and the empirical research of Tizard and Townsend were all part of this movement.[39] Second, there was concern over the place of children in the long-stay hospitals which reached its climax in the second half of the 1970s with the publication of the Court and Jay Reports, Maureen Oswin's study and the work of the National Development Group for the mentally handicapped.[40] At its starkest, the Jay Committee considered the mental handicap hospital 'quite unacceptable' for children and advocated in its place a model of care that offered families a whole range of professional services, and long term care in a suitable family where that was not possible. Finally, there was a range of practical pressures from the mid-1950s. Overcrowding had become a serious problem. Because of their age, many mental hospitals were in a serious state of disrepair and the finance available for their modernisation or rebuilding was extremely limited. Moreover, there was a crisis in staffing: the supply of unmarried women who had staffed much of this type of residential care was declining because of their retirement and the new employment opportunities available to women workers in the expanding service sector.

The obstacles to change, however, have been equally formidable. Community care has undergone a redefinition from 'care in' to 'care by' the community,[41] thereby raising an ideological debate about family, other care-givers and the state, which will be discussed in the next section. Community care also implies a shift of responsibility within the statutory sector, predominantly from the NHS to the SSDs; but joint planning and joint finance arrangements have only served to highlight the difficulties inherent in more collaborative professional practice. Because of the difficulty of resolving pressures in both these areas Means and Smith have portrayed community care as one of the symbolic policies which are 'designed to reassure the public about good intentions but which are never intended to be appropriately resourced in relation to their far-reaching objectives.'[42]

The implementation in 1993 of quasi-market arrangements is the most recent redefinition of community care. It was principally a reaction to the financial implications of changes in the supply of residential care for older people. In the mid-1970s, local authorities still met demand for such care principally from their own stock of residential accommodation; but by 1990 the private sector had become the major provider. This change was occasioned by both an increasing demand from an ageing population and a reduction in local authority spending consequent on macroeconomic decisions about public spending. It was also doubly paradoxical because incentives offered through the *public* social security system underpinned the expansion in the *private* supply of residential care and created a 'perverse incentive' towards residential care at the time when government rhetoric was increasingly directed towards the alternative of community care. Whatever the intended or unintended consequences of the decision, however, it was expensive. It also served to perpetuate a long-standing stereotype about the appropriate location of care for older people – although one which still only applies to a minority.

THE SHIFTING BOUNDARIES OF WELFARE

The creation of quasi-markets and the expansion of the private market in child minding and nursery provision, as well as in residential care for older people, is one example of the re-negotiation of responsibility for personal welfare in the mixed economy of the 1980s. The two other major examples of shifting boundaries were family and communal responsibility, and between the voluntary sector and the state.

In relation to the former, Moroney has written: 'Historically most social welfare programmes were developed on the premise that the family and the immediate neighbouring environment constituted the first line of responsibility when individuals had their self-maintaining capacities impaired or threatened.'[43] In the Poor Law such responsibilities were based not just on piety or affection but on the concept of 'liable relatives', which was the means by which the notion of family obligation was legally enforced. The coercive measures of the poor law 'failed to call forth sufficient informal support',[44] and the obligation was finally abolished in 1948 except for that between spouses, and between parents and immature children.

Its abolition, however, made it easier for commentators to claim that the services of the welfare state were undermining family care. The threat of potential bed blockages in hospitals, for example, was blamed on relatives refusing to offer a home to elderly patients. Such a belief, and its support within government in the 1950s and 1960s, according to Means, 'helps to explain the slowness to give local authorities the legal power to provide a full range of domiciliary services ... The great fear was that the wider availability of domiciliary care would be used by carers ... to abandon elderly relatives to the state'.[45] Much the same argument can be made about the ambivalent attitude towards day care for children. Broadly the state's assumption has been that parents, and mothers especially, will care for young children during the day – an assumption which postwar theories of child development conveniently reinforced.

Over the past three decades, however, research has clearly demon-strated that the feared abandonment of relatives to the state was largely unfounded, especially in relation to older and disabled people. Family care has persisted despite the changes in family life and the successive expansion and contraction of the statutory sector. This research has heightened awareness of the costs of care, borne especially by women – though men, once 'the forgotten carers', are now receiving increased attention.[46] It has also indicated the variety of emotions both among carers – duty as well as affection[47] – and those receiving care who, as one recent study has suggested 'do not want to rely on their relatives for extensive help', let alone feel that they can demand it. That finding is of particular significance for, as has been argued: 'the more that govern-ments try to redraw the boundaries between the state and the family and to extend the range of responsibilities which they assume will be taken by kin, the closer we come to reviving the idea of "liable relatives"'.[48]

What, finally, of the changing responsibilities between the state and the voluntary sector over the past fifty years? The accepted view has been that the voluntary sector shrank in influence and supply in the era of the positive state that followed the Second World War. More recent studies have questioned this interpretation.[49] As Deakin, for instance, has argued, 'the Labour Party and its leaders were far less statist in their attitudes towards welfare than has sometimes been sug-gested'.[50] If so, it is even more important to recognise the divergent attitudes towards the voluntary sector that existed in the postwar Labour government. One strand clearly remained suspicious. No one expressed these reservations more forcefully than Richard Crossman, though in the 1970s he was to offer a very different view of the volun-teer in modern social service. Of his earlier attitude he wrote, 'We all disliked the do-good volunteer and wanted to see him replaced by pro-fessionals and trained administrators in the socialist welfare state of which we all dreamed.'[51] Attlee, with his earlier experience of East End settlement work, took a different view:

> Alongside everything done by the local authority and the state there
> are people who want to do a bit more... I believe that we shall always
> have alongside the great range of public services, the voluntary ser-
> vices which humanise our national life and bring it down from the
> general to the particular.[52]

For Herbert Morrison, Lord President in the postwar Labour govern-ment, the issue was less about the nature of a democratic society, and more about co-operation between the statutory and voluntary sectors. Here too earlier experience was important. Morrison as chairman of the London County Council had encouraged a number of successful examples of statutory–voluntary collaboration during the 1930s. Not surprisingly the issue for him in the late 1940s was one of identifying areas 'where statutory and voluntary effort can co-operate efficiently';[53] though, as Jane Lewis's chapter in this volume suggests, partnership has been susceptible to widely differing definitions over time.

The parameters of such partnership were already established in the inter-war years, and in certain respects persisted after the war was over. Braithwaite's study *The Voluntary Citizen* published in 1938 showed that the sources of charitable funding were changing. Voluntary donations played a less important role, while payments by the central or local state for services rendered by agency arrangements were increasing.[54] The provision of services for blind people introduced by the 1920 Act provides one such example. What is interesting about the 1940s is the way such arrangements persisted to a greater degree in the personal welfare sector compared to other parts of the welfare state. As Brenton notes: 'The more importance attached to the need for universal provision, for basic guaranteed levels of service and for legally established rights rather than charity, the more likely the service was to be taken into the public sector entirely.'[55]

In personal welfare the statutory–voluntary partnership was a negotiated responsibility that had benefits to both parties, even if the relationship increasingly assumed a superior–subordinate form. The voluntary organisations received some measure of financial security by the availability of public funds, while central and especially local government received the continuing expertise of the voluntary agencies and their staff. This was particularly the case in the care of older, infirm and handicapped people. In those sectors, a Ministry of Health circular pointed out, voluntary organisations 'have much special knowledge and experience which would be helpful to local authorities in preparing their schemes'.[56] The developments and changes in the statutory sector in the 1960s, described earlier, necessarily impacted upon the structure and style of this statutory–voluntary relationship; but it was only in the 1970s that the continuing autonomy of the voluntary sector began to be called into question. The introduction of special schemes for unemployed people, such as the Job Creation Programme, provided voluntary organisations with central government funding to employ people on community projects for a year. In this way, voluntary organisations 'set up for social welfare or community purposes found themselves turning into employment and training agencies'.[57] In the process, partnership was again being redefined, with voluntary agencies becoming in effect a service delivery arm of the state.

More recent changes have tended to reinforce that role. The centrality of contracting in the new community care arrangements highlights both the difference of size and status between voluntary organisations and threatens the sector's role of independent campaigning and advocacy. It also raises 'the question of how different voluntary organisations that enter the contract culture will look from public or even private sectors, a question that has already achieved prominence in the United States'.[58] Conformity to contract represents a new and different aspect of complementarity for both the statutory and the voluntary sector of personal welfare. And it is at least pertinent to inquire how far it represents a return to the agency arrangements of half a century and more ago.

CONCLUSION

This chapter has begun to identify a number of emergent themes which need to be addressed in further historical analysis of the sector of individual welfare. The first is risk. How can historical study contribute, for example, to an understanding of the changing notions of vulnerability, the varied repertoire of caring strategies, the socially structured dependencies of childhood, disability and old age as well as the experience of the past fifty years which suggests that the risk of threats to welfare has been a feature of care environments as well as domestic circumstances?

The second is relationships. The historical analysis of the mixed economy of welfare so predominant in the personal social services suggests the need for closer exploration of the interrelationships between the sectors, the tensions that have been created and the ways in which they have been resolved. Power-holding, professionalism, financial arrangements and political decisions may all constitute an agenda for such an analysis of the interface that characterises the mixed economy.

The final issue is that of responsibility which, in a variety of aspects, has been one of the central themes of this chapter. On a broader – but related – canvas David Thomson has suggestively argued that 'the history of social welfare in Britain in recent centuries must be seen as a series of shifts to and fro between two loci of responsibility'. These he characterises as 'the individual and his or her immediate family' on the one hand and 'the wider community of non-kin' on the other.[59] In reviewing the period of the past 50 years in the sector of personal welfare, this chapter suggests that historical analysis urgently needs to explore the changing balance not only between but also within these different loci of responsibility.

Notes

1. R. Lowe, *The Welfare State in Britain since 1945* (Basingstoke: Macmillan, 1993), p. 261.
2. M. Hill, *The Welfare State in Britain* (Aldershot: Edward Elgar, 1993), p. 38.
3. M. Evandrou et al., 'The Personal Social Services: "Everyone's Poor Relation but Nobody's Baby"' in J. Hills (ed.), *The State of Welfare* (Oxford: Oxford University Press, 1990), p. 213.
4. G. Finlayson, 'A Moving Frontier: Voluntarism and the State in British Social Welfare 1911–1949', *Twentieth Century British History* 1 (1990), pp. 183–206.
5. D. Thomson, 'Welfare and the Historians' in L. Bonfield (ed.), *The World We Have Gained* (Oxford: Blackwell, 1986), pp. 365–6.
6. Evandrou, 'Personal Social Services', p. 209.
7. Cmnd 3703, *Report of the Committee on Local Authority and Allied Personal Social Services* (London: HMSO, 1968).
8. B. Davies, *Social Needs and Resources in Local Services* (Oxford University Press, 1968); S. Sainsbury, *Registered as Disabled* (London: Bell, 1970).
9. J. Baldock, 'The Personal Social Services: The Politics of Care' in V. George and S. Millar (eds), *Social Policy towards 2000* (London: Routledge, 1994), p. 170.
10. P. Barclay, *Social Workers: Their Roles and Tasks* (Bedford: NCVO, 1982).
11 R. Griffiths, *Community Care: Agenda for Action* (London: HMSO, 1988).
12. R. Means and R. Smith, *The Development of Welfare Services for Elderly People* (London: Croom Helm, 1985), p. 136.
13. R. A. Parker, 'The Gestation of Reform: The Children Act 1948', in P. Bean and S. Macpherson (eds), *Approaches to Welfare* (London: Routledge & Kegan Paul, 1983), pp. 205–213.
14. E. Younghusband, *Social Work in Britain: 1950–1975* volume 1 (London: Allen & Unwin, 1978), p. 286.
15. E. Younghusband, *Social Work*, pp. 38–9.
16. M. Payne, *Power, Authority and Responsibility in Social Services* (London: Macmillan, 1979), p. 22.
17. H. Glennerster, *British Social Policy since 1945* (Oxford: Blackwell, 1995), p. 64.
18. P. Hall, *Reforming Welfare* (London: Heinemann, 1976).
19. J. Cooper, *The Creation of the Personal Social Services 1962–74* (London: Heinemann, 1982).

20. Cmnd 1191, *Report of the Committee on Children and Young Persons* (London: HMSO, 1960), para 37.
21. Hall, *Reforming*, p. 19.
22. R. Crossman, *The Diaries of a Cabinet Minister*, vol. 3 (London: Hamish Hamilton/Jonathan Cape, 1977), various references.
23. Cmnd 3703, para 637.
24. Hall, *Reforming*, p. 83.
25. Public Record Office Kew: MH 102 1382.
26. L. Challis, *Organising Public Social Services* (London: Longman, 1990), p. vii.
27. Hill, *The Welfare State*, p. 81.
28. M. Langan and J. Clarke, 'Managing in the Mixed Economy of Care', in J. Clarke et al. (eds.), *Managing Social Policy* (London: Sage, 1994), p. 73.
29. G. Wistow et al., *Social Care in a Mixed Economy* (Milton Keynes: Open University Press, 1994), p. 65.
30. R. A. Parker, 'Children' in Ian Sinclair (ed.), *Residential Care: The Research Reviewed* (London: HMSO, 1988), p. 60.
31. Evandrou, *The Personal Social Services*, p. 259.
32. Roy Parker, 'Elderly People and Community Care' in Ian Sinclair et al. (eds), *The Kaleidoscope of Care* (1990), p. 19.
33. Audit Commission, *Making a Reality of Community Care* (London: HMSO, 1986), p. 15.
34. Cmnd 6922, *Report of the Care of Children Committee* (London: HMSO, 1946), para. 370.
35. J. Packman, *The Child's Generation* 2nd edn (Oxford: Blackwell, 1981), pp. 34–5.
36. P. Townsend, *The Last Refuge* (London: Routledge & Kegan Paul, 1962).
37. L. F. Harding, *Family, State and Social Policy* (Basingstoke: Macmillan, 1996), p. 163.
38. N. Parton, *Governing the Family* (Basingstoke: Macmillan, 1991), p. 196.
39. See, for example, R. D. King et al., *Patterns of Residential Care* (London: Routledge & Kegan Paul, 1971); P. Townsend *Last Refuge*; P. Townsend, 'Foreword', in Pauline Morris *Put Away: A Sociological Study of Institutions for the Mentally Retarded* (London: Routledge & Kegan Paul, 1969); E. Goffman *Asylums* (New York: Anchor Books, 1961).
40. M. Oswin, *Children Living in Long Stay Hospitals* (London: Heinemann, 1978); Cmnd 6684, *Fit for the Future: the Report of the Committee on Child Health Services* (London: HMSO, 1976); Cmnd 7468, *Report of the Committee of Enquiry into Mental Handicap Nursing and Care* (London: HMSO, 1979).
41. Cmnd 8173, *Growing Older* (London: HMSO, 1981).
42. R. Means and R. Smith, *Community Care* (London: Macmillan, 1994), p. 44.
43. R. Moroney, *The Family and the State* (London: Longman, 1976), p. 4.
44. H. Qureshi and A. Walker, *The Caring Relationship* (London: Macmillan, 1989), p. 24.
45. Robin Means, 'Older People and Personal Social Services', in David Gladstone (ed.), *British Social Welfare* (London: UCL Press, 1995), p. 202.

46. See, for example, S. Arber and N. Gilbert, 'Men: The Forgotten Carers', *Sociology,* 23 (1) (1990), pp. 111–18; M. Fisher, 'Man-made Care: Community Care and Older Male Carers', *British Journal of Social Work* 24 (1994), pp. 659–80.
47. See, for example, J. Finch and D. Groves (eds.), *A Labour of Love* (London: Routledge and Kegan Paul, 1983); J. Lewis and B. Meredith, *Daughters Who Care* (London: Routledge, 1988).
48. J. Finch and J. Mason, *Negotiating Family Responsibilities* (London: Routledge, 1993), p. 180.
49. G. Finlayson, *Citizen, State and Social Welfare in Britain 1830–1990* (Oxford: Clarendon, 1994); N. Deakin, 'The Perils of Partnership: The Voluntary Sector and the State 1945–1992' in J. Davis Smith et al. (eds), *An Introduction to the Voluntary Sector* (London: Routledge, 1995).
50. Deakin, 'Perils' p. 40.
51. R. H. S. Crossman, 'The Role of the Volunteer in the Modern Social Service', in A. H. Halsey (ed.), *Traditions of Social Policy* (Oxford: Blackwell, 1976), pp. 264–5.
52. Cited Finalyson, *Citizen* p. 281.
53. Cited Deakin, 'Perils' p. 44.
54. C. Braithwaite, *The Voluntary Citizen: An Enquiry into the Place of Philanthropy in the Community* (London: Methuen, 1938).
55. M. Brenton, *The Voluntary Sector in British Social Services* (London: Longman, 1985), p. 18.
56. Ministry of Health Circular 87/46.
57. M. Taylor, 'Voluntary Action and the State' in David Gladstone (ed.), *British Social Welfare*, p. 228.
58. J. Lewis, 'Developing the Mixed Economy of Care: Emerging Issues for Voluntary Organisations', *Journal of Social Policy* 22 (2) (1993), pp. 190–91.
59. D. Thomson in Bonfield, *World*, p. 365.

4 The Voluntary Sector and the State in Twentieth Century Britain
Jane Lewis

CONCEPTUALISING THE VOLUNTARY SECTOR AND ITS RELATIONSHIP WITH THE STATE

For historians and social scientists alike, it has proved extremely difficult to reach any working definition of 'the voluntary sector'. Differences between voluntary organisations often seem to be as great as the differences between, say, service providers in the voluntary and public sectors. Considerable effort has gone into trying to establish a typology of voluntary organisations[1], but the task is widely acknowledged to verge on the impossible. Large-scale service providing agencies, such as the National Society for the Prevention of Cruelty to Children or the Family Welfare Association (prior to 1942, the Charity Organisation Society), often have long histories, but small, local self-help groups have often been much shorter-lived. The pre-war period was dominated by service organisations and by mutual-aid societies, such as the friendly societies; since the war the sector has probably become more diverse and recent decades have seen an explosion in self-help groups.

At the most general level, it is agreed that there is something different about the voluntary sector. In Britain, for example, Hatch has suggested that voluntary organisations are more than informal groups, yet they are not established by statute or controlled directly by statutory authority, nor are they commercial in the sense of profit-making.[2] In seeking to distinguish them, he has thus sought to identify characteristics that might serve to differentiate voluntary organisations from both the state and the private sector (in the sense of both the informal and the commercial sectors). However, as others have pointed out, the boundaries between the sectors have been and remain blurred, although the extent and the nature of the blurring is disputed. Billis has argued for example, that voluntary organisations have bureaucratic, informal and associational aspects and that it is precisely this mixture of characteristics that makes them distinctive.[3]

Economists in the United States, where the voluntary sector is particularly large, have tried to go beyond description in seeking an explanation for the existence of the voluntary sector, although, their exemplars have usually been service providing organisations, which reflects the relative importance of such organisations in the USA. Again, their theories have focused on the nature of the relationship between the voluntary sector, and both the commercial sector and the state. Hansmann has argued that non-profit organisations have arisen in situations in which there are information asymmetries between producer and consumer, that is in situations in which the consumer feels unable to evaluate the quantity and quality of a service and therefore seeks additional protection from the provider.[4] In contrast, Weisbrod has stressed the importance of government rather than market failure and has suggested that voluntary organisations have grown up to meet minority demands that have been ignored by the state.[5]

In these theories, the relationship between the voluntary sector and the state amounts to a zero-sum game. There is little place for co-operation or indeed blurring between the sectors. Salamon has taken issue with such an approach and has emphasised instead the possibility of voluntary sector failure, an emphasis which has the advantage of recognising that historically the voluntary sector has not always been viewed as the residual sector.[6] He lists voluntary sector weaknesses as insufficiency, particularism, paternalism and amateurism, which have been enough to bring in the state. Thus, he argues, it may be appropriate to see the state and the voluntary sector as compensating for each other's failure.

Most recently, increasing numbers of commentators have begun to insist that the pattern of voluntary organisation has been shaped as much or more by socio-political variables as by economic efficiency criteria and they have stressed the importance of an historical understanding as to how voluntary organisations have become embedded in particular societies.[7] It may be, as Gronbjerg has suggested for the USA, that the pattern of relations between the state and the voluntary organisations has been very different in different service sectors; for example she describes the field of child welfare as having been characterised by co-operation, health care by accommodation, education by competition and housing by symbiotic development.[8]

Sceptics may wonder whether the effort to distinguish the voluntary sector from the state and/or the private sector is worth the effort. However, voluntary organisations have played a large role in the making of modern welfare states, although whether the amount of money flowing through them ever exceeded state expenditure on welfare is a matter of debate.[9] Recent efforts to produce typologies of modern European welfare states[10] have arguably been fundamentally flawed by a failure to examine the different roles of voluntary organisations cross-nationally. More than that, the proper nature of the relationship between the voluntary sector and the state has long been a subject of considerable concern to those involved in the actual development of social policy. The Webbs famously distinguished between 'the parallel bars' they believed to exist in the early part of the century and the 'extension ladder' that they felt *ought* to exist.[11] Such commentaries have been as much or more about the role of the state as about voluntary organisations, and they have by no means accurately described the *reality* of the voluntary/statutory relationship, which has usually been very varied depending on the type of voluntary organisation. Nevertheless, it is possible to see ideas about the 'ought' of statutory/voluntary relations moving through distinctive phases in Britain during the twentieth century. This chapter will seek to chart these in broad-brush fashion. It will also indicate how the general shifts in ideas about the appropriate nature of the relationship had significant effect on one kind of voluntary organisation, service providers,[12] especially as their financial dependency on the state increased.

Finlayson referred to the voluntary/statutory relationship as 'a moving frontier'.[13] This may describe relationships on the ground rather well. However, the term most commonly used in the literature describing the 'ought' of the relationship, certainly from the 1920s, was that of 'partnership'. The point that will be made in this chapter is that this term has been susceptible to widely differing meanings over time.

SEPARATE SPHERES: 1900–1914

Voluntary organisations providing personal social service, and often – notwithstanding their principles to the contrary – alms, occupied a position of considerably greater influence in relation to the state than their counterparts in the late twentieth century. It may be argued that the nature of social welfare organisation was particularly favourable to voluntary effort at the turn of the century, but influential opinion within the personal service societies was also concerned to stake out the necessarily distinctive contribution of charity. While there was every intention to co-operate with the state, it was believed that the world of charity should remain separate from it and ideally should take the lead in social action.

Harris has pointed out that in nineteenth-century Britain it is more accurate to see voluntary organisations as part of the way in which political leaders conceptualised the state. She has described the aim of Victorian governments as being 'to provide a framework of rules and guidelines designed to enable society very largely to run itself'. This did not amount to rank atomistic individualism: 'the corporate life of society was seen as expressed through voluntary associations and the local community, rather than through the persona of the state'.[14] Nineteenth-century Britain had effective central government institutions, but a small central bureaucracy and a strong desire to limit the activities of central government. In this arrangement, voluntary organisations may best be conceptualised as part of a range of 'buffer institutions' that developed between the central state and the citizen and which were conceived of as part of the fabric of the state. They were not, as Thane has remarked, 'the fortuitous corollary of the limited state but [were] integral to the conceptualisation of that state by its leaders'.[15]

At the turn of the century, much state social provision was locally financed and locally administered. The Poor Law was controlled by locally elected Boards of Guardians and education by locally elected School Boards. But in the years before World War I, matters of social policy gradually became the stuff of 'high politics',[16] prompted in large part by the rapid increase in the financial burden experienced at the local level. Rates in London, for instance, rose between 30 and 50 per cent in the period between 1891 and 1906. Thus the welfare reforms of the Liberal Government of 1906–14 came to rely on a quite different pattern of finance: taxation in the case of old age pensions and contributory insurance against sickness and unemployment (which also required a state contribution out of taxation). However, in respect of its administration, national insurance in particular represented an attempt to reconcile state compulsion with mutual aid voluntarism; trade unions and friendly societies were invited to administer the policy.

The fact that social provision was local made it easier for a measure of welfare pluralism to exist. As the role of central government in social provision grew, however, so the balance between the voluntary and statutory sectors shifted. During the 1980s and 1990s the New Right has hankered after 'little battalions',[17] that is, social provision determined by community and neighbourhood. However, such an idea was arguably more feasible in the late nineteenth century than now because the central state left local territory relatively free from control. Ware has also suggested that as the growth of the market expanded social relations beyond smaller communities after 1900, so it drew local elites away from local concerns (this was certainly something that bothered Octavia Hill[18]) and weakened reciprocal and impersonal altruism.[19]

The social, political and economic conjuncture at the turn of the century was therefore conducive to a large role for the voluntary sector. In addition, leading members of the world of social action believed strongly in the social purpose of charity and in charity as a fundamental social principle, whose practice offered the only possibility of achieving real and sustainable social progress. C. S. Loch, the influential secretary of the Charity Organisation Society from 1875 to 1914, insisted that charity was not philanthropy. The goal of charity was the promotion of a sense of membership in society and its practice was centred on the nature of the obligations attaching to that membership and the ways in which a particular individual could be enabled to participate as a citizen. The basic conditions of membership, or citizenship, were that an individual must become socially efficient, that is self-sustaining and morally competent.[20] Furthermore, the fulfilment of citizenship obligations in an ethical state had to be voluntary, which was why charity and not the statutory authorities was accorded such importance. People had to act morally of their own free will; by definition they could not be forced to do so. Those working with people in need had therefore to give their time voluntarily and they had to be able to persuade those they worked with to change their behaviour so that they became self-supporting.

This was the central creed of the Charity Organisation Society, but the importance of voluntary personal social service as a means of achieving social change was more widely shared. According to Loch, the key to the practice of true charity lay in the principle of reciprocity: 'As price is the measure of economic exchange, so at the time or ultimately a rise in the standard of membership [of society] is the measure of the social exchange, which we call reciprocity.'[21] This view stressed the social interdependence of people, their need for service, friendly dealing and 'social solidarity'. The better off performed their obligations as citizens when they voluntarily offered to help those less fortunate than themselves, not just by giving alms, but by providing the kind of personal service (or social work) designed to promote self-maintenance and fully participative citizenship. The poor fulfilled their duties as citizens by responding to whatever plan was proposed to restore them to self-maintenance. The principle of reciprocity guarded against purely selfish actions on the part of the rich. It lifted charity above the narrow concerns of political economy and gave it ethical purpose.

The circumstances of the founding of the Charity Organisation Society in 1869 illustrate the way in which charity was to be accorded a place from which to take forward its social work. From the beginning, the COS's sphere of action was defined in relation to the Poor Law. The Goschen Minute on the Relief of the Poor in the Metropolis, issued by the central Poor Law Board in 1869, set out the relationship between the Poor Law and voluntary action and was welcomed by the members of the Council of the London COS as being in complete harmony with their approach.[22] Goschen stated his anxiety about the rise in pauperism (that is, in destitution as distinct form poverty) and the effect it might have on the public, increasing their concern and their indiscriminate giving. In face of this possibility, he was anxious to promote an agreed set of limits on charitable and Poor Law relief. His main concern was to hold the line on Poor Law relief. The role he consequently set out for charity was to assist those on the verge of destitution, in other words to prevent them becoming a public charge, while the state was conceptualised as a provider of last resort. Sidney and Beatrice Webb referred to this as the 'cowcatcher' theory of charitable action.[23] Goschen thus advocated co-operation between the statutory and voluntary sectors on similar tasks, while maintaining separate spheres of action. This appealed to the COS not least because the scheme accorded charity the leading position. In theory, it was the COS that would decide who would be dealt with by charity (the deserving) and who by the Poor Law (the undeserving) and the organisation eagerly set out to co-operate at the local level with Boards of Guardians. The fact that in practice such a partnership for the most part failed to develop did not in any way change the ideal.[24] Leaders of the organisation remained convinced that the only way to achieve social progress was to change individual behaviour, and the only way to do that in a democratic society was via voluntary endeavour.

Other personal service societies that became prominent during the Edwardian period – the Guilds of Help and the Councils of Social Welfare – were very critical of COS practice, but continued to believe that charity should take pride of place in social service provision. Nevertheless, these organisations took a very different view of how to draw the boundary line between the voluntary sector and the state. In the view of Hancock Nunn, who founded the Hampstead Council of Social Welfare: 'What is needed is, not that there should be anything like parallelism between Statutory Relief and Voluntary Assistance, but that exactly opposite relations should subsist. Parallel lines are lines that never meet'.[25] Given that the state and the COS had failed to organise relief working separately, he felt that it was logical to argue that more joint working was needed. In Hampstead, he set up a joint committee consisting of five members of the COS, five guardians and five local councillors. After 1903, the Board of Guardians agreed to refer all cases to the committee, which became the Council of Social Welfare. To Hancock Nunn, this seemed to represent the proper working out of the Goschen Minute of 1869. However the guilds and councils varied in the extent to which they were prepared to see voluntary work tied to that of the state via joint machinery, or, even more especially, via financial aid.

The new personal service organisations put considerable emphasis on co-operating with democratically elected local bodies. They were determinedly civic-minded.[26] They also put an even greater premium than had the COS on personal social work, such that the majority began to develop a new partnership with the state which involved a division of labour rather than a division of client group. The voluntary agencies would provide friendly visiting and co-ordinate charitable and state efforts by drawing up mutual registers of those assisted and the like, while the state provided a national minimum level of relief.

The guilds insisted that any citizen could be helped and refused to draw a line between Poor Law and charity clients. They insisted that no one was undeserving or unhelpable and stressed the undesirability of the COS practice of abandoning people who were declared ineligible for assistance.[27] This effectively undermined the division of labour between charity and the Poor law which had been derived from the principles of deterrence and, even if many guilds did not want to be subservient in any way to the statutory authorities, heralded the beginnings of a more complementary partnership. The Bradford Guild of Help responded positively to the 1906 legislation on school meals, and while the COS continued to regard all the social welfare reforms of the Liberal Government as a totally undesirable extension of state intervention and a threat to charity as a social principle, the new organisations welcomed them.

Leading members of the COS feared that the new pragmatism regarding cooperation with the state would reduce voluntary action to personal social work in the service of the state. Certainly, the redefinition of the partnership between the voluntary sector and the state that was crafted by the guilds and councils was above all pragmatic; the vision of the role of charity that had sustained the COS disappeared and personal social service societies were in the inter-war years more at risk of having their role defined by the state.

COMPLEMENTARY OR SUPPLEMENTARY: 1918–1980

In 1937, Llewellyn Smith spoke of a 'borderland' rather than a borderline existing between the voluntary and statutory sectors.[28] Major commentaries on the role of the voluntary sector during the inter-war years attempted to reconceptualise the relationship between the voluntary organisation and the state. It was part of this rethinking that many people no longer viewed financial support of voluntary endeavour by the state as problematic.

Constance Braithwaite, who admitted that she was trying to reconcile her faith in the voluntary sector with her commitment to socialism, came out in favour of a 'national minimum': 'my conclusion is that the relief of poverty should be the responsibility of the State and not of charity, but that charitable relief will and should continue as long as poverty exists which is not adequately relieved by the state'.[29] This left voluntary organisations, in her view, with a supplementary role, and an experimental or pioneering role. Macadam took a similar position in her influential analysis of the 'new philanthropy' and the 'new partnership', in which she called for closer co-operation between the state and voluntary organisations. She welcomed the Webbs' idea of the 'extension ladder' as a prescription for voluntary/statutory relations, the idea being that voluntary organisations would influence and supplement public services, but no longer aim to be the first line of defence for social services. Macadam reserved special criticism for the COS, calling on it to 'frankly recognise' that the future could not lie in trying to supersede the state.[30] T. S. Simey, a lecturer in public administration at Liverpool University, followed Macadam's lead in seeing nothing beyond a supplementary role for the voluntary sector.

These were only prescriptions for voluntary organisations and not accurate descriptions of actual patterns of voluntary activity, which remained very unpredictable. For example the voluntary sector retained monopoly control of district nursing until as late as 1948.[31] But most writers conceptualised voluntary organisations as pioneers or as providing supplementary services and by the end of the inter-war years one of the chief justifications for voluntary endeavour had become the idea that voluntary organisations were useful for doing what the state could not manage to do. Macadam felt that voluntary effort was most appropriate for schemes that were experimental, for activities that called for flexibility or highly individualised work, or for specialised 'watchdog' activities. Thus, personal service was still considered a suitable task for voluntary action. Beveridge sought to reassure the members of the COS that since what the state provided had to be the same for all citizens, there would always remain scope to provide individual care for those who needed something more or different. He too used the word 'supplementary' in his writing on voluntary action to describe the work of voluntary organisations in relation to the state. However Beveridge continued to insist on the importance of the 'spirit of service' and invoked voluntary action as an important counterweight to the business motive and, like many others in the wake of fascism, a fundamental ingredient of modern democracy.[32]

In 1948 Parliament abolished the Poor Law, and in the postwar welfare state, personal service societies increasingly had to define their work in relation to new statutory services. In the case of the COS, which became the Family Welfare Association in 1946, it focused on the provision of in-depth family casework, and as its social workers became professionalised so it also became increasingly reliant on local authorities to fund the service. In the immediate postwar years, the FWA could argue that it was in fact providing a complementary service to that of the local authority welfare departments. However, as local authority personal social services grew in size and scope, this position became harder to sustain.

The 1959 Younghusband Report for the Ministry of Health on local authority social workers recommended a huge increase in their numbers[33] and the 1968 Seebohm Report on personal social services recommended the creation of unified social services departments.[34] The Seebohm Committee explicitly addressed the role of voluntary organisations, suggesting that they would continue to have a major role 'developing citizen participation in revealing new needs and in exposing shortcomings in the services'.[35] The Committee thus offered the voluntary sector the role of pioneer and watchdog. But in the case of an organisation like the FWA, its highly professional service offered to but a few clients was likely to be increasingly regarded as a luxury. As the 1978 Wolfenden Report pointed out, local authorities varied considerably in the support they were prepared to give voluntary organisations.[36] In the 1950s, 1960s and 1970s, many local authorities and Labour politicians were suspicious of the activities of many voluntary organisations, especially some of the older personal service organisations which were fatally tarred with the 'charity' brush. It was not until 1976 that Richard Crossman as the leading Labour Party spokesman on the social services, for example, came to the view that voluntary action was to be valued for its idealism and had a role to play in humanizing state bureaucracies.[37]

During the immediate postwar decades, voluntary action was generally viewed as in some way secondary. However, as doubt about the responsiveness of large state bureaucracies began to grow in the 1970s, so new arguments in favour of giving a greater place to voluntary providers of social services came from both the political right and left.[38] In 1979, Gladstone argued for a 'preference-guided society' in which government would retain a major responsibility for financing welfare and thus secure equity, but the voluntary sector would take over much of the service delivery.[39] The 'welfare pluralists' argued that greater participation by voluntary organisations in the delivery of social services would also mean the possibility of greater choice for users and representation of a wider spectrum of interests. For these writers, participative decentralised pluralism was closely allied to ideas about empowerment and the importance of local democracy and in their vision of welfare provision, the voluntary sector became integral, rather than a supplementary or complementary partner.[40]

On the political right, the Conservative Government that came to power in 1979 expressed a commitment to the trinity of the market, the voluntary sector and the family in addition to a determination to limit the activities of the state. The main point of difference between Conservative doctrine and the welfare pluralists lay in motivation: the Conservatives were concerned above all with economy and efficiency, the welfare pluralists with participation. In addition, whereas the welfare pluralists favoured a slow transition to a devolved, differentiated and participative system of service delivery, the Conservatives wanted to see as rapid a transition as possible. There were nevertheless significant points of agreement, in terms of both the common desire to elevate the needs of the consumer above professional opinion and the faith in the capacity of the voluntary sector to expand and deliver.

ALTERNATIVE PROVIDERS? 1980s–1990s

A more 'mixed economy of welfare' received massive encouragement during the 1980s and 1990s, but in the context of a voluntary sector heavily reliant on paid as well as unpaid workers and a strongly centralising state. Late twentieth century voluntary effort is not autonomous from that of the public sector, the lines have been blurred in terms of the use of paid staff and the receipt of state funding.

Thus the conditions under which the voluntary sector might once more assume a greater role are very different from those at the turn of the century. The 'tight/loose' organisation pioneered by private sector firms in the 1980s, involving the decentralisation of production and the centralisation of command, has been parallelled in the 'new public management' of the public sector. Since 1988 'quasi-markets' have been introduced in all the social services – in health, housing, education and community care, the voluntary sector becoming a major provider in housing and community care, the private sector a bigger provider in education, while health has remained more of an internal market. Unlike earlier in the century, the fiscal conditions have been firmly set by central government and because postwar service-providing agencies have been funded primarily by government, their room for manoeuvre in the new situation is limited.

In respect of social care, the Government's aim has been to turn local authorities into enablers, who purchase more than they provide, so promoting a mixed economy of care. This has been seen as central to the achievement both of user choice and of services that are simultaneously high quality and cost effective.[41] It is the idea of separating finance from provision that has been labelled a 'quasi-market' by academic researchers. Le Grand has described the introduction of quasi-markets as a response to two sets of critics: those on the political right, who charged that welfare bureaucracies were wasting resources on excessive administration and protecting their own interests at the expense of those of users, and second, those concerned with equity as well as with efficiency. The latter set of arguments suggested that the welfare system was particularly unresponsive to the needs and wants of the very people it was set up primarily to help, the poor and disadvantaged.[42]

There are significant implications for voluntary organisations in the implementation of a 'purchaser/provider split' in social care as well as in the process of contracting that follows from it. Social services departments have been asked to establish the level of need and then to decide how much of what kind of service is required in consultation with other statutory authorities, voluntary organisations, users and carers. This effectively means that what voluntary organisations can offer enters a broader local authority purchasing strategy. Thus voluntary organisations must offer something that the purchaser wishes to buy. Since the Second World War, voluntary organisation service providers have usually been supported by grant aid from local authorities. These grants were never unconditional, but most organisations used them to support both service and campaigning work, as well as core administrative activities. Under the new approach, the statutory authority takes the lead in deciding exactly what kid of activity it is prepared to contract for. This is likely to result in a narrowing of voluntary work (it is, for example, unlikely that a local authority will pay for campaigning work), and more say for the statutory authority over the nature of the activity (for example, in respect of which client group is to be served).

These political developments amount to a substantial change in the relationship between local authorities and voluntary organisations. Voluntary action is no longer regarded as supplementary or complementary, but is potentially an alternative to state provision. Indeed, Harrold has shown how in the areas of mental health and caring for elderly people, the voluntary sector has already been asked to fill the gaps left by the withdrawal of direct state provision.[43] The trend is thus away from voluntary organisations providing services *in addition* to the state, and towards voluntary provision *instead* of the state.

When Government issued its draft guidance on the 1990 community care legislation, it suggested a firm functional split between purchaser and provider functions for social services departments along the lines of the changes taking place in health authorities. Both local authorities and the voluntary sectors reacted strongly against this idea. The Association of Metropolitan Authorities acknowledged that all the factors linking local authorities and voluntary organisations 'will require a rethink', but insisted that local authorities should avoid making a rigid purchaser/provider split, seeking instead to achieve 'a redefined form of partnership'.[44] The National Council of Voluntary Organisations also deplored any move to contracting on the basis of price-based competition. 'A critical question in this debate is "who does what best?" The concept of partnership needs to be preserved, even if the award of a particular contract has to be made with due regard to financial proprieties.'[45]

The revised government guidance substantially modified the earlier impression of a model imported from the private sector. The document acknowledged the importance of trust and stated that one of the chief strengths of the relationship between the statutory and voluntary sectors was the closeness of contact between local authority and community providers. It concluded that the new relationship was best conceived as 'being a contract culture involving close ongoing relationships with providers, rather than being based upon anonymous short-term price competition'.[46]

The introduction of contracts has effectively formalised the relationship between local authorities as funders and voluntary agencies. Recent research has shown that partnership via contract forces greater professionalisation on the part of the voluntary agency, has an impact on governance and accountability, and also has an impact on the goals of the organisation.[47] Meeting detailed specifications often requires more professional staff, while volunteers are unlikely to take kindly to the additional bureaucratic requirements associated with running a contract. Additional technical complexity also tends to threaten broad-based governance. The unpaid management committee, that might be considered to be one of the key defining features of the voluntary sector, finds itself unable to cope with the pace of change. Finally, in respect of goals, the organisation may face difficulty in finding the money to carry forward its own chosen programme.

Self has suggested that: 'the massive use of contracting introduces a new type of relationship between governments and private organisations, which changes the behaviour of both parties, increases their interdependency and blurs the traditional distinctions between them'.[48] Taylor and Hoggett also consider that there is potential for remaking contractors in the image of the purchaser, in other words for the voluntary sector losing its distinctive characteristics.[49]

CONCLUSION

Voluntary organisations were never wholly able to call the tune in respect of social provision, although particular spokesmen achieved a position of considerable influence at the turn of the century, when central government broadly agreed with the kind of relationship set out by leaders of the COS. This was never achieved in practice, but the idea of a partnership with shared goals, founded on a respect for Poor Law principles, and separate spheres of operation in respect of client groups was widely accepted. Thus the idea of co-operation between the statutory and voluntary sectors was not new in the inter-war period, but rather represented a change in the content of the idea of partnership.

During the late 1980s and 1990s it has been too easy to romanticise the post- Second World War relationships between the voluntary and statutory sector, which in practice ranged from the positive through neutral to hostile. However, while most service providing voluntary organisations lost a major part of the financial autonomy, they did retain, via grant aid, their ability to determine the nature of the supplementary or complementary activities they undertook. The recent development of quasi-markets and contracting have been conceptualised yet again as a rewriting of the partnership between the voluntary and statutory sectors, but it poses new threats. Contracting as a mechanism puts voluntary organisations into a purchaser/provider relationship that is likely to result in voluntary agencies being treated as equals in the sense of alternative providers, but which at the same time tends to assume them to be the same form of organisation as the purchaser. Billis has warned of the dangers of an instrumental use of the voluntary sector which emphasises only those attributes that are of direct use to government.[50] However, as we saw at the beginning of this chapter, voluntary organisations are inherently different in the mix of bureaucratic and associational features they present. The term partnership has served to gloss over the problems inherent in a relationship between a formal bureaucratic statutory organisation and one that is more ambiguous. The new basis for partnership may be firmer in so far as voluntary organisations may come to adopt more bureaucratic features, but this also implies a significant change in the nature of voluntary organisations that may not be cost free.

Notes

1. For example, David Gerard, *Charities in Britain: Conservatism or Change?* (London: Bedford Square Press, 1983); Hugh W. Mellor, *The Role of Voluntary Organisations in Social Welfare* (London: Croom Helm, 1985).
2. S. Hatch, *Outside the State* (London: Croom Helm, 1980).
3. David Billis, *Organising Public and Voluntary Agencies* (London: Routledge, 1993).
4. H. Hansmann, 'Economic Theories of Non Profit Organisations', in W. W. Powell (ed.) *The Non Profit Sector. A Research Handbook* (New Haven: Yale University Press, 1987).

5. B. S. Weisbrod, *The Non Profit Economy* (Cambridge, Mass.: Harvard University Press, 1988).
6. L. M. Salamon, 'Partners in Public Service: The Scope and Theory of Government-Nonprofit Relations', in W. W. Powell (ed.), *The Non-Profit Sector. A Research Handbook* (New Haven: Yale University Press, 1987); 'the Non-Profit Sector and Government in the US', in H. K. Anheier and W. Seibel (eds) *The Third Sector: Comparative Studies of Nonprofit Organisations* (New York: de Gruyter, 1990).
7. For example, S. Kuhnle and P. Selle (eds) *Government and Voluntary Organisations* (Aldershot: Avebury, 1992); and A. Rathgeb Smith and M. Lipsky, *Nonprofits for Hire. The Welfare State in the Age of Contracting* (Cambridge, Mass.: Harvard University Press, 1993).
8. K. A. Gonbjerg, 'Patterns of Institutional Relationships in the Welfare State: Public Mandates and the Nonprofit Sector', in S. A. Ostrander and S. Langton (eds), *Shifting the Debate. Public/Private Sector Relationships in the Modern Welfare State* (New Brunswick: Transaction Books, 1987).
9. R. Humphreys has suggested that nineteenth-century medical charities and philanthropic public works accounted for a substantial part of Victorian voluntary endeavour, but has argued that any claim that charity provided more in poor relief than the Poor Law must be treated with suspicion ('The Poor Law and Charity. The COS in the Provinces, 1870–1890', unpublished PhD. thesis, University of London, 1991).
10. See especially G. Esping Andersen, *The Three Worlds of Welfare Capitalism* (Cambridge; Polity Press, 1990).
11. S. Webb and B. Webb, *The Prevention of Destitution* (London, 1912).
12. Focusing on service providing organisations obviously slants the analysis. If a different kind of voluntary organisation were to be used as the basis for the analysis, for example, mutual aid societies, a quite other series of shifts would probably be observed.
13. G. Finlayson, 'A Moving Frontier: Voluntarism and the State in British Social Welfare', *Twentieth Century British History* 1 (2), 1990.
14. J. Harris, 'Society and State in Twentieth Century Britain', in F. M. L. Thompson (ed.), *The Cambridge Social History of Britain, 1750–1950*, vol. 3 *Social Agencies and Institutions* (Cambridge: Cambridge University Press, 1990).
15. P. Thane, 'Women in the British Labour Party and the Construction of State Welfare', in S. Koven and S. Michel (eds), *Mothers of a new World. Maternalist Politics and the Origins of Welfare States* (London: Routledge, 1993).
16. J. Harris, *Private Lives Public Spirit. A Social History of Britain, 1870–1914* (Oxford: Oxford University Press, 1993).
17. D. Willetts, *Modern Conservatism* (Harmondsworth: Penguin, 1992).
18. See J. Lewis, *Women and Social Action in Victorian and Edwardian England* (Aldershot: Edward Elgar, 1991).
19. A. Ware, 'Meeting Needs through Voluntary Action: Does Market Society Corrode Altruism?', in A. Ware and R. Goodin (eds), *Needs and Welfare* (London: Sage, 1990).

20. C. S. Loch, *A Great Ideal and its Champion. Papers and Addresses by the late Sir C. S. Loch* (London: Allen & Unwin, 1923).
21. Ibid., p. 47.
22. *Twenty Second Annual Report of the Poor Law Board, 1869–70*, Appendix A, no. 4, C. 123, 1870.
23. Webb and Webb, *Prevention of Destitution*, p. 229.
24. J. Lewis, *The Voluntary Sector, the State and Social Work* (Aldershot: Edward Elgar, 1995).
25. T. Hancock Nunn, *A Council of Social Welfare. A Note and Memorandum of the Report of the Royal Commission on the Poor Law and Relief of Distress as to the functions and Constitution of the new Public Assistance authority and its Local Committees* (London: no publisher, 1909), p. 70.
26. K. Laybourn, *The Guild of Help and the Changing Face of Edwardian Philanthropy* (Lampeter: Edwin Mellen Press, 1994).
27. For example, N. Masterman, 'The COS of the Future', *Charity Organisation Review*, June 1906; and W. Milledge, 'Guilds of Help', *Charity Organisation Review*, July 1906.
28. H. Llewellyn Smith, *The Borderland between Public and Voluntary Action in the Social Services*, Sidney Ball Lecture (London: Oxford University Press, 1937).
29. C. Braithwaite, *The Voluntary Citizen. An Enquiry into the Place of Philanthropy in the Community* (London: Methuen, 1938), p. 16.
30. Ibid., p. 67.
31. Enid Fox, 'District Nursing and the Work of District Nursing Associations in England and Wales, 1900–1948', unpublished PhD. thesis, University of London, 1993.
32. W. Beveridge, *Voluntary Action. A Report of Methods of Social Advance* (London: Allen & Unwin, 1948).
33. Ministry of Health and Department of Health for Scotland, *Report of the Working Party on Social Workers in the Local Authority Health and Welfare Services* (London: HMSO, 1959).
34. *Report of the Committee on Local Authority and Allied Personal Social Services*, Cmnd 3703, 1968.
35. Ibid., para 495.
36. Wolfenden Committee, *The Future of Voluntary Organisations* (London: Croom Helm, 1978).
37. R. Crossman, 'The Role of the Volunteer in the Modern Social Services', in A. H. Halsey (ed.), *Traditions of Social Policy. Essays in Honour of Violet Butler* (Oxford: Blackwell, 1976).
38. Maria Brenton, *The Voluntary Sector in British Social Services* (London: Longman, 1985); Marilyn Taylor, 'The Changing Role of the Nonprofit Sector in Britain: Moving Toward the Market', in B. Gidron, R. Kramer, and L. M. Salamon (eds), *Government and the Third Sector: Emerging Relationships in Welfare States* (New York: Jossey Bass, 1992); and Barbara Waine, 'The Voluntary Sector – the Thatcher Years', in N. Manning and R. Page (eds), *Social Policy Review* 4 (London: Social Policy Association, 1992) all provide overviews.
39. F. Gladstone, *Voluntary Action in a Changing World* (London: Bedford Square Press, 1979).

40. See also Hatch, *Outside the State*.
41. Department of Health, *Community Care in the Next Decade and Beyond, Policy Guidance* (London: HMSO, 1990); Dept of Health and Price Waterhouse, *Implementing Community Care. Purchaser, Commissioner and Provider Roles* (London: HMSO, 1991).
42. J. Le Grand, 'Quasi-Markets and Social Policy', *Economic Journal* 101 (September, 1991); and *Quasi-Markets and Community Care* (Bristol: School for Advanced Urban Studies, 1993).
43. S. Saxon Harrold, 'Competition, Resources and Strategy in the British Non-Profit Sector', in H. K. Anheier and W. Siebel (eds), *The Third Sector: Comparative Studies of Non-Profit Organisations* (New York: de Gruyter, 1990).
44. Association of Metropolitan Authorities, *Contracts for Social Care. The Local Authority View* (London: AMA, 1990).
45. National Council of Voluntary Organisations, *Working Party Report on Effectiveness in the Voluntary Sector* (London: NCVO, 1990).
46. Department of Health and Price Waterhouse, *Implementing Community Care. Purchaser, Commissioner and Provider Roles* (London: HMSO, 1991).
47. J. Lewis and H. Glennerster, *Implementing the New Community Care Policy* (Buckingham: Open University Press, 1996).
48. P. Self, *Government by the Market? The Politics of Public Choice* (London: Macmillan, 1993). p. 123.
49. M. Taylor and P. Hoggett, 'Quasi-Markets and the Transformation of the Independent Sector'. Paper given at the Quasi-Markets in Public Sector Service Delivery Conference, Bristol, School of Advanced Urban Studies, 22–4 March, 1993.
50. Billis, *Organising Public and Voluntary Agencies*.

5 From 'Problem Family' to 'Underclass', 1945–95

John Macnicol

INTRODUCTION

When they look back at the 20th century, future historians may well view the 1950s as its least typical decade. Peacetime full employment and steady economic growth may be seen as aberrations in a century characterised by recession, unemployment and military conflict. Yet today there is a tendency – of which both political right and left have been guilty – wilfully to misrepresent the 1950s. Conservatives indulge in a mythologising, idealising, 'reinvention of tradition' process, whereby that period is portrayed as a laissez-faire paradise before the 1960s ushered in permissiveness and a welfare explosion. The left have been equally guilty of depicting the 1950s as a time of Butskellite torpor, in which social policy issues were little discussed. According to this scenario, the social work profession is said to have been paralysed by a mindless 'psychiatric deluge' mentality; poverty remained undiscovered; substantial class and gender inequalities in access to good secondary education were tolerated; and the National Health Service complacently ignored all those important issues that were to come back and haunt it in the 1980s and 1990s.

To be sure, the existence of virtual full employment in the 1950s glued families and communities together, and gave economic hope to young people. We should not be surprised that, as a result, discussion of social problems was relatively muted. But there *was* discussion, even if its linguistic construction and analytical focus was different. This paper will explore the concern over a different kind of poverty from that which exercised the minds of British poverty warriors in the 1960s and 1970s. The 1950s debate on 'problem families' was highly contested, was at times sociologically quite challenging, and in several respects was a rehearsal for the 'underclass' debate of the 1980s and 1990s. Looking back at it reveals some striking continuities in the evolution of an 'underclass' discourse; but it also shows how much in

69

British society has changed over the last fifty years. The biggest difference of all is, of course, the changed structure of the labour market.

THE ORIGINS OF THE 'PROBLEM FAMILY' CONCEPT

Broadly speaking, the debate over the 'problem family' arose from
two obvious sources. The first, immediate, one was the evacuation of
schoolchildren at the start of the Second World War, an episode
which gave rise to considerable middle-class concerns over the existence of an incorrigible 'submerged tenth' within the population. The
famous quotation from the Women's Group on Public Welfare's study
of evacuation, *Our Towns* (1943) – which was widely read and
absorbed – encapsulates this concern:

> The effect of evacuation was to flood the dark places with light and
> bring home to the national consciousness that the 'submerged
> tenth' described by Charles Booth still exists in our towns like a
> hidden sore, poor, dirty, and crude in its habits, an intolerable and
> degrading burden to decent people forced by poverty to neighbour
> with it. Within this group are the 'problem families', always on the
> edge of pauperism and crime, riddled with mental and physical
> neglect, a menace to the community, of which the gravity is out of
> all proportion to their numbers.[1]

The historical evidence of the condition of evacuee children is tanta-
lisingly elusive because that evidence was filtered through the distorting lens of middle-class-prejudiced social observation. Most accounts
of the evacuation experience – and certainly those that passed into
popular folklore – are anecdotal, impressionistic and emotionally
charged (reflective of a number of factors, including the collective ner-
vousness felt within British society at the start of the War). The
stereotypical image of the inner-city evacuee child as a lice-ridden,
incontinent, foul-mouthed, 'street urchin' was not substantiated by
systematic Government medical inspections in later waves of evacuation (which showed that such cases were a small minority), though in
these later waves the children were probably better prepared for their
ordeal.[2]

Two opinion lobbies were particularly influential in launching the
'problem family' concept by offering up their own analysis of the
evacuation experience. The first was that loose grouping of voluntary

organisations, predominantly female and middle class, that helped evacuees to settle into their new surroundings in reception areas. These helpers were over-inclined to place the worst possible construction on the temporary symptoms of emotional distress displayed by the evacuee children. It was these highly-charged, class-prejudicial accounts of the children's behaviour that gave the impression that a large section of the British working class were the 'great unwashed', living lives of dirt, disorder and incorrigible irresponsibility, their bodies riddled by headlice and impetigo, lacking elementary domestic manners, and culturally alienated – in short, urban savages of the worst kind.

The second influence was the Pacifist Service Units (PSU). These were teams of conscientious objectors (often Quakers) who, during the War, performed social work with bombed-out families, instead of serving in the Armed Forces. Pacifist Service Units had been formed in 1942–3 initially in Liverpool, Manchester and Stepney, East London. Much of PSU work was practical and non-judgemental – for example, physically moving a family to a new home, redecorating it, and finding replacement furniture – and arose directly from bomb destruction rather than family dysfunction. But there was a section within the PSU movement which was particularly disturbed by the 'discovery' of inner city poverty. During the War the Units worked with 'difficult' families, for whom billets were hard to find (for example, those with maladjusted children). Spurred on by the anecdotal revelations of evacuation, more conservative spirits within the PSU began to clarify and define the *raison d'être* of their work – particularly when the decision was made to continue such work after the War, taking on (in 1947) the name 'Family Service Units' (FSU) and merging it into mainstream social work practice.

But the evacuation experience and its aftermath were really only the catalyst: in eugenic circles, concerted attempts were made to present 'problem families' as the descendants of the hereditary 'social problem group' of the 1930s which, in turn, was believed to have developed out of the 'residuum' before the First World War. This certainly was the view of the most enthusiastic propagandists of the 'problem family' idea. Most notably, Dr C. P. Blacker (General Secretary of the Eugenics Society) adopted the technique currently deployed by New Right think-tanks in Britain and America: that of endlessly repeating an idea (in self-sponsored publications) in the hope that repetition will confer upon such an idea the status of a self-evident truth. Hence on numerous occasions Blacker and other eugenic enthusiasts insisted that 'problem families' possessed a clear collective pedigree. Their ancestors had been 'periodically exposed to the limelight of publicity', and concerns over the existence of such a group were traceable back to Charles Booth's *Life and Labour*, the 1909 Report of the Royal Commission on the Poor Laws, the 1913 Report of the Royal Commission on the Care and Control of the Feeble-Minded, the 1929 Report of the Wood Committee on Mental Deficiency, the researches of E. J. Lidbetter and David Caradog Jones in the 1930s, and so on.[3] In *Problem Families: Five Enquiries* (1952), Blacker devoted several pages to an outline of these long-term origins.[4]

Others argued – as commentators in the USA were to argue in the 1960s – that full employment, economic growth and a comprehensive welfare state had brought about exactly that state of affairs dreamed of by inter-war 'reform eugenists', such as Leonard Darwin: the creation of such a high quality environment that the genetic or behavioural defects of the social problem group were now sharply revealed like beached driftwood at low tide. 'Comprehensive medical services and comprehensive National Insurance will necessarily draw further attention to this group', wrote Blacker, and Seebohm Rowntree observed that:

> As the economic level of the poorest class is raised and their standards of welfare are improved, the problem families stand out more clearly as a minority who do not benefit from the improved conditions, but remain a menace and a disgrace to the community.[5]

Indeed, it became something of a cliché in social work literature that problem families were, quite simply, those who very obviously failed to utilise all the new services of a comprehensive welfare state.

THE 'PROBLEM FAMILY' SURVEYS

By the late 1940s, three broad opinion groups had become extremely interested in the 'problem family' idea – the Eugenics Society, the Family Service Units, and some local medical officers of health. There was a natural convergence of interest between these three groups, but each brought its own agenda to the study of the problem and this, as we shall see, was to create considerable tensions in the research work and was to weaken enormously the viability of the 'problem family' concept.

The decision to undertake systematic research into 'problem families' was taken in 1946–7, just about the time that the Pacifist Service Units changed their name and began a conscious campaign to attain greater respectability within the social work profession. Inside the portals of the Eugenics Society, a leading spirit seems to have been Dr Fred Grundy, MOH for Luton, whose espousal of a genetic model of mental deficiency went back to the early 1930s, and who suggested to Blacker that the Society's long-standing research into the social problem group could profitably be re-activated in this new form. At about the same time (early in 1947), David Jones (Secretary of the FSU Executive Committee) corresponded with Blacker on the desirability of mounting a co-operative investigation.[6] Accordingly, a Problem Families Committee was formed in 1947, and supervised research in six areas: these were later reduced to five – North Kensington, Bristol, West Riding, Rotherham and Luton. The Committee was chaired by Blacker, with C. G. Tomlinson as organising secretary; it included Lord Horder, David Jones, Richard Titmuss (who appears to have discreetly dropped out at some point), and the local medical officers of health who were to co-ordinate the fieldwork.

For the Eugenics Society, the 'problem family' research was an important effort in self-rehabilitation. The outbreak of the Second World War seemed to have fatally discredited the eugenics movement, given that Britain was fighting the most crudely eugenic regime in world history. The social disruptions of wartime also temporarily dispersed the small but highly influential network of London-based social intelligentsia who ran the Eugenics Society and kept up its propaganda. But hardline eugenics (stressing negative eugenics) was being diluted anyway in the 1930s with the emergence of a more cosmetically-acceptable 'reform eugenics' that stressed positive eugenics rather than more controversial negative eugenic policies (such as sterilisation). The reincarnation of the 'social problem group', phoenix-like, from the ashes of its own discredit in the late 1930s was thus not entirely surprising, for the 'problem family' concept was a logical outgrowth of 'reform eugenics' and was to reawaken all the dilemmas and ambiguities contained within the latter.

Bedecked in new sociological clothing, the broad idea of an hereditary 'underclass' was resurrected in a form more acceptable to the postwar world. Anxious to re-establish its waning academic credibility, the Eugenics Society tried to build bridges with 'legitimate' research enterprises, such as the London School of Economics project on the social grading of occupations: the arch-eugenist David Caradog Jones helped with this project, and Sir A. M. Carr-Saunders, David Glass and, later, Richard Titmuss (all key Eugenics Society members) acted as intellectual conduits. The eagerness with which Eugenics Society leaders returned to the task of ascertaining the underclass of its day is an indication of how blissfully untouched they had been by the supposed 'egalitarian consensus' of the War years, and of how insubstantial and impermanent that consensus actually was.

The second group contributing to the 'problem family' debate was the Family Service Units which, as we have noted, were the wartime Pacifist Service Units renamed. The FSU were avowedly un-ideological in outlook, stressing the importance of practical, non-judgemental intervention. As Sir John Wolfenden was to comment later, FSU work involved 'continuous long-term casework with the family as a whole and continuous compassion'.[7] What such language symbolised was a peculiarly British, home-grown trend in social work thinking that acted in opposition to the scientism of Freudian psychiatric social work (much more dominant in America in the 1950s). If in retrospect PSU sentiments strike one as nebulous in the extreme, it is because they deliberately sought to minimise jargon and mystification: the emphasis was on the 'ordinary', taking pride in the intimacy of human relations between caseworker and client, uncluttered by grand theory. At times, this gave 'problem family' discussions a touch of the bizarre – as, for instance, when one social worker suggested that the answer was to give a family lessons in barn-dancing, and another spoke proudly of supplying a home help who cooked appetising puddings for the husband ('since the time that the home help had been there, he had eaten every one').[8] Rather more perceptively, Tom Stephens remarked (of the early Pacifist Service Units):

> The Units approached social work as willing amateurs: few of their members had relevant experience or theoretical training, and these had to be acquired as the work progressed. They came to it with little more than open minds, a willingness to learn and an enthusiastic devotion to the job.

Interestingly, Stephens suggested that, as pacifists (some of whom had served prison sentences for their beliefs during the War), the Unit members

> had a particular sympathy for the outcast, and in rejecting the suggestion that any family could be abandoned as beyond redemption

they were giving expression to their fundamental belief in the value of the individual.

He acknowledged, however, that subsequently 'a professional outlook', involving 'some theoretical training' did develop.[9] FSU thus sought to mount evaluative research studies that would demonstrate the success of this directly interpersonal approach. Their purpose in researching problem families was to 'undertake intensive and comprehensive welfare work' among them; such work 'would be *experimental*, endeavouring to develop suitable methods of rehabilitation and assisting such families'.[10] Hence FSU definitions of a 'problem family' frequently contained revealing phrases such as 'needing special assistance', 'hard to reach' or 'inability to raise themselves by unaided efforts'. Thus in pushing the 'problem family' concept, some FSU leaders were clearly engaged in a process of professionalising their work and trying to set up a casework method at odds with mainstream psychiatric social work.

The third group involved in the 'problem family' debate of the 1950s consisted of a number of local medical officers of health. During the War, medical officers had become more closely involved with the social and human consequences of bombing, evacuation and all the attendant social problems. For example, as the government department with the major responsibility for the evacuation scheme, the Ministry of Health had to organise the billeting arrangements for 'difficult' children (those needing special care or supervision, such as child guidance), including the establishment of special hostels for them, and ensure that local medical officers carried out such instructions.[11] The War brought medical officers into closer contact with the very poorest, inner-city families; after the War, a number of them published articles highlighting the existence of 'problem families', and these were eagerly seized upon by the Eugenics Society leaders. In its 'problem family' research, the Society worked in close co-operation with several local medical officers. It is significant that the period 1945–8 was the starting-point for systematic 'problem family' research, for this was the period of the National Health Service's establishment. Not unnaturally, medical officers of health were seeking to carve out an influential new role in the forthcoming Service. Ultimately, they were to see their functions usurped by, on the one hand, high-technology hospital medicine, and, on the other, the expanding social work profession. But in the late 1940s and early 1950s their foray into the 'problem family' debate was partly a defining of professional interest.

CONFLICTS OF PERSPECTIVE

Each of these interest groups brought to the 'problem family' debate its own perspective; and this immediately gave rise to conflict, particularly between the Eugenics Society and the Family Service Units. (As Barbara Wootton remarked, the construction of 'problem family syndromes' reflected 'not only the objective facts of problem family life, but also in equal measure the subjective interests of the investigators concerned'.)[12] The most important source of conflict was the FSU conviction that 'problem families' could be socialised back into respectability by intensive rehabilitation. This conviction is hardly surprising, given that the principal *raison d'être* of the FSU was just such rehabilitative social work. Thus the FSU pamphlet *Problem Families* contained lurid descriptions of domestic squalor, and implied that such families represented the continuance of the 'social problem group' identified by the Wood Committee and Caradog Jones in the inter-war years. One part of the analysis was thus infused by a pessimistic, hereditarian determinism, hinting that defective germ plasm was to blame. But the analysis then concluded on an optimistic note, implying behavioural causes that could be remedied:

> In the light of five years' experience among these problem families in Liverpool and Manchester, it can be stated quite definitely that their condition of life, both material and spiritual, can be improved.[13]

Likewise, in another publication the FSU declared that 'the essence' of its work among such families was 'a personal relationship, tirelessly patient, rejecting no situation as hopeless',[14] and when the FSU prepared a film strip on problem families, for use at public meetings, the emphasis in the accompanying script was on the transforming effect of intensive social work with such families. The implication was that a dramatic change of environment could effect an equally dramatic change in behaviour:

> The bedroom – once squalid and fouled, now clean and inviting. Though poorly furnished with only the barest necessities it is a room in which new found pride and respect are evidenced.[15]

Indeed, the frequent reliance on the definition of 'problem families' as those unable to take care of themselves 'without special assistance' is indicative of this self-promotion by the FSU.[16] By contrast, a central definition used by the Eugenics Society was 'intractable in-educability', a concept which, if viable, would have rendered pointless the optimistic, rehabilitative approach of the FSU. At the core of eugenics as an ideology was the conviction that human beings were irredeemably programmed by their genetic endowment from the moment of conception. Thus the FSU always preferred to see the problem as one of *family* malfunctioning, whereas the Eugenics Society was, as always, anxious to prove that 'problem families' con-stituted a coherent intergenerational *class*, composed of genetically deficient individuals.[17]

Finally, we should note that the FSU showed scant concern for the process of searching for causes, whereas for the Eugenics Society this was everything. Generally, FSU social workers were uninterested in the construction of long-term eugenic pedigrees – indeed, on one occasion A. F. Philp went so far as to declare that 'before the War no-one talked about problem families'[18] – preferring to define the condition of the families and then evaluate the remedial power of intervention precisely tailored to the needs of those individuals within such families. For the FSU, evaluative research was all-important; by contrast, the Eugenics Society really had nothing to evaluate.

'EASY TO RECOGNISE, BUT HARD TO DEFINE': METHODOLOGICAL PROBLEMS

The results of the Eugenics Society's research were published in 1952 as C. P. Blacker's *Problem Families: Five Enquiries*. (A volume devoted to Bristol was also published separately by R. C. Wofinden.)[19] Space does not permit a detailed account of this work, other than in the general points made below. It is sufficient to say that the results were, at best, tentative, and, at worst, little more than pure speculation. Frequently, Blacker had to apologise for the incompleteness of the findings, and at the outset rather lamely announced that 'these inquiries are to be regarded not as exhaustive factual reports but as experiments in method'.[20] Only a small proportion warranted having the 'problem' label attached to them: North Kensington, 0.26 per cent of all families; Bristol, 0.14 per cent; West Riding, 0.12 per cent; Rotherham, 0.35 per cent; Luton, 0.62 per cent. This accorded with estimates by other medical officers, which generally quantified 'problem families' as containing roughly one per cent to two per cent of the total population.

The greatest difficulty encountered by Blacker was that of opera-tionalising the many impressionistic accounts of 'problem families' that existed, and ensuring that there was some consistency of definition across the five areas surveyed. A with today's 'underclass' debate, many social observers in the 1950s agreed that an undeniable 'problem' existed in the form of a new, disturbing and very visible kind of family poverty; but there was considerable disagreement over whether it could be measured by objective indicators, and, more importantly, over its causes.

All hardline proponents of the 'problem family' idea faced enor-mous difficulties created by the economic and social conditions of postwar Britain. The most important of these was the fact that improved economic circumstances in the postwar world had destroyed 'unemployability' as a viable defining characteristic, whereas it had been accorded great prominence in the litany of social failures attrib-uted to the inter-war 'social problem group'. During the Second World War, many citizens previously marginal to the labour market were drawn into employment. Considerable attention has been paid to the temporary wartime work of women.[21] Less research has been done on the sudden increase in labour force participation by men and women aged 65 or over, and still less on the way in which groups of people who previously had been extremely marginal to the labour market, for reasons of ill-health or disability, were re-industrialised. One such group was the mentally handicapped (or 'mentally defec-tive', as they had been known in the 1930s). During the War, there took place, in effect, a natural experiment, the results of which con-vincingly refuted the standard pre-war 'social incompetence' definition of mental deficiency: the mentally handicapped proved that they could be economically self-sufficient, and even behaved in such thoroughly capitalist ways as opening bank accounts. As one observer recorded:

The higher grade mentally defective adult in the community became a national asset instead of a liability almost overnight, and this extended to a number of the lower grade. It became relatively easy to place in employment those leaving schools for the educa-tionally subnormal.[22]

The 1950s also saw considerable advances in the care and treatment of the mentally handicapped: for example, it was shown that intensive therapy could improve the intellectual performance of 'higher grade' defectives.[23] If the hard core of the 1930s 'social problem group' could vanish so quickly, then those inhabiting the periphery were even more remediable.

The continuation of full employment in the 1950s presented a potentially serious difficulty, for no longer could it be argued that labour market failure was caused by poor genetic endowment. Full employment also made it impossible to use the simple and easy definition used by proponents of the 'social problem group' concept of the inter-war years – that of welfare dependency (or, in E. J. Lidbetter's case, Poor Law 'chargeability'). This essentially 'administrative' definition had been open to considerable criticism (notably, that the size of the social problem group depended in great measure upon the eligibility criteria for receipt of state benefits), but it had the advantage of producing a quick and easy quantification. No longer was this possible: Blacker's survey found that fully 46.3 per cent of 'problem family' households investigated contained male heads in regular employment, and 28.1 per cent in casual employment; only 10.2 per cent were unemployed.[24] Thus researchers tended to rely upon the much more ephemeral indicator of contact with a range of local social services, or upon vaguely condemnatory descriptions of social incompetence.

We can see this if we briefly examine some of the instant definitions of 'problem families', for all of them implied social incompetence without being able to offer any precise quantitative measure of it, and did so in language that verges on the surreal or the tautological: families presenting 'an abnormal amount of subnormal behaviour over prolonged periods, with a marked tendency to backsliding' (C. O. Stallybrass); 'rudderless barques with flapping sails drifting on the social tide, driven hither and thither by any momentary gust of emotion' (C.O. Stallybrass); those 'who, for their own well-being and for the well-being of others... for reasons unconnected with old age, accident, misfortune, illness or pregnancy, require a substantially greater degree of supervision and help over longer periods than is usually provided by existing services' (C. G. Tomlinson); 'a family becomes a problem when it really cannot, itself, cope with its own problems' (E. Stephenson).[25]

But what unpalatable modes of behaviour were represented by such loose definitions, and what concealed meanings were contained therein (such as the militaristic metaphor of 'backsliding')? In practice, the focus of concern usually shifted sideways from the male breadwinner to the 'domestically incompetent' mother. It is striking how frequently, in 'problem family' literature, women were blamed more than men, this even extending to the biologisation of social failure. For example, Blacker's survey found that half of male heads of 'problem families' were below normal intelligence, but fully two-thirds of housewives were. This, he concluded, was 'in general accordance with expectation, though it is possible that the intelligence of house-wives may have been underestimated through their frequent ill-health and their not infrequent condition of depression or rejection'.[26]

However, maternal incompetence was difficult to measure in an era of intact families, high marriage rates and low illegitimacy ratios. Here is an interesting contrast to today's debate on the underclass, in which single parenthood figures prominently. A major contributory factor to today's high ratio of out-of-wedlock births has been the declining rate of marriage, which has meant that a decreasing proportion of premarital conceptions are regularised by marriage before the birth of the baby: basically, the 'shotgun wedding' is a less frequent occurrence. In the late 1940s, marriage rates were high. Thus although nearly 30 per cent of all mothers conceived their first-born child out of wedlock (this proportion being as high as 42 per cent for those aged under 20), these pre-marital conceptions were overwhelmingly regularised by subsequent marriage.[27]

What, then, *was* 'family failure'? Clearly, it was not illegitimacy, for Blacker found only 14 per cent of 'problem family' households had one or more illegitimate children, and fully 77.5 per cent of their housewives were married. Average family size was 4.5 children (and not necessarily completed fertility). High fertility was seen by Blacker as a defining characteristic of such families. But this hardly constituted 'family failure'; if anything, it was the reverse. Nor could it be encap-sulated by a precise legal definition. There was, in fact, an interesting tension between legalistic and therapeutic definitions: most FSU social workers were unwilling to identify 'problem families' as those so incor-rigible as to have their children classified as 'neglected', and thus fall foul of the law. Despite the previously-quoted statement by the Women's Group on Public Welfare that such families were 'in and out of the courts for child neglect', child-neglecting families were gener-ally not seen as the same as problem families. To have conflated the two would have simplified the definitional process considerably, and reduced problem families to a tiny number; also, the possibility of re-socialising them back into respectability would have been judged as remote. The FSU liked to think that they possessed the power to intervene and *prevent* a family falling foul of the courts. Problem fami-lies were thus seen as occupying a niche above 'child neglecting' fami-lies but below the lowest stratum of the 'respectable' working class.

Nor was a 'problem family' one in which children were deprived of love. Proponents of the concept had to give grudging acknowledgement to the fact that parental affection was evident in such families, even if it was expressed in 'rough' behaviour foreign to the more restrained middle-class family dynamic. The difficulty of reconciling both male breadwinning and parental affection with the overall judgement of social and familial failure is well summed up in the following convoluted passage:

Real poverty is not the primary cause of their condition, but all the symptoms of poverty may arise out of their fecklessness and apparent inability to learn. Although sometimes possessed of low cunning, it is generally found that one or both parents are of a mental stature below normal. If this is the breadwinner, he is usually unfit for any but the unskilled and relatively low-paid tasks... Carelessness and irresponsibility rather than a wilful disregard of his duties are his common characteristic, and when cruelty arises out of this conduct it is seldom intentional, for there is usually a strong, if misdirected, affection between parents and children. For example, the father will quite unnecessarily lose a day's work to accompany the mother and a child with a minor ailment to the hospital or clinic.[28]

Faced with a solid phalanx of intact families, 'problem family' researchers focused instead on sexual promiscuity, underlying marital conflict, mis-spending of household income and, most of all, domestic disorder and squalor. At the epicentre of this whirlpool of domestic chaos was said to be the incompetent mother. However, here researchers faced more difficulties. Dirt and uncleanliness could be held up as emblems of social failure, but measuring them was another matter. (Incredibly, Blacker hinted at one point that a certain Edgar McCoy, of Manchester University, had devised a methodology for quantifying household squalor.)[29] Proponents of 'problem family' concept thus tended to rely upon cultural judgements that looked highly suspect. In short, most of the definitions of 'problem families' were essentially *descriptions* of household squalor, piled high one on top of the other. This was a point made by critics: that the definitional process merely described symptoms, and never revealed causes. As Philp and Timms commented, these descriptions involved 'amalgamation of traits taken from several different families rather than actual cases'[30] – a kind of composite social work nightmare. The construction of such ethnographic stereotypes produced some remarkably lurid passages. The most famous, by R. C. Wofinden, is long, but worth quoting in full, as it is a classic of its kind:

> Almost invariably it is a large family, some of the children being dull or feeble-minded. From their appearance they are strangers to soap and water, toothbrush and comb; the clothing is dirty and torn and the footgear absent or totally inadequate. Often they are verminous and have scabies and impetigo. Their nutrition is surprisingly average – doubtless partly due to extra-familial feeding in schools. The mother is frequently substandard mentally. The home, if indeed it can be described as such, has usually the most striking characteristics. Nauseating odours assail one's nostrils on entry, and the source is usually located in some urine-sodden, faecal-stained mattress in an upstairs room. There are no floor coverings, no decorations on the walls except perhaps the scribblings of the children and bizarre patterns formed by absent plaster. Furniture is of the most primitive, cooking utensils absent, facilities for sleeping hopeless – iron bedsteads furnished with fouled mattresses and no coverings. Upstairs there is flock everywhere, which the mother assures us has come out of a mattress she has unpacked for cleansing. But the flock seems to stay there for weeks and the cleansed and repacked mattress never appears. The bathroom is obviously the least frequented room of the building. There are sometimes faecal accumulations on the floors upstairs, and tin baths containing several days' accumulation of faeces and urine are not unknown... The children, especially the older ones, often seem to be perfectly happy and contented, despite such a shocking environment. They will give a description of how a full-sized midday meal has been cooked and eaten in the house on the day of the visit, when the absence of cooking utensils gives the lie to their assertions... One can only conclude that such children have never known restful sleep, that the amount of housework done by the mother is negligible, and that the general standard of hygiene is lower than that of the animal world.[31]

This positively elegiac passage is fascinating for its internal contradictions, unjustified assumptions and disconnected reasoning, which even the most elementary textual critique reveals. The symbols of household disorder are striking. Even more interesting is the obsession with incontinence as a metaphor for social failure – as if anal retention were a symbol of capital accumulation – and general household squalor. (Clearly, coals were not the only thing being kept in the bath.) Blacker's rationalisation of such purple passages – that they could be 'a guide to field-workers in what to look for'[32] – was disingenuous. In decoding such passages we are in the territory so brilliantly explored by Mary Douglas's *Purity and Danger* (1966).[33]

It is clear that such 'ethnographic overload' was a product of the impossibility of constructing agreed indicators of 'problem family' membership. Fifty years later, we cannot peer into these family homes and compare our reactions with those of contemporary social workers and researchers, many of whom were clearly disturbed by what they found. But one text did offer some photographic evidence – Tom Stephens's *Problem Families: an Experiment in Social Rehabilitation* (1945). Most of the photos were of appalling housing conditions, and the obvious conclusion to be drawn was that the 'problem' under scrutiny was environmental and economic. However, one photo was of a 'problem family' (minus the male breadwinner and two of the children). (It is a tribute to the values of the time that a client's photograph could be published for public scrutiny in such a way. This level of intrusion – and violation of social work professional confidentiality – would be unthinkable today.) The caption accompanying the photo reads:

> Mother. The child in her arms is nearly four and cannot walk or talk; the other child is almost beyond control. In addition, her eldest child is mentally defective and the baby is in hospital with rickets. Living in one room at a rent of twelve shillings.

Yet it is possible to interpret the photographic message in an entirely different way: the mother is bright-eyed, feistily defiant, and seems to have taken trouble with her appearance (she is wearing a ribbon); clearly, personal appearance matters to her, for the room boasts a mirror; the younger child who allegedly cannot walk is wearing shoes with worn soles (admittedly they could well be hand-me-downs); the older child has the mother's spark in her eyes. All in all, it is the backdrop scene of late-1940s British slum housing (in Salford) that strikes one as the 'problem'. Nowhere in the commentary is it explained why a family of six people is living in one room at a rent of twelve shillings a week – roughly half as much again as the equivalent National Assistance Board rent allowance.[34]

THE SURVEYS

These methodological problems were clearly revealed when the Problem Families Committee constructed a research design. Local MOHs were to liaise with a wide range of statutory and voluntary authorities, and prominent individuals, in the targeted areas, with a view to compiling a list of families 'presenting various problems'. These authority figures included head teachers of schools, school medical officers, NSPCC inspectors, health visitors, district nurses, chief constables, borough treasurers, and so on: in other words, those who staffed the infrastructure of the local state and its attendant quasi-state bodies. Suggestions made by these would produce a 'primary list' of possible 'problem families' (details of which would be entered on standard forms). Some families would then be removed, until a 'consolidated list' of chronic 'problem families' was left:

> The list would then be pruned until it finally contained a residuum consisting of the authentic problem families as generally agreed by persons of experience viewing the subject from different angles.[35]

In this process of pruning, the scope for arbitrary judgement was enormous. The first distorting factor was the degree of efficiency of these surveillance authorities: the better developed (or better resourced) they were, the more widely would their net be cast. This has always been a problem in all underclass definitions, involving the conflation of behavioural or genetic defining characteristics with essentially artefactual, 'administrative' ones. Seizing upon this very point, Philp and Timms protested that 'administrative definitions in general depend so much upon the state of public administration at a particular time and place that they must be considered very limited'.[36] As Blacker himself weakly conceded on one occasion, 'the number of problem families deemed to exist in any community will depend on where the line is drawn by definition'.[37]

A second difficulty was that eugenists were no nearer to separating nature from nurture than they had been twenty years before. The primary list would inevitably include

> families whose predicaments have been brought about by circumstances largely outside their own control, such as accident, chronic illness, death of wage-earner and similar misfortune. Such families

should be excluded from the final list. The decision as to exclusion may in some cases be doubtful.[38]

In *Problem Families: Five Enquiries* (1952), Blacker thus felt obliged to contribute a long passage on this age-old sociological conundrum, wearily concluding that 'the interaction of nature and nurture is here so close as to make it exceedingly difficult to distinguish the separate effects of each'.[39]

A third difficulty was that of ascertaining families with 'multiple' social problems. In practice, 'multi-problem' families were defined as those known to several local agencies (again, an administrative rather than a sociological definition), and the impressionistic descriptions of problem families usually contained the confident statement that they (and their ancestors) were known to a wide range of local bodies. But empirical evidence of this was unconvincing. For example, Dr William Barr's survey of Rotherham ascertained 78 suspected problem families. Of these, only one had been mentioned by four local bodies; ten had three mentions; twelve had two mentions; and fully 55 had only one mention each. No notifications at all were received from seven bodies: intriguingly, these included the police, probation officers and Barr's fellow medical officers.[40]

Nor were the principal defining characteristics chosen by the Problem Families Committee much help. At the heart of a problem family's condition was said to be the 'mental backwardness' and 'temperamental instability' of the parents, which were said to compound three other features. The first of these was 'intractable ineducability'. (As has already been noted, such fatalism jarred with the FSU's optimistic standpoint.) In order to make this definition as elastic as possible, it was to comprise 'more than an inability to progress at school: it embraces the wider idea of failure to learn how to behave in the home and in the community'. Thus could the subjective judgements of the investigators be factored in. The second characteristic was 'a squalid home wherein dirt and chaos reign'; again, this was conveniently open to interpretation. Third was the birth of numerous 'unwanted children' as well as 'high wastage-rates' (miscarriages and still-births); the question of what was or was not a 'wanted child' was entirely at the say of the investigator.[41]

Blacker hoped that several stages of consultation would reduce the scope for subjective and arbitrary judgements. The initial 'primary' list of families in each area was to be vetted by C. G. Tomlinson in order to produce some kind of consistency of judgement. Then Blacker and

Caradog Jones made a further scrutiny. The difficulties they faced can be judged from an exchange of correspondence between the two men – very revealing of the private unease beneath their public confidence. Having gone through the 'problem family' case studies, Caradog Jones was assailed by doubts. He wrote:

> Of the 24 sample cards from Bristol, I should say that No. 10 is definitely *not* a problem family now. *If* it ever was one, it deserves further study, because we have always rather assumed that the problems arose as a result of innate, and therefore rarely curable, defect.
>
> I am also disposed to query Nos. 2, 3 and 14. Evidence about condition of home in 2 is conflicting. The same applies to 3; most of the trouble here may be due to the husband's drinking habits with consequent discouragement to an unintelligent and weakly wife. In 14 the trouble again is due to the husband – ill-controlled temper, which reacts on the wife so that she looks ill.[42]

In reply, Blacker reassured his colleague that:

> Minor difficulties of interpretation are bound to arise and I have no doubt that differences of opinion are possible on what families should be included and excluded from the final list of 'authentic' families.[43]

There was a great danger that, in practice, judgements would be made according to middle class social norms and expectations. Though Blacker was aware of this danger, other eugenists were not. Sir A. M. Carr-Saunders believed that the Society should investigate both ends of the social scale – 'promising' families and well as 'problem' ones. He wrote confidently:

> Given good sense, experience and the opportunity for observation, it is not at all difficult to identify the promising family. If in any small community the parson, the midwife, the schoolmaster and the nurse put their heads together – in any country village for instance – they would easily pick out the promising as they would the problem families. There would be of course the difficulty of where to draw the line between the worthy and the promising, as there is between the poor and the problem. And this is because the line must be arbitrary.[44]

In the localities, the investigators also faced difficulties. R. C. Wofinden found that, in Bristol, an additional dozen problem families came to light after the investigation, and had doubts about the methods of ascertainment.[45] E. O. Lewis (who had conducted a survey of mental defectives for the Wood Committee in the late 1920s, and whose views were thus considered important) felt that, apart from Bristol, the surveys had been 'far from thorough'. He concluded that MOHs had 'but partial knowledge of the social conditions generally in their areas'.[46]

GROWING CRITICISMS

It would be quite wrong to see the 'problem family' concept as wholly dominant in the world of 1950s social work. As has already been noted, psychiatric social workers tended to distance themselves from the cheerful amateurism of the FSU; but they were equally anxious to discredit the biological determinism of the eugenists, and instead offer salvation through psychotherapy. An example of this was Elizabeth Irvine's review of Blacker's *Problem Families* in the *British Journal of Psychiatric Social Work* for May 1954. Irvine attacked Blacker's methodology as slipshod, and focused on the greatest weakness in all his writings on social questions – the tendency to draw confident conclusions from evidence that was incomplete and allusive. She pointed out that Blacker had used the essentially subjective judgements of local authority staff, she criticised the imprecision of defining characteristics like 'temperamental instability', and she suggested that it was quite wrong to see all such socially defective families as suffering from 'a unitary pathological condition': in fact, there was probably a great variety of personality disorders at work, at the root of which was emotional immaturity. Irvine thus viewed the domestic disorders in 'problem family' homes – and even the lack of toilet training – as indicators of the emotionally-retarded, childlike personalities of their inhabitants. Caustically, she warned:

If concepts and hypotheses are not clearly understood and defined, and if the greatest care is not taken to secure factual data of the highest possible reliability, the subjection of these data to statistical techniques will only yield a pseudo-science.[47]

The unease felt by many family caseworkers was illustrated by David Donnison's *The Neglected Child and the Social Services* (1954), a study in Manchester and Salford of 118 families whose children came into public care. Donnison's meticulous analysis of the families' circumstances revealed an enormous variety of causal factors (most of the families having suffered a fairly obvious misfortune) and high-lighted the success of practical intervention, from planning family budgets to scrubbing floors, washing children and redecorating the home. Like many at the time, Donnison seems to have felt some ambi-guity towards the broad 'problem family' idea: for example, he praised the work of Family Service Units 'among families whose squalid and disorderly lives make them a burden on the community', but insisted that child neglect was 'often a symptom of the extreme apathy bred by poverty, ignorance, poor health, bad housing, low intelligence, and other handicaps'.[48] Another detailed study into 52 allegedly 'problem' families was carried out by Harriett Wilson, who concluded that they displayed a wide heterogeneity of social conditions; with considerable sophistication, she explored the enormous difficulties involved in meas-uring their apparent failure to live up to 'normal' social behaviour.[49]

The most powerful sociological critique came from Noel Timms who, more than anyone else, injected a dose of heavy scepticism into the 'problem family' debate throughout the 1950s. Drawing upon the sociologist Robert Merton's work (and anticipating Hyman Rodman's idea of the 'value stretch'), Timms suggested that an observable gap existed between the cultural goals sought by the members of a 'problem family' and their means to achieve those goals – what Merton called 'retreatism'. Examining a group of clients of a social work agency, Timms found clear evidence of what today would be called 'mainstream aspirations':

We found that rarely, if ever, was there a clear indication that the standards of conformist behaviour had been completely abandoned. Even at the lower end of the scale, the usual norms and codes of respectability, cleanliness and discipline are frequently reproduced at the slightest provocation.

But in observing the families' behaviour, it was necessary to distin-guish between 'real' and 'nominal' standards: lip-service would be paid to the latter, by the frequent use of 'nominal clichés'. Timms noted that 'lofty ideals and strict rules, particularly concerning children, are often stressed despite the most glaring failure to live up to such values.' Thus an investigator should not conclude – as many pro-ponents of the 'problem family' idea had concluded – that domestic disorder was an indication of a lack of standards: instead, the blocks to achieving those standards should be investigated, and these were often caused by poverty, ill-health, low vitality, lack of personal initiative or 'subnormal intelligence'.[50]

By the early 1960s, the 'problem family' had been subjected to a series of devastating critiques. Most notably, Philp and Timms, in *The Problem of 'The Problem Family'* (1957), had placed all component parts of the concept under the most intense sociological scrutiny, and found them wanting. When Philp returned to the subject in 1963, his analysis reflected the shifts that were taking place in sociology: it stressed the economic difficulties of 'multiple problem' families, and their attendant complications (such as lower health status, or overcrowded housing conditions), and saw their personal failings as stemming from deficiencies of personality rather than hereditary weakness.[51]

THE 'UNDERCLASS' DEBATE

By the mid-1960s the 'rediscovery of poverty' was effecting yet another of several paradigmatic shifts in poverty studies over the course of the 20th century. According to one account, this had begun partly as a reaction against the way that psychiatric social workers like Elizabeth Irvine had labelled low-income families as 'emotionally immature'.[52] The 'problem family' thus slipped from public scrutiny. But two related ideas did resurface again – the 'culture of poverty' in the late 1960s, and then in the 1970s, the 'cycle of deprivation'. In what respects is it legitimate to see a linear development from 'problem family' to 'underclass', 1945–95?

Certain continuities can certainly be observed. The 1950s saw the demonisation of an apparently new and different kind of poverty – a poverty of lifestyle rather than a poverty of income, and one seen as sharply at odds with prevailing cultural norms. As in today's 'underclass' debate, the identification of 'problem families' involved a process of social distancing, or fear of 'the other', based upon class, gender and age (race had not yet entered the equation). Whereas today the focus is upon degraded lifestyles in 'underclass estates', or condemnatory accounts of 'welfare mothers' (involving what has been called 'the eroticisation of social problems'), in the 1950s it was household disorder and maternal incompetence that came under scrutiny. The idea of the 'problem family' was pushed strongly by a small but active pressure group – the Eugenics Society – in a way very similar to today's 'new right' think-tanks such as the Institute of Economic Affairs and the Manhattan Institute. Like the underclass debate of today, the 'problem family' concept relied upon the conflation of essentially artefactual, administrative definitions with behavioural ones; and, in practice, this usually amounted to quasi-ethnographic descriptions of degraded lifestyles. A complex variety of human conditions was reduced to one unitary category. In the 1950s, as in the 1990s, most thoughtful observers agreed that a very visible 'problem' existed. But there was substantial disagreement over its causes, ranging from poor housing conditions to unalterable genetic defect.

Yet in many respects the 1950s were in a different era. Re-stimulated by the Second World War, the old heavy industries were able to deliver jobs to the mass of the male workforce. Now the labour market does not do that, and there is real concern for the plight of unskilled young males. Correlated with declining male labour market opportunities there has occurred a set of inter-related changes in demographic and family-formation behaviour. Whether or not one accepts all the apocalyptic implications of the arrival of a 'post-industrial' society based upon 'disorganised' capitalism, it is clear that, if these still-minority trends continue, they will constitute a significant new phase of the demographic transition. The 1990s 'underclass' debate has been frequently driven by an empirically simplistic, political agenda that seeks to blame 'over-generous' welfare payments. Viewed as a consequence of the transition to a more globalised, 'postindustrial' economic base, however, the current concerns about widening social polarisation are very disturbing. The old FSU remedy of scrubbing floors and painting walls will do little to prevent the growth of a permanent 'two-thirds/one-third' society. In that respect, the 1950s do appear to be years of optimism and hope.

Notes

1. Women's Group on Public Welfare, *Our Towns: a Close-Up* (London: Oxford University Press, 1943), p. xiii.
2. John Macnicol, 'The Effect of the Evacuation of Schoolchildren on Official Attitudes to State Intervention', in Harold Smith (ed.), *War and Social Change: British Society in the Second World War* (Manchester: Manchester University Press, 1986), pp. 3–31.
3. C. P. Blacker, 'Social Problem Families in the Limelight', *Eugenics Review*, Vol. XXXVIII, No. 3, Oct. 1946, p. 17.
4. C. P. Blacker, *Problem Families: Five Enquiries* (London: Eugenics Society, 1952), p. 9–12.

5. Blacker, 'Social Problem Families', op. cit., p. 17; Foreword by Rowntree, in Tom Stephens (ed.), *Problem Families: an Experiment in Social Rehabilitation* (London: Pacifist Service Units, 1945),p. vii.
6. Jones to Blacker, 4 Feb. 1947, Contemporary Medical Archives Centre (CMAC) Eug/D168 (London: Eugenics Society Archives, Wellcome Institute).
7. 'Foreword', in A. F. Philp, *Family Failure: a Study of 129 Families With Multiple Problems* (London: Faber, 1963), p. 7.
8. Comments by Miss E. Stephenson and Mrs P. Stead, in: County Councils Association, Association of Municipal Corporations and London County Council, *Welfare Conference, Held on 24th and 25th February, 1955: Report of Proceedings* (London: County Councils Association, Association of Municipal Corporations and London County Council, 1956), pp. 39, 45.
9. Stephens, op. cit., p. 45.
10. Memo, 'Family Service Units: Outline of Proposed Organisation' (1947), CMAC Eug/D168.
11. Ministry of Health, *Hostels for 'Difficult' Children* (London: HMSO, 1944).
12. Barbara Wootton, *Social Science and Social Pathology* (London: Allen & Unwin, 1959), p. 55.
13. Family Service Units pamphlet, *Problem Families* (n.d., c. late 1940s).
14. Family Service Units pamphlet, *Will You Help?* (1947).
15. Film strip script, 'Problem Families' (n.d.) CMAC Eug/D173.
16. Memo, 'Family Service Units: Outline of Proposed Organisation', op. cit.
17. See, for example, David Jones, 'Family Service Units for Problem Families', *Eugenics Review*, Vol. XLI, No. 4, Jan. 1950, p. 171.
18. *Family Failure*, op. cit., p. 15.
19. R. C. Wofinden, *Problem Families in Bristol* (London: Eugenics Society, 1950).
20. C. P. Blacker, 'Preface', in Blacker, *Problem Families*, op. cit.
21. For example, Penny Summerfield, *Women Workers in the Second World War* (London: Croom Helm, 1984).
22. Olive Bowtell, 'The Historical Background', in Margaret Adams (ed.), *The Mentally Subnormal: a Social Casework Approach* (London: Heinemann Medical, 1960), p. 12.
23. A. F. Philp, op. cit., p. 97.
24. Blacker, *Problem Families*, op. cit., p. 15.
25. C. O. Stallybrass, 'Problem Families', *The Medical Officer*, Vol. LXXV, 9 March 1946, p. 89; Stallybrass, 'Problem Families', *Social Work*, Vol. 4, No. 2, April 1947, p. 35; C. G. Tomlinson, *Families in Trouble: an Inquiry into Problem Families in Luton* (Luton: Gibbs, 1946), p. 11; E. Stephenson, in *Welfare Conference*, op. cit., p. 35.
26. Blacker, *Problem Families*, op. cit., pp. 64–5.
27. Sheila Ferguson and Hilde Fitzgerald, *Studies in the Social Services* (London: HMSO and Longmans, Green, 1954), p. 90.
28. Robert Oxen Black, 'Problem Families', typewritten article extract, 21 Jan. 1949, CMAC Eug/D169.

29. Blacker to Caradog Jones, 17 Oct. 1951, CMAC Eug/C193.
30. Philp and Timms, op. cit., p. 7.
31. R. C. Wofinden, 'Problem Families', *Public Health*, Vol. LVII, No. 2, Sept. 1944, p. 137.
32. Blacker, *Problem Families*, op. cit., p. 15.
33. Mary Douglas, *Purity and Danger: An Analysis of the Concepts of Pollution and Taboo* (London: Routledge, 1966).
34. Stephens, op. cit., p. 1 and facing.
35. Memo, 'Problem Families. Proposed Pilot Inquiries', Nov. 1947, CMAC Eug/D169.
36. A. F. Philp and Noel Timms, *The Problem of 'The Problem Family'* (London: Family Service Units, 1957), p. 6.
37. Blacker, *Problem Families*, op. cit., p. 21.
38. Memo, 'Problem Families', op. cit.
39. Blacker, *Problem Families*, op. cit., p. 28.
40. Barr to Blacker, 22 Aug. 1951, CMAC Eug/D170.
41. Blacker, *Problem Families*, op. cit., pp. 16–17.
42. Jones to Blacker, 25 Nov. 1949, CMAC Eug/C193.
43. Blacker to Jones, 1 Dec. 1949, ibid.
44. Note by Carr-Saunders, 'Proposed Galton Trust', 27 Nov. 1949, CMAC Eug/C58.
45. Wofinden to Blacker, 21 May 1951, CMAC Eug/D171.
46. Lewis to Blacker, 1 Feb. 1952, ibid.
47. Elizabeth E. Irvine, 'Research into Problem Families: Theoretical Questions Arising from Dr. Blacker's Investigations', *British Journal of Psychiatric Social Work*, Vol. 9, May 1954, pp. 24–33.
48. David Donnison, *The Neglected Child and the Social Services* (Manchester: Manchester University Press, 1954), esp. p. 89.
49. Harriett Wilson, *Delinquency and Child Neglect* (London: Allen & Unwin, 1962).
50. W. Baldamus and Noel Timms, 'The Problem Family: a Social Casework Approach', *British Journal of Sociology*, Vol. IV, No. 4, Dec. 1955, esp. pp. 319–23.
51. Philp and Timms, op. cit. See also, Barbara Wootton, op. cit., pp. 54–62.
52. See comments to this effect by Harriett Wilson in: Rodney Lowe and Paul Nicholson (eds), 'The Formation of the Child Poverty Action Group', *Contemporary Record*, Vol. 9, No. 3, Winter 1995, p. 614. For the original controversy, see: Harriett C. Wilson, 'Problem Families and the Concept of Immaturity', *Case Conference*, Vol. 6, No. 5, Oct. 1959, pp. 115–24, and Elizabeth E. Irvine, 'Some Notes on Problem Families and Immaturity', *Case Conference*, Vol. 6, No. 9, March 1960, pp. 255–8.

6 Democratic Socialism and Equality
Lord Plant

The aim of this chapter is to try to pin down and analyse the conception of equality favoured by C. A. R. Crosland, who was the pivotal intellectual figure in defining a role for social democracy in Britain once the first stage of the social democratic transformation of British society had been achieved by the 1945–51 Labour governments. Basic industries and the Bank of England had been nationalised and the National Health Service had been established, but as Richard Crossman was wont to argue, one of the major problems facing the Left by 1951 was that it seemed as though it had run out of ideas. So much had been achieved, particularly following the rigours of war, but it was not clear where the Left should go next, particularly since the vast bulk of the Labour Party did not wish to follow the forms of socialism being established in Eastern Europe or the type that had been established in Russia. There was a need to find a clear social democratic alternative to both European communism and pre-war capitalism but which equally held out a vision of a society more enticing and more compelling than one in which basic industries had been nationalised and a Health Service established.

By 1956 Crosland had published *The Future of Socialism* which synthesised a vast range of material from economics, sociology, social politics, psychology, and political science in the service of the idea that democratic socialism/social democracy has to serve the cause of greater social equality. This book had a salience which few books of political thought and doctrine have achieved in the UK. It filled the intellectual vacuum on the Left and it gave a great deal of confidence to non-Marxist social democrats and it fitted very well into the approach of the new Party leader, Hugh Gaitskell, who had himself come to believe independently in the 1940s that the next stage of democratic socialist advances had to be in defence of greater equality. Given the significance of this work in the intellectual climate of mid-century politics, it is important to try to become as clear as possible what Crosland meant by equality and what he took to be the strategy for achieving it. Before moving to this task however, it is important to set the issue of equality in a wider political context for both the Left and Right.

LEFT, RIGHT AND SOCIAL JUSTICE

Unlike many of their political opponents, democratic non-Marxist socialists have to be very sensitive to the moral values on which their political attitudes and policy prescriptions rest. The traditional Conservative may, following the advice of Michael Oakeshott,[1] eschew the pursuit of rationalism in politics – the self-conscious pursuit of ideas such as equality and social justice – and prefer instead to pursue the 'intimations' present in the existing tradition of political activity. He may claim to follow what he tendentiously regards as common sense and practical experience and not be unduly bothered by the security of the moral basis of his position. However, this cannot be a position which can appeal to the radical. To the radical socialist, 'common sense', 'experience' and 'tradition' are likely to be seen as persuasive honorific titles given to privileged special pleading.

Modern Conservatives, more influenced by Hayek than by Oakeshott, may equally abandon the search for just principles to govern the distribution of benefits and burdens in society. Taking the view that any attempt to constrain the market in the interests of 'the mirage of social justice' is likely to be totalitarian, they manage, as Hirsch argues, to take the issue off the political agenda:

> One broad solution which is propounded by the economic libertarian school of Hayek and Friedman is to deal with the distributional issue by taking it off the agenda… The economic outcome is legitimised, not as just but as unjustifiable. Those who have drawn trumps in the existing allocation of economic endowments are merely fortunate, those who have drawn blanks unfortunate; all will be damaged by attempts to get a legitimated distribution by deliberate adjustment.[2]

Again here there is no need to worry about the moral basis of the distribution of benefits and burdens following on market transactions. In arguments with the traditional or the radical Right, a clear view about the nature of the egalitarianism to be defended by democratic socialists and its moral basis would seem to be at a premium.

Equally, the democratic socialist, unlike the Marxist, has to give a central place to his/her values in his/her political life. Marx in his mature writings seems to have been very clear that his critique of capitalism did not depend on moral assumptions but on historical and economic analysis. In Marx's mind, at least from the time of writing *On the Jewish Question*, moral values and corresponding social and political attitudes were rooted in material economic interests with the corollary that there can be no political appeal which can act as a countervailing power to those interests, challenge them and transcend them. Indeed, in his *Critique of the Gotha Programme*, Marx criticised democratic socialists precisely on the grounds that they did not see issues of social justice and equality as being fully determined by the existing productive relations and the class interests based upon them. For the Marxist, the pattern of ownership of the means of production determines the character of the distribution of goods and services in society and there is no role at all for an independent appeal to values such as justice and equality to criticise the pattern of distribution. In this sense, there is a certain amount of common ground between Marxists and the radical Right.[3] It is no accident therefore that the founder of revisionist socialism, Edward Bernstein, made the *moral* demands of socialism central to his thought.[4] The importance placed upon moral values and political principles is an explicit affirmation of the role of democracy in democratic socialism: people have to be persuaded and convinced, arguments put and visions of society defended if the democratic process is to work and the Marxian tie between values and material interests is to be broken. Crosland in response to this placed the *ideals* of democratic socialism at the centre of the political agenda:

> We have to have either more equality or less, or the present amount: and politicians, in deciding which of these is the correct objective cannot but make some supposition about the welfare of the community. They have no excuse merely because these can be shown to be of an ethical nature for avoiding this responsibility.[5]

An egalitarian principle of distributive justice was central to Crosland's socialist vision. He saw the principle as constituting the main dividing line between socialists and non-socialists,[6] and as a principle which is likely to remain at the very centre of the political arena because problems of distribution will cease only with the abolition of scarcity. It is arguable that scarcity is a fundamental feature of human social life given the positional character of many of the goods which human beings desire,[7] so that the possibility of human relationships assuming an altruistic co-operative form is not a serious political option. In a situation of scarcity, individuals are always going to be concerned with the pattern of distribution of goods which prevails and the nature of the justification of that pattern. To that extent, therefore, Crosland is right to see problems about equality and social justice as endemic to political and social life.

Equality is, of course, a highly complex and contested social ideal and discussion of it can soon become very elusive. For my purposes here I shall distinguish three types of equality: equality of opportunity, equality of result and democratic equality. In *Socialism Now*, Crosland points out that he and other revisionists 'adopted the "strong" definition of equality – what Rawls has subsequently called the "democratic" as opposed to the liberal conception of equality of opportunity'.[8] This is an important statement because Crosland has often been taken as endorsing without qualification equality of opportunity. For example, Norman Birnbaum in an early reaction to *The Future of Socialism* took this view in *Socialist Commentary* in September 1959 and this misconception was repeated more recently by Steven Lukes in his *Essays in Social and Political Theory*.[9] It is also important, as we shall see, because Crosland links his own views on equality with those developed by John Rawls in his *A Theory of Justice* and in the course of this chapter we shall have cause to look more closely into this relationship.

EQUALITY OF OPPORTUNITY

The 'liberal' conception of equality as both Crosland and Rawls call it is fairly clear: it is straightforward equality of opportunity. Such a conception of equality would allow for fair competition for scarce social resources, income, status, power and so forth; certainly Crosland sees such a view as having an important place in his vision of a social democratic society on the grounds that it would make for a mobile dynamic society and this would have a disturbing effect on the class structure. Equality of opportunity represents the meritocratic policy of widening the social basis of recruitment to positions of privilege in society. The aim is to provide equality of competition even if this leads to inequality of outcome. In *The Future of Socialism* Crosland gives a good description of the positive aspects of equality of opportunity:

The essential thing is that every citizen should have an equal chance – that is his democratic right, but provided that the start is fair let there be maximum scope for individual self-advancement. There would be nothing improper in either a high continuous status ladder... or even in a distinct class stratification... since opportunity for attaining the highest status or topmost stratum would be genuinely equal.[10]

Such a view certainly appears radical. It rejects the idea of recruiting to scarce social positions from an hereditary class, it is efficient as a way of matching skills to jobs and would lead to a continuous crossover in class membership. Some have taken the view that such a society would be marked by extreme insecurity and ought to be rejected on the basis of the psychological damage it would be likely to do. Crosland rejects this picture painted by some sociologists and psychologists as unduly pessimistic.

However, there are some difficulties with the notion of equality of opportunity taken on its own which make it in his own words 'not enough' for socialists. The major difficulties lie in attempting to equalise starting points, so that the competition for privileged positions is in fact fair, and in justifying those privileged positions in a manner consistent with socialist principles. On the latter point it is argued by some critics that the idea of privilege is inconsistent with the equality of respect which is owed to each individual in virtue of his or her common humanity and that equal respect points towards greater equality in the conditions of life, that is wealth, income, status and power. According to this view the socialist should be concerned not with opening up recruitment to privileged positions to wider sections of the population but rather with narrowing as much as possible the differences in the conditions of life between individuals. Instead of a hierarchical society based upon recruitment by merit, those who believe in equality of outcome wish to argue in favour of a progressive narrowing of hierarchy. The justification of equality of outcome can emerge from the discussion of equality of opportunity in another way. The whole basis of equality of opportunity depends upon the start of the competitive race being fair, but there are very clear limits within which this is possible. First of all, granted that the family is the basic social institution in our society, the influence of any action taken in the field of health, education and welfare is going to be mediated through the family with all the differentiating effects this will have upon the start of particular children in life. Moreover, studies of education inequality and attempts by governments to correct these through programmes of positive discrimination have suggested that such programmes are less successful than had been hoped. Reflections such as this have led one major researcher in this field to argue that, 'instead of trying to reduce people's capacity to gain a competitive advantage over one another, we will have to change the rules of the game so as to reduce the rewards of competitive success and the cost of failure'.[11] There are therefore these twin supports for a conception of equality in terms of greater and greater equalities in outcomes: inequalities, even when fairly competed for, are inconsistent with socialism and in any case the competition can never be made fair.

There are, however, difficulties with placing equality of outcome at the centre of a socialist framework of values. It may well be inconsistent with political and civil liberties and it embodies very weak demands in terms of efficiency. The first of these points has been well put by a proponent of such a view of equality. As Frank Parkin says in *Class Inequality and Political Order*:

socialist egalitarianism is not readily compatible with a pluralist political order of the classic western type. Egalitarianism seems to require a political system in which the state is able to continually hold in check those social and occupational groups which, by virtue of their skills or education, might otherwise attempt to stake claims to a disproportionate share of society's rewards. The most effective way of holding such groups in check is by denying them the right to organise politically or in other ways to undermine social equality.[12]

For social democrats, such a conclusion renders the conception of equality which requires such drastic curtailments of political liberty suspect. The other aspect of equality of outcome is one on which Crosland has much more to say and which leads on to the third conception of equality, what he and Rawls call the 'democratic conception' of equality. Equality of outcome fails to recognise that certain inequalities may have essential economic functions. It is concerned to ensure a single status society on the basis of equality of respect but neglects the fact that without differential rewards certain jobs, the performance of which is to the benefit of everyone, may not get done. Democratic equality attempts to do justice to some of the arguments directed against mere equality of opportunity while at the same time being sensitive to the fact that there may be the need to pay differential rewards.

Crosland goes some way with those who wish to argue that equality of opportunity is suspect as a socialist idea. He takes the view, which Rawls was later to develop, that not only does equality of opportunity lead to the development of a hierarchy of merit but the qualities which such a hierarchy may reward are arbitrary from the point of view of the moral demands of distributive justice. High rewards are given on the basis of merit to talents and abilities which are to a very large extent morally arbitrary in the sense that the individual is not fully responsible for them and they are in large part the result of genetic endowment and fortunate family background. In *The Future of Socialism* he puts the argument without equivocation: 'No one deserves either so generous a reward or so severe a penalty for a quality implanted from the outside and for which he can claim only a limited responsibility.'[13] The point is repeated in *Socialism Now*: 'By equality, we meant more than a meritocratic society of equal opportunities in which the greatest rewards would go to those with the most fortunate genetic endowment and family background.'[14]

DEMOCRATIC EQUALITY

Thus equality of opportunity is not a sufficiently rich conception on its own for a socialist view of equality, but equally he rejects equality of outcome because of its indifference to the fact that greater economic rewards for some may have a vital economic function. On the face of it, his position appears paradoxical. He rejects pure equality of opportunity and its resultant meritocracy and yet is in favour of differential rewards rather than equality of result. However, the resolution of the paradox is to be found in the justification he gives for differential rewards. Departures from equality are to be justified not by appeals to merit or desert but rather on the basis of a rent of ability – the amount of money (or for that matter non-material incentives) which would be necessary for individuals to perform tasks without which the whole community would suffer. There is a trade-off to be found between equality and incentive but it must be a real trade-off based upon a rent of ability and not on the basis of merit. Such differential inequalities need not lead to hierarchies such as were found to be characteristic of meritocracies because what the tasks are which will require incentives will depend upon circumstances and will vary. Because of this, it is impossible to say in advance what inequalities will be functional in an economy and at what level they will have to be set: 'How large this should be is of course impossible to lay down in general terms. If we believe in equality we can only say that we shall balance the possible loss to equality against the possible gain from exploiting the ability. The balance of loss and gain will depend upon the supply price of different grades of ability.'[15] On the basis of considerations of this sort we could say as an approximation that Crosland had a belief in equality, with inequalities being justified if, and only if, differential rewards work to the benefit of the community as a whole and we can assume that access to jobs which command differential rewards would be on the basis of genuine equality of opportunity. Of course, not all incentives or differential rewards are properly to be regarded as increasing inequality. Some socially important tasks may well involve considerable welfare costs for those who perform them. They may for example be dangerous or done permanently at night and extra payments for the performance of such tasks might be better seen not as *increments* of income but more as *compensation* for the 'dis-welfare' suffered in doing the job. The extra payments bring the worker up to the level of welfare experienced by others and as such the differential payment is a way of securing equality of welfare rather than being a departure from it. However, it is of course true, and Crosland takes the point, that most differential payments do involve a trade-off between equality and economic efficiency and as such he has to make assumptions about the necessity for incentives, that there is a need for a rent of ability which will create inequalities – otherwise socially important tasks will remain undone. At this point, egalitarians of result have criticised those who have made a case for differential and inequality producing payments. It is quite central to the case of those who believe in complete equality of result that incentives are ultimately unnecessary and the need for them is merely the effect on human motivation of the competitive ethos of capitalist society. Lukes, in defending egalitarianism of result makes this point:

> A further weakness of the theory [of democratic equality] is its assumption that unequal rewards are the only possible means of mobilising qualified individuals into adequately performing important jobs. It leaves out of account the intrinsic benefits of different positions in relation to the expectations, aptitudes and aspirations of different individuals... and it fails to consider functional alternatives to a system of unequal rewards such as intrinsic job satisfaction, the desire for knowledge, skills and authority, of public service etc.[16]

Certainly any egalitarian who cares about the possible range of inequalities which the rent of ability criterion would set up has to be interested in the possibilities which Lukes suggests. At the same time, though, the fact that these are not material incentives does not mean that they do not embody inequalities of life conditions and are morally speaking in much the same position as material incentives. It must also be said that the evidence cited by Sen in *On Economic Inequality* about the success of the application of non-material incentives in China during 'the Great Leap Forward' is not encouraging.

Presumptive equality with inequalities justified in terms of a rent of ability is a distinctive view of equality which falls between equality of opportunity and equality of result. It is a view of equality which enables Crosland to answer a persistent question put by Conservative critics of the egalitarian ideal: how much equality ultimately? In his book, *Inside Right*, Ian Gilmour put the question thus:

> In constantly demanding more equality, while refusing to specify how much, the revisionists are like a general continually ordering his troops to move east irrespective of whether the terrain is flat or mountainous, fertile or barren, well drained or swamp, and ignoring the casualties they suffer or inflict and the amount of equipment they may lose. But then ideologists do not make good generals.[17]

This is really a rather unsubtle criticism. The question should not be 'how much equality?' but 'how much inequality?' Democratic equality (presumptive equality combined with a theory about justified inequalities) cannot specify in advance and for all time the range and nature of the inequalities which will be made legitimate by the rent of ability criterion. Differential rewards are to be paid after empirical investigation of the economic function of a particular task and the supply price of the skills to fulfil it. This will clearly vary from time to time and place to place, depending upon the kinds of natural advantages and disadvantages which a society may incorporate and the stage of its economic development. The idea that this could be specified in other than piecemeal and empirical terms and subject to constant scrutiny and revision is ludicrous. It would make as much sense to ask a market-oriented Conservative how much competition precisely he is willing to allow in the market. Usually he will answer that occasionally the national interest or whatever will require intervention in the market but, of course, he could never say in advance and in detail what this would amount to. Similarly, the democratic egalitarian cannot say in advance and for all times what divergences from equality are to be justified in his terms.

MORALITY AND EQUALITY

So far I have contrasted three conceptions of equality and have argued that Crosland comes closest to asserting a principle of presumptive equality coupled with a view about the range of justifiable inequalities which are required as a rent of ability if important economic functions are to be performed. I now want to turn to the moral justification of such a principle. In *The Future of Socialism* Crosland does not spend very much time on this issue and I will argue that what he has to say is inadequate, but the issue is not of marginal importance. What matters in society is not the sheer fact of inequality but how these inequalities are perceived, in particular whether they are perceived as fair or unfair, just or unjust. If a particular set of unequal rewards can be defended on the basis of their fairness or justice, then the resentment which is directed towards them by those who do not share them is illegitimate. On the other hand, if this cannot be shown, then the resentment is justified. We need an argument based upon some kind of theory of justice to distinguish between legitimate and illegitimate resentment and to answer the criticism that the pursuit of equality in order to lessen social resentment is the politics of envy. Among social theorists Runciman has asked this question most pertinently: 'Is it legitimate to speak of people's perceptions of inequality as "distorted" or to describe a disproportionate awareness of inequality as "envy"? Or is there no criterion which could be brought to bear by which the use of any such term could be better justified than any other?'[18] This is not merely an academic, philosophical issue because it is at least arguable that issues of this sort play a major role in industrial and social discontents which are important in restricting economic growth and not only this, it is of central importance to the coherence of Crosland's own intellectual position. Colin Welch, in a vehement attack, has pointed out the issue which Crosland has to face here:

> To achieve any sort of durable financial success in such a world were it possible, is to expose oneself not only to Mr Crosland's icy disapproval but, more important, to the envy and resentment of the masses – ugly and unconstructive sentiments which, so far from

rebuking, he fully endorses, tries even to share, and proposes to assuage by levelling down the objects of envy. Did it not cross his mind that the greater the relative equality prevailing, the more all surviving inequalities (and he permits some) will be resented?[19]

This kind of assault can only be countered by an argument which shows that the inequalities are unjust and the resentment legitimate.

However, the difficulty goes deeper than this. Crosland held the view that social resentment was a disruptive force in industrial relations and that the elimination of the objects of resentment would itself help Britain's economic performance. Such a view seems to underlie his endorsement of something like an early version of the Social Contract in a speech in Copenhagen in 1971 in which he developed the view that an incomes policy would only work in a society in which greater social equality is being pursued.[20] An incomes policy introduced against a background of *unjustified* inequalities is not going to command the assent of workers. The same point has been made powerfully by John Goldthorpe in a number of studies in which he suggests that: 'the existence of inequality, of an extreme, unyielding and largely unlegitimated kind, does militate seriously against any stable normative regulation in the economic sphere because it militates against the possibility of effective value consensus on the distribution of economic and other resources and rewards.'[21] Unless the structure of inequalities does have some accepted moral basis, workers are unlikely to moderate wage claims. The so called 'wages jungle' is one part of a wider system of inequality which lacks justification. Inequality may be a brute fact: what matters is our perception of its legitimacy and justice and this is why, as Crick points out in the epigraph to this chapter, socialist theories must rest upon some kind of moral philosophy, in this case a theory of justice.

It is perhaps worth noting in passing that Conservatives are going to have to face up to this issue at some point. Under the influence of Hayek, and more remotely Hume, the tendency has been to try to argue that since there is no basis for agreement over the distribution of economic rewards, we should depoliticise the distributional issue, abandon the search for justice in the pattern of reward and leave it to the market place. However, this is probably unrealistic and is inconsistent with Toryism's traditional outlook, as has been well explored by Irving Kristol in his essay 'When Virtue Loses All Her Loveliness'.[22] To legitimise market outcomes is to neglect notions such as merit and desert (Hayek and Hume are clear about this) but it is precisely notions such as these which are dear to many Conservatives. Those who doubt this should read Welch's *Encounter* essay discussed above.

The difficulty with Crosland's position on this basic moral point is that he takes the view that his conception of equality is in some sense arbitrary and that it is far from being a consensus value. He argues that conceptions of equality lack objective validity, are not amenable to proof or disproof and must be accepted or rejected according to 'the moral predilections of the reader'.[23] In an article in *Encounter*, Vaizey points out that Crosland's egalitarianism was arbitrarily determined, without pointing out the problems to which this gives rise. A moral appeal which relies on the moral predilections of the reader is all very well, but it will hardly suit the radical because the predilections of the majority may well be in another direction. Indeed Crosland goes out of his way to emphasise this. The point is made repeatedly when he claims in many of his writings that the position of the worst off can only be significantly improved in a situation of economic growth because only then will those better placed be able to maintain their standard of living in absolute terms while allowing for relative improvements in the position of the worst off. This implies that egalitarianism is not a central consensus value otherwise this would not be necessary.[24] In addition, he draws an explicit distinction in *Socialism Now* between consensus values and egalitarian ones.[25] So a sheer appeal to the moral predilections of his readers is on his own account not likely to take us all the way. On the one hand, we need to see the distribution of benefits and burdens as legitimate and just in order to minimise social resentment; on the other hand, we have no clear moral basis to underpin the conceptions of justice and equality invoked.

RAWLS AND CROSLAND

Earlier I mentioned the fact that Crosland linked his view of equality, 'democratic equality', with the work of John Rawls whose *A Theory of Justice* has had such a profound effect in Britain and the United States. In *A Theory of Justice* Rawls attempts to construct an argument which will provide an objective basis for democratic equality but which seeks to relate to, and, in a sense theorise our ordinary reflective moral consciousness. In this sense it claims not to stand apart from everyday moral reflection but to stand in reflective equilibrium to it. Obviously a project of this sort must have a fascination for a social democrat and some commentators have noticed the need for precisely this kind of work. Stuart Hampshire, for example, in his review of Rawls's work in *The New York Review of Books*, argues as follows: 'In England, books about the Labour party's aims, for example those by Douglas Jay and Anthony Crosland since the war, needed just such a theory as this stated in its full philosophical generality.'[26] The need for such a project to round out Crosland's own intellectual position I hope already to have shown; others have noticed the importance of a Rawlsian perspective to his work.[27] Despite limitations of space and the problems with the theory, I hope to say something about the salience of this relationship.

In *A Theory of Justice* Rawls points out the extent to which our everyday views about the justice of a particular distribution of benefits and burdens will be influenced by our interests, the particular stake which we will have in a particular pattern of distribution. An argument which merely appeals to the unreflective predilections of the public is likely just to reflect these interests. In order to break out of this subjectivism, which is not likely to support radical proposals, we must stand back from our interests. The most appropriate way in which this can be done would be in terms of a hypothetical social contract in which we try to envisage what individuals in a state of hypothetical equality and in ignorance of their own talents and abilities would choose as principles to govern social life. To make a claim about justice, as opposed to a subjective claim about where one's own interests lie, means on this model that it would have to embody a principle to which the person making the claim would have to have subscribed without knowing in advance whether he or she would be a beneficiary or a loser under the operation of the principle. In this model Rawls's individuals are compelled to choose principles of distributive justice in total uncertainty of how the principles will apply to them. The model tries to translate into cash terms what we mean by fairness when we use the term in adjudicating various claims. In Rawls's view, the contractual model is the best device for elucidating fair and impartial judgement. Granted the model, Rawls argues that his hypothetical individuals would adopt a 'maximin' strategy, choosing from among all the principles the best of the worst possible outcomes they could experience under the operation of various possible principles. Utilising this strategy, Rawls argues that the 'contracting parties' would choose principles of justice to which he gives the name 'democratic equality', the view with which Crosland allies himself in *Socialism Now*. Rawls's two principles of justice are:

1   Each person to have the most extensive system of equal basic liberties compatible with similar liberties for all;
2   Social and economic inequalities to be arranged so that they are (a) to the greatest advantage to the least advantaged consistent with a just savings principle, and (b) attached to offices and positions open to all under conditions of fair equality of opportunity.

The first principle secures co-extensive principles of liberty, so central to democratic socialist thought; the second is a principle of presumptive equality with inequalities being justified if, and only if, they are to the benefit of the least advantaged members of society. Again we see the point which Crosland made much of, namely that differential rewards may be necessary and where they are necessary they are to be paid not on the basis of personal merit or desert but rather on the grounds that they are functionally necessary to the economy and to the benefit of the least advantaged members of society. Of course, it is impossible to do justice to the immense subtlety and complexity of Rawls's theory here, but what he is claiming is that it is possible to develop a model of rational decision making which will correspond to our reflective notions of fairness and impartiality and that this model is rich enough to yield substantive principles of distributive justice of a democratic egalitarian sort which will provide a benchmark for assessing the justice or otherwise of a particular set of rewards. Only a procedure of this sort will enable us to break out of a purely subjective approach to problems of distribution, which means that it is impossible to escape from the charge of pursuing the politics of envy without merely resorting to a relabelling of one's own attitudes. Only some kind of theory of justice which develops our intuitive, but not worked out, notion of fairness or impartiality will enable socialists to demonstrate in principle what kinds of grievances are to be regarded as legitimate and what pattern of inequalities are to be regarded as just. This is central to the intellectual coherence of democratic socialism and practically important in handling the problem of resentment against inequalities which as we have seen may be crucially important in incomes policy.

The trouble is, of course, that all of this does look far too academic. Samuel Brittan has pointed to the intractable nature of the problem faced here. He admits that some kind of justification has to be given to the structure of distribution and that it is important to develop a moral consensus over this, but equally the kinds of moral arguments deployed seem very remote from the general moral consciousness of individuals: 'if the rational arguments for accepting a system that does not aim at complete distributive justice are too abstract or sophisticated to command assent; and if there is an emotional void that cannot be met merely by rising incomes and humanitarian redistribution unrelated to "merit", then the outlook for liberal democracy is a poor one'[28] The Rawlsian answer is that the contractual model does develop ordinary reflective notions of fairness, but this can be doubted as can the logic of the arguments in favour of the two principles at least as developed by Rawls. This is by no means a closed question, but Brittan's point still remains true; such arguments and devices *appear* too abstract. Are we then left with an appeal to the moral predilections of the electorate, which, as Crosland clearly realised, are quite frequently not of an egalitarian sort? It is just not possible to string together a set of consensus attitudes towards legitimate inequalities because the basis of the legitimation is just not there. Indeed, if we follow Goldthorpe, the development of consensus about a legitimate pattern of distribution *depends* upon moral values and does not itself exist apart from them:

> Such consensus in turn cannot be achieved without the distribution of economic resources and rewards, and indeed the entire structure of power and advantage becoming in some way principled – becoming that is, more capable of being given consistent rational and moral justification ... In other words, the advancement of social justice has to be seen not as some lofty and impracticable ideal ... but rather as an important *precondition* of mitigating current economic difficulties.[29]

Crosland placed equality at the heart of the agenda of socialism and insisted that it and increasing growth and welfare are inextricably linked. What democratic socialists still require are the intellectual resources to provide the rational and moral justification for the reward structure they favour, resources which can be translated into a political language which is accessible to all and not the rarefied language of political philosophers. This is why it is perhaps important to look at some middle-range justifications which could be given to democratic equality rather than to the vast overarching theory developed by Rawls.

IN DEFENCE OF DEMOCRATIC EQUALITY

In the first place there are good grounds for rejecting the Hayekian view that social justice is a mirage and its pursuit should be taken off the agenda of politics. His view that goods and services, benefits and burdens are not *distributed* by some identifiable human agency but rather by the impersonal forces of the market may be true but is irrelevant. Hayek wishes to draw the conclusion that because there is no distributor or agency there can be no injustice, and the outcomes of exchanges have to be accepted for better or worse as *unjustifiable*. However, what is just and unjust is the way in which society reacts to the distribution. The misfortune of having a physical handicap is not an injustice, but justice comes into the picture in the way in which others react to those who have suffered such misfortune. In the same way as we seek to mitigate the effects on individuals of misfortunes in this sense, so we can seek to redress the misfortunes which are socially distributed and nurtured. The pursuit of social justice and the attempt to constrain the market in its interest is not a mirage and in a world of scarce resources, both physical and social, it is unlikely that the question of who is to get what and on what principle will ever become irrelevant to the political agenda.

There are other Hayekian arguments which can also be doubted. He argues that market outcomes in respect of the worst off and the poor are not unjust because they are unintended. Injustice has to be provided by intentional action. In a market people buy and sell for intentional reasons, but the outcome of all that buying and selling produces a pattern of income and wealth which was not intended by anyone and, as a result, this outcome is not unjust whatever the degree of poverty and inequality to which it might lead.

This argument is very dubious. Even if one accepts that injustice is a matter of something being caused intentionally (and I have suggested earlier that this may not be so), we can nevertheless be held responsible for the foreseeable even if unintended consequences of our action. Given this it is possible to argue that we do bear collective responsibility for the foreseeable but unintended consequences of extending the market to new areas. If those who enter such markets with least are likely to leave it with least and if this is a foreseeable consequence, then we could legitimately be held responsible for it. We cannot put the issue of distributive justice off the agenda of politics just by focusing on the role of intention in markets.

Democratic equality also seems to be well defended against attacks on the Left from those who believe more strictly in equality of result. Equality of result is often justified, as we have seen, in terms of notions of common humanity and the respect owed to an individual. However, it is arguable that it is irrational, if one takes respecting individuals seriously, to prefer strict equality of result to democratic equality with its commitment to the idea of inequalities being justified if they help the whole community, including the worst off. Granted that differential rewards are being paid on the basis of rent of ability rather than desert, there is no disrespect towards those who do not achieve such differential rewards and in addition they can see that the rewards embody a principle which it is in their own interest to accept. The only ground on which it might seem rational to prefer equality of result would be some overriding commitment to community and social solidarity: that the gains in levels of welfare which might accrue from paying differentials would not offset the decline in social solidarity which the distancing effect of the differential payments would have. However, the advocate of democratic equality can counter this argument because one of the advantages of the theory is that it does attempt to give some content to the rather vague notion of community. Rawls has developed this point quite cogently:

> The difference principle [the second of the two principles of justice]... does seem to correspond to a natural meaning of fraternity. Namely the idea of not wanting to have greater advantages unless this is to the benefit of others who are less well off. The family in its ideal conception and often in practice is the one place where the principle of maximising the sum of advantages is rejected. Members of a family commonly do not wish to gain unless they can do so in ways that can further the interests of the rest. Now wanting to act on the difference principle has precisely this consequence. Those better circumstanced are willing to have their greater advantages only under a scheme in which this works out for the benefit of the least fortunate.[30]

Differential rewards need not create social distance and destroy the sense of community in a society if they are paid on the basis set out in the difference principle and in terms of a rent of ability, and if those who are paid the differential rewards do not turn themselves into a self-perpetuating elite. However, changing social circumstances are always likely to *change* the groups of individuals to whom such rewards are paid.

Democratic equality seems well defended against the libertarian Right and the communitarian Left and it is equally clear why such a conception of equality should appeal to the worst-off members of society and why a society organised on the basis of such a principle should command their allegiance. Democratic equality is clearly in their interests and will secure their welfare. The real difficulty, however, as Crosland's remarks about the difficulties of redistribution in periods of low growth make clear, is to provide reasons why the better endowed should feel loyalty to and vote in favour of a society organised on democratic egalitarian lines. This is clearly the basic moral problem here: how to justify egalitarian distributive principles to persons each of whom has a fundamental interest in receiving the greatest possible share of distributed goods. If there is no resolution to this problem any system of democratic egalitarianism is going to be relatively unstable because only the worst-off members of society are going to have an incentive to support such a system and they are not going to be numerically significant enough (particularly if one adopts a relative view of poverty) to ensure the stability of a system of egalitarian distribution of the sort envisaged. However, there are two arguments here which are rather similar and could give reasons of self-interest to the better off to support a system of democratic egalitarianism.

It could be argued in the first place that the well-being of the better endowed as well as that of the worst off members of society rests upon mutual co-operation. In order for the better endowed to be able to exercise their talents, capacities and powers and to derive satisfaction from doing so, there has to be a scheme of social co-operation. The surgeon can only operate if certain more menial tasks are performed; the philosopher can only think if he has a university and libraries, which again depend upon the services of a great many other people. Such co-operation can only exist between parties who recognise their mutual dependence only if they see the terms of their co-operation as fair. If this is not so there will be resentment and lack of co-operation. A fair agreement may not be optimal for any individual, but it is a necessary contract to ensure the smoothness of the relationship. The critic will of course argue that while this may be true, the concessions made by the better-off under conditions of democratic equality seem to be much greater and indeed the system seems to be geared to optimising the position of the less well off. The answer to this surely is to take up Crosland's point about merits and deserts. If, as he argues, we bear only very limited responsibility for our assets (these being the result of genetic endowment and fortunate family background), then it is reasonable to ask those with these assets to better themselves only under a system in which so doing will help those who are less well off and whose less fortunate position is by parity of reasoning not fully their responsibility. Granted the point that society is a co-operative venture, if fate has stepped in and penalised some participants who use the assets they have got, then it may seem only fair that the advantages of the fortunate should be used in ways which help them and the less well off.

The other argument would be more direct appeal to self-interest. It is the view that individuals will see the advantage of the pooling of natural talents in a scheme of mutual benefit, for the better off as well as for the worst off. Individuals will be aware that the community will support them in time of need whether in health, education or welfare, in exchange for an agreement between individuals to share their talents in a way which benefits others as well as themselves. Although this may seem to evade the problem posed earlier about the significance of the numbers of those who are poor and disadvantaged, the fact is that with the contingencies of life being what they are no individual could ever be sure that he or she would not have to draw upon this kind of help and therefore the better off would have an incentive to support it. There is a good deal of evidence that this is in fact the way people do feel about welfare institutions, particularly the NHS, and Titmuss in his *Gift Relationship* discusses this attitude in some detail.[31]

CONCLUSION

While I have tried to give a favourable constructionist reading of Crosland's view of equality, largely by utilising Rawls (with whom Crosland allies himself), as a basis for flushing out some of the less clear aspects of Crosland's theory, nevertheless there are some points about the political consequences of his view of equality that deserve attention and to which Crosland was not sufficiently sensitive. The first is an argument due to Hayek and also elaborated by Samuel Brittan. The claim here is that once the state takes on a role in distribution in a pluralistic society in which there is no clear consensus about distributive principles, then interest groups will arise the aim of which will be to obtain for themselves, as for other groups which they claim to champion, what from their own sectional point of view they regard as their just share of social resources. This will lead to a bleak zero-sum game in politics in which coalitions of powerful interest groups will be able to extract from Government particular distributive concessions. On this view distributive politics encourages rank-seeking behaviour. The central point here is that this will happen in the absence (necessary in a pluralist society) of a clear consensus about social justice as a basis for distribution. This problem is made worse because Crosland wants to argue that his egalitarian conception of justice is not a consensus one, while at the same time arguing that it can be achieved through oblique means via economic growth, fiscal dividends and increased public expenditure. The Hayek/Brittan argument almost exactly reverses the points cited from Goldthorpe. For Goldthorpe an orderly society depends upon a distributive consensus. For Hayek the search for a distributive consensus in a pluralist and modern society is a mirage and will in fact lead to the zero-sum interest group competition.

Given that Crosland was rather blasé about what one must take to be the social and moral base for his view of equality he might be criticised for not taking the Hayek/Brittan view more seriously. This relates to another lacuna in his position. If there is a response to Hayek and Brittan about the difficulty of pursuing distributive politics in a pluralist culture, then I believe that it has to lie in a more open and transparent form of democracy in which difficult distributive claims are weighed and accepted or rejected in terms of procedures which are believed to be fair and legitimate by those disadvantaged by them. For someone who wanted to use the powers of the state to a high degree to produce social outcomes that he wanted, Crosland paid very scant attention to issues about political legitimacy and the quality of British representative government and of its associated bureaucracies. This led to a major defect for someone who places so much emphasis on politics. If we go back to where we started and the contrast between Crosland's position and that of the Hayekian neo-liberal on the one hand and the Marxist on the other, we can see how important this defect is. The neo-liberal does not take too much account of the nature and legitimacy of government. What matters is limited government which will provide the legal framework for the market, external defence, and other public goods, together with a minimal welfare state. Politics and government is nomocratic, dealing essentially with rules and procedure. It is not the aim of government to produce particular social outcomes. Equally the Marxist sees government as representing economic interests in the final analysis and so not too much weight can be put on political initiatives as Marx's *Critique of the Gotha Programme* showed. The search for a moral basis for political legitimacy is an ideological illusion. So in very different ways the neo-liberal and the Marxist are sceptical about politics. This cannot be so for Croslandite social democrats and this puts into relief their failure to consider the nature of the state both in its representation and bureaucratic functions to enable it to serve.

Notes

1. Michael Oakeshott, *Rationalism in Politics* (London: Methuen, 1962).
2. Fred Hirsch, *The Social Limits of Growth* (London: Routledge & Kegan Paul, 1977), p. 182.
3. Robert Nozick, *Anarchy, State and Utopia* (Oxford: Blackwell, 1975).
4. Edward Bernstein, *Evolutionary Socialism* (New York: Schocken Books, 1961). Reference may also be made to R. Plant, 'Continental, Social and Political Thought 1900–18' in C. B. Cox and A. E. Dyson (eds), *The Twentieth Century Mind* (Oxford: Oxford University Press, 1972).
5. C. A. R. Crosland, *The Future of Socialism,* revised edition (London: Jonathan Cape, 1964), p. 137.
6. C. A. R. Crosland, *Socialism Now and Other Essays* (London: Jonathan Cape, 1974), p. 15.
7. See Hirsch, *The Social Limits to Growth*, op. cit. Hirsch's account is crucial because it stresses the endemic nature of scarcity not because of the supposed exhaustion of natural resources but because the positional nature of some goods means that the more they are consumed the less they are 'goods'. When all stand on tiptoe none may see; many social goods are like this. They have an intrinsic positional dimension, not everyone can consume them, whatever the rate of growth. Because of this, it is of vital importance that those who do consume positional goods do so legitimately in the eyes of those who do not. Social scarcity of this sort is going to give rise to problems about social justice and equality however much the standard of living generally increases. Hirsch's subtle argument puts into doubt some of the optimism of the final pages of *The Future of Socialism*. (See also chapter 10, note 1.)
8. *Socialism Now*, op. cit, p. 15.
9. S. Lukes, *Essays in Social Theory* (Basingstoke: Macmillan, 1977). See particularly the essay 'Socialism and Equality'.
10. *The Future of Socialism*, op. cit, p. 150.
11. C. Jencks, *Inequality* (Hammondsworth: Penguin, 1974), p. 25.
12. Frank Parkin, *Class Inequality and Political Order* (London: Paladin, 1971), p. 183.
13. *The Future of Socialism*, op. cit, p. 168; see also p. 144, 'It seems unjust and unwise to penalise people to quite such a prodigious extent for inherited characteristics'.
14. *Socialism Now*, op. cit, p. 15.

15. *The Future of Socialism*, op. cit, p. 145.
16. Lukes, op. cit, p. 140.
17. Ian Gilmour, *Inside Right* (London: Hutchinson, 1977).
18. W. G. Runicman, *Relative Deprivation and Social Justice* (Harmondsworth: Penguin 1972).
19. Colin Welch in 'Crosland Reconsidered', *Encounter*, January 1979.
20. *Socialism Now*, op. cit, p. 249.
21. John Goldthorpe, 'Social Inequality and Social Integration', in Wedderburn (ed.), *Poverty, Inequality and Class Structure* (Cambridge: Cambridge University Press, 1974), p. 228.
22. Irving Kristol, 'When Virtue Loses All Her Loveliness', in I. Kristol and D. Bell (eds), *Capitalism Today* (New York: Humanities Press, 1971).
23. *The Future of Socialism*, op. cit, p. 140.
24. John Vaizey in *Encounter*, August 1977, 'Remembering Anthony Crosland', p. 87. Vaizey sees this feature of Crosland's work as indebted to the analysis of moral judgement developed in A. J. Ayer, in *Language, Truth and Logic* (London: Gollancz, 1946).
25. *Socialism Now*, passim.
26. Stuart Hampshire, 'A New Philosophy for the Just Society', *New York Review of Books*, 24 February 1972.
27. See Vaizey and Bell in 'Anthony Crosland and Socialism', *Encounter*, August 1977.
28. Samuel Brittan, *The Economic Consequences of Democracy* (London: Temple Smith, 1977), p. 272.
29. John Goldthorpe, 'Social Inequality and Social Integration', in Wedderburn (ed.), op. cit, p. 231.
30. John Rawls, *A Theory of Justice* (Oxford: Clarendon Press, 1972) p. 105. I have tried to discuss these themes in 'Community: Concept, Conception and Ideology', in *Politics and Society*, Vol. 8, No. 1, 1978, and in *Political Philosophy and Social Welfare* (London: Routledge & Kegan Paul) 1980.
31. R. M. Titmuss *The Gift Relationship: From Human Blood to Social Policy* (London: Allen & Unwin, 1970).

7 The National Assistance Board and the 'Rediscovery' of Poverty

John Veit-Wilson

INTRODUCTION

This chapter reports for the first time on a unique review of the adequacy of the United Kingdom's social assistance benefit levels, carried out in the early 1960s. Even before the foundation of the Child Poverty Action Group (CPAG) in 1965, an increasing number of reports were publicly 'rediscovering' the persistence of poverty. They were also suggesting that the incomes of recipients of National Assistance (NA) were inadequate, in the sense that they were insufficient to meet national standards of minimal social participation.[1] The review was the means by which the National Assistance Board (NAB) privately sought to test these criticisms. Its singularity is that it is the only empirical study of adequacy ever carried out by officials within a government department, as opposed to external researchers. Perhaps because it confirmed that the social reforms of the 1945 Labour Government had not abolished poverty, the report was neither published nor subsequently referred to.[2] No further attempt to test the adequacy of income maintenance benefits, or even to set adequacy standards, has been made by any UK government to the present day.

The review was carried out by two groups of NAB officials. One group (chaired by Allan Beard) considered the NA scale rates for children; another (chaired by Robert Windsor) carried out a more complex survey of adult NA scale rates. I shall refer to their reports by their names: Beard Report (BR) and Windsor Report (WR). They reported to the National Assistance Board itself, the committee which ostensibly had executive power to run the NA system and make recommendations to the Minister for Pensions and National Insurance (MPNI), who in turn was answerable for it in Parliament (and who, in

116

reality, took the overarching policy decisions). Their work was innovative because it acknowledged the social relativity approach to defining poverty rather than simply the subsistence approach adopted by the Beveridge Committee in 1942.[3] However, their task was not to carry out a sociological enquiry into the nature of poverty but to use methodologically defensible criteria to test the minimal adequacy of NA by conventional and politically credible standards and to report on their findings.[4]

CHANGING ATTITUDES IN THE NAB

The appointment of a new Secretary, Sir Donald Sargent, to the National Assistance Board in 1959 after the retirement of Sir Harold Fieldhouse, who had been Secretary since 1948, marked a change in the acceptability of new ideas in the NAB. Fieldhouse had represented old-fashioned Poor Law assumptions, with their emphasis on less-eligibility, minimum subsistence, the class-cultural stratification of standards of claimant needs and administrative 'tone'.[5] Sargent was appointed at a time when government had just abandoned the minimum subsistence rationalisation of National Assistance benefits and decided instead to uprate them in line with 'increasing national prosperity'.[6] Geoffrey Beltram, an official in the NAB at the time, recalled that Sargent 'had a very difficult job of letting in some fresh air, which he did very effectively, and he responded to a lot of the criticism of the scale rates and of the failure of the old people to claim and so on in a positive way'.[7] The traditional view held by administrators was, Allan Beard recalled, to avoid embarrassment to the government at all costs and, 'if ministers could not find more money, to put up arguments for leaving things as they were'. For traditionalists to admit that the scales were inadequate was implicitly to condemn their own stewardship. Consequently, they would not ask for increases in the scales over inflation, 'whereas Sargent's view was different. If he thought the rates were inadequate, then he'd bang on people's doors'.[8]

Sargent started by encouraging purposive enquiry into issues of actual or potential interest to policy-makers. Up to this time, the functions of the department had been seen as merely administrative, the policy changes amounting to little more than uprating the scales in line with inflation. For instance, the enquiries into the adequacy of the scale rates in 1934 and 1948 had been paper exercises, concerned primarily with providing a politically viable subsistence rationale for less-eligible benefit scales. Instead, Sargent initially commissioned Kenneth Stowe (who later became Permanent Secretary of the DHSS) to carry out a review of the history of the Poor Law benefits. Stowe recalled in 1988 how this had first impressed on him the continuing truth of the assertion made by the UAB officials in 1934, that there was little scientific basis for the level of the scale rates:[9]

> That would be true now. There isn't a scientific basis, there never has been, and no-one has ever succeeded in establishing one. I am not saying that there cannot be; I'm saying that as a matter of historical record there never has been a scientific basis. And it never has, in my view, been seriously pursued as an option. I've been in and around that department for 36 years and I never heard anybody seriously suggest that we should set up a scientific study to discover what the adequate basis for the scale is to be. There were no real reviews of adequacy. The Social Security Review initiated under Norman Fowler did not address adequacy. It took the framework as it was and started necessarily from the standpoint of cost.[10]

In fact, we shall see that Sargent later commissioned two major studies of the adequacy of the scale rates, but Stowe saw these as being more pragmatic then scientific.

Partly as a result of the raising of the scale rates in 1959, the problem of the wage stop became salient:

> The wage stop deduction, as a proportion of the total entitlement of a family, had been getting bigger because of what happened in 1959. This share of national prosperity led to a very substantial percentage increase for married couples, an 18 percent increase if I recollect correctly. This was applied pro rata to the subordinate scale rates, which meant that in the case of a family with three (or more) children the aggregate increase occasioned by the 1959 uprating was very high. It also had a repercussion on wages. From that point on, people like Frank Cousins and other trade union leaders came to perceive that the Conservative government had given them a very useful stick with which to beat employers, namely that the wages were now manifestly too low, a big step down from adequacy by comparison with the NA scale rates for a family of four or six.
>
> The wage stop problem with which we were concerned was getting acute; there was a lot of anecdotal evidence that these families with children were having a very hard time. Donald Sargent was

concerned about it. It was as simple as that. You had a Permanent Secretary who thought that 'I'm not happy – let's find out what's going on' – a straightforward concern about the poverty of families with children. This concern had many ways of surfacing, from meetings of the Area Office managers and Regional Controllers in London, cases coming in, general conversation; it bubbled in the administration; it was perceivable in the centre. It's the antennae saying 'this isn't right'. Donald Sargent was very good with antennae. That's what started it.[11]

At the outset, the departmental Information and Research Unit which Sargent set up in 1960 consisted of Kenneth Stowe and Stanley Evans. 'The Board welcome the increase in general awareness that more knowledge is essential to the development of sound policies for improving their [the poor's] lot', it reported.[12] This desire for reliable information was not, of course, a matter of philanthropy alone. The department needed information of its own to respond to or even anticipate the assertions of a new generation of academic specialists in social policy, many of them in the London School of Economics and under the influence of Richard Titmuss,[13] who were beginning to make a public impact. 'There was constant pressure, there was constant criticism', Beltram recalled, 'the Titmice had been nibbling away for years, there had been a constant barrage of attack'.[14] Although there was resistance by some older NAB officials to accepting the new ideas about poverty and need:

nevertheless it was registering inside, there was a lot of discussion going on, especially the younger administrators who were firmly repressed by the old guard. But when Sargent came in the repression was lifted. Sargent was quite a sagacious man – he spotted straight away the drift of events, and he also spotted that Ken Stowe was an exceptional person, so he pulled out Ken Stowe and used him, and people like Bob Windsor, who was in some ways a different kind of person. He was sage, conservative and also entirely honourable in not subordinating facts to political expediency. Sargent was responding to the pressure for change in the teeth of opposition from the old guard who were still there, but with the support and enthusiasm of the slightly younger guard.[15]

The pressure for a different approach was political as well as academic. In the party political sense, for instance, Stowe recalled:

Richard Titmuss was very active at this time; he was held in very considerable respect. I remember going down with Allan Beard to listen to a debate at the House of Commons, and the Opposition was winning all the arguments. Fed by the Titmice, they were coming out with the facts and figures which made the Ministers' answers look thin.[16]

It was Richard Titmuss's estimates of the numbers of poor in Britain, some seven to eight million, which the officials gave the Minister in their briefing for the Commons debate on the NI Bill and NA Amendment Regulations in November 1960, and it was Richard Crossman, a Labour politician and member of the same intellectual circle, whom they reported as saying that there were some eight million 'living on or near the poverty line, or one in seven of the affluent society'.[17] Labour attacks were likely to increase with the maturing of several research projects. Lynes was preparing his critique of the 1959 scale rate increases, *National Assistance and National Prosperity*, in which he questioned whether the increase had really kept pace with average incomes. Abel-Smith and Townsend were working on their re-analysis of Family Expenditure Survey data for 1953–4 and 1960, which showed that the number and proportion of the poor had increased during this period if measured by a standard based on the changing NA scales.[18]

The NAB notes added that there was no firm evidence of how many lived just above the poverty line of the NA scale rates, and complained that the number of the poor increased every time the scales were raised. This latter point raised the broader issue that the NA scales did not constitute an independent measure of poverty. But what should be used? In January 1960, the Chairman of the NAB, drafting a paper on 'The Question of Increased Reliance upon National Assistance', had complained that the standards of what was subsistence kept changing.[19] This anticipated a letter from Townsend and Lynes in *The Guardian* in which they pointed out that the government had abandoned the subsistence basis of NI and NA but without putting an alternative standard in its place.[20]

This political challenge highlighted two problems: not only the paucity of the existing standards used but, even worse, their disregard in the wage stop. The Chairman of the NAB himself felt that 'it is manifestly not satisfactory that the Board should in so many cases ... reduce payments below the scale fixed by themselves to give a reasonable standard of subsistence'.[21] Apparently the matter was becoming seen as politically serious, and Sargent wrote to the Permanent Secretary of the MPNI, Sir Eric Bowyer:

> For the first time, I believe, since the war an attack on the Board seems to be developing about the wage stop clause … Quite independently of the outbreaks of public criticism, we have ourselves been feeling increasingly troubled about the position. We have no doubt about the rightness of the wage stop policy – and indeed I think most responsible opinion outside would agree with it in principle. And we are quite sure it would not be right to be deterred by wage stop difficulties from making justifiable improvements in the scale rates. Necessary as the wage stop is, we cannot but feel very unhappy at restricting a family's income to some pounds below what, according to our scales, it should be.[22]

While the NAB therefore did not regret the improvements in the scale above low wages, it wanted to know what might be done to diminish the wage stop problem.[23] Sargent consequently opened discussions with the MPNI on proposals such as increased family allowances for larger families and 'the abolition of the ban on paying national assistance to men in full-time employment'.[24]

The period at the end of the 1950s and the beginning of the 1960s was thus one of change: changing perspectives on the adequacy of the scales themselves, and changing political and administrative awareness of the need for defensible independent standards of adequacy of level and tone. Further information was required, particularly on the needs of children. In December 1962, therefore, Sargent commissioned his Information and Research Unit team to carry out a study 'to examine the children's rates, their general level in relation to the adult rates, the age banding and the relativities between the different age bands'.[25] The next section deals with its approach and findings.

In this and the later enquiry into adult rates, Sargent and Stowe were both clear that 'science' had only a limited role to play. Sargent reported at the time that:

> It could not, of course, be claimed that when a piece of work of this kind had been done it was possible to deduce from it a scientific answer to the question of what action, if any, was called for. The answer must still be a matter of judgement, but he was certain that better results were obtained if judgement was exercised on the basis of a full assessment of the relevant facts and considerations: and he

had no doubt of the worth-whileness of a study of this kind on the grounds of strict practical usefulness. In addition it was, he thought, necessary to take account of the fact that studies of this kind were increasingly being made in the social service field by outsiders ... [H]e felt that, in addition to the consideration of practical useful-ness, the Board would be liable to find itself at a disadvantage if it was not in a position to make it clear, if necessary, that basic deci-sions were based on a thorough study of the relevant facts, includ-ing practice in comparable fields.[26]

Stowe, too, saw policy relevance as a barrier to 'science'. A 'profound' study meant 'really going deep into the science' of needs, but:

We took the empirical path of asking, what do [the scales] actually buy? There is no science; you are going to have to make a judge-ment on whether or not this, in the climate of the times, is a reason-able sum for a family to live on, ... the local [NAB] offices didn't think it was: Exceptional Needs Grants going up, discretionary additions going up, with no underlying rationale. It was the rule book being blown by the local staff because they felt it wasn't fair.[27]

The studies of children's and adult scales were, in essence, not pro-voked by existing academic critiques of the scales but by the view that the facts needed to be collected. Much of the academic research still remained to be published, and the Child Poverty Action Group was not founded until both reports were completed. Beard could recall no outside influences of that kind on his report, insisting that 'the essence of Sargent's approach was that he would have an objective study with no political influences and then present the results to his masters'.[28] But there was a measure of political calculation in identifying the masters: the studies were commenced after twelve uninterrupted years of Conservative government and:

Sargent could see that Labour might come in, and he could see that it wasn't good enough to be in the old reactionary rut. He was col-lecting evidence and setting up a situation where, to an incoming Labour government, he could say 'Look, we've been doing all this work, and this is the direction it points in.'[29]

The following sections, which report on the two studies, suggest that the disclaimer of science was perhaps over-modest.

THE STUDY OF THE CHILDREN'S SCALE RATES CHAIRED
BY ALLAN BEARD

The question of the adequacy of the children's scale rates exercised the Board in the context of the wage stop. If less-eligibility held the NA rates for a married couple to below low wages, could not family allowances and the NA children's rates be used to meet the additional needs of children in the family? Civil servants had, however, tradition-ally countered such criticism by the argument that children's benefits were only one element among several in the family's total income and should not be seen in isolation.[30] The immediate reason for Sargent's establishment of the study was, therefore, a different debate within the Board about whether the scales for older children were enough in themselves and had the appropriate relativities to the other scales. It minuted that when next there was a review of all the scales, there might be a case for proposing a higher increase for children between 11 and 15. The explicit aim of the study was therefore 'to examine the case for this increase'.[31]

The study was carried out by Stowe and three other officials; he and four colleagues (one of whom was Beard, the head of the group[32]) then evaluated the material and wrote the report. It was commissioned on 20 December 1962 and reported a year later in December 1963. Two internal surveys were carried out. The first examined how some 300 families with children, who had received NA for a year or more, were managing; the second was concerned with the duration of receipt of NA by families with children, and how far their basic benefits were supplemented by Exceptional Needs Grants and Discretionary Allowances. Data was also collected from the Family Expenditure Survey, from sociologists ('with discretion') and medical authorities, from the Ministry of Health and from local authorities and voluntary organisations (such as those operating second-hand clothing stores).

The group was aware that, given greater resources of staff and time, more could have been done in amassing information about the situ-ation of all families with children, non-poor as well as poor.[33] But in spite of this, the report claimed that 'sufficient material had been assembled ... to clarify the questions which needed to be considered and to provide a reasonable corpus of material with which to frame the answers and draw some conclusions'.[34] Beard's memorandum to Sargent covering the final report stated that 'as far as I am aware, this is the first time that information on this subject has been assembled in such quantity and detail in one document'.[35] However, the group did not express its conclusions as formal recommendations. Instead, it referred to 'some possible lines of development'[36] and to principles by which the scales might be evaluated.

It is not relevant here to expand on the methods or general conclusions of the study, but to consider in what ways and how far the report reflected the state of departmental thinking about needs. The issue for the officials was to find a defensible current definition of the minimum needs of children, expressed in cash terms. As common sense and political opinion raised the question of whether children of different ages had different needs in cash terms, this had to be investigated.[37]

The group initially considered the history of the children's scale rates. It recalled that 'under the Poor Law it had been customary to have a flat rate for each child, regardless of age' and that age banding had been introduced by the Unemployment Assistance Board, which originally provided for four age bands for children up to 14 (then the normal school leaving age for the working class) and one from 14 to 18. The report noted the lack of scientific basis for the UAB's scales, but its reiteration in 1963 is worth remark:

> There is no evidence to show whether or not the amounts of children's scale rates were fixed on any scientific basis. Whilst it is not possible to ascertain the basis on which the age-banding was decided it was said in a note of 25th June 1934 to the Treasury that ' ... it could be justified if necessary by reference to dietary studies such as that of Cathcart and Murray'. Nevertheless, the Parliamentary debates ... indicate that the children's scale rates received a large measure of acceptance ... [and] were recognised as an improvement on the Poor Law rates generally, and the principle of age-banding was well-received. Criticism was based largely on the fact that the proposed children's scale rates were low in relation to the food standards recommended by the BMA and to the general standards recommended by the Children's Minimum Committee ... These were answered by reference to the Board's discretionary powers and to the fact that the children's scale rates should not be looked at in isolation but as part of the total family income.[38]

The traditional civil service approach was therefore one of deciding on the level of the scales (almost determined, one might say, by the less-eligibility principle) and then finding *post hoc* rationalisations in terms of a different and publicly hard-to-dispute discourse, that of nutritional science. But what was to be the new approach in 1963?

The group's starting point was the admission that the children's scale rates in 1946 had been set below the Beveridge recommendations (which themselves were acknowledged to be inadequate), and that there had been no clear statement of what they were intended to cover. The general assumption was that the rates for children 'were regarded as having only the same elements in them as the Beveridge rates (viz. food, clothing, fuel, and light).'[39] For children, about four-fifths of the rate was for food, three-twentieths for clothing and the remaining one-twentieth for fuel and light. The Beveridge standards had been dispensed with by the Assistance Board (AB) after the war because the available foodstuffs did not match the recommended minimum diet, and the Ministry of Health had then admitted that the scale rate for men of working age was inadequate.[40] 'Beveridge had considered, following Cathcart and Murray, that as much or more should be allowed in food for children over five as for a single pensioner; the 1948 allowance for a single pensioner (11s 6d) was, however, higher than the whole of the children's scale rate for the 11–15 age group, 10s 6d.'[41] The report appended the Assistance Board memoranda of 1945 and 1948, which reiterated the political nature of the judgement, but it avoided the simple assertion that the NAB baseline for children was inadequate, turning instead to an examination of the external standards by which the official measures might be judged.[42] 'The Beveridge standard was the last test of adequacy applied by the Board to the children's scale rates', and:

> the pre-1948 studies of the cost of maintaining a child were all directed to establishing *the minimum subsistence* cost. Subsistence for a child was considered to comprise only a sufficiency of food and a bare standard of clothing. Provision for fuel was added on a family basis by Rowntree but on a personal basis by Beveridge.[43]

Food costs for children were simply based proportionately on adult estimates. Beveridge's addition for clothing and fuel came from the 1938 survey of working class household expenditure. Revaluing these estimates at 1963 prices suggested the NA scales provided 'substantial margins' above these minimum subsistence authors' estimates of the cost of a child.[44]

The group also examined contemporary studies. On food needs, it used British and US medical data and accepted that children of 11 upwards needed as many calories as adults doing light work. Costings were derived from the Ministry of Health's nutritional expert (Dr W. T. C. Berry), the National Food Survey data and Dr T. Schulz[45] of the Oxford Institute of Statistics ('she found no correlation in these surveys between income and quantity and quality of food consumed comparable to the close correlation in pre-war years'). On clothing needs, it was noted that in adolescence, age was not much use as a guide to height, and that over the age of about 13 'children mostly wear clothing from the adult price range'.[46] The FES data examined for the years 1957, 1961 and 1962 gave an indication of the incremental costs of children in families of different sizes and income levels. The random sample of 300 families who had received NA for a year or more showed, *inter alia*, that nearly two-thirds were single parent households; that 'housewives had little idea of the cost of maintaining their children, budgeting always being on a family basis'; that heating expenditure varied by the number of adults but not children; and 'the investigators gained the impression that clothing caused the greatest amount of worry to families with children'.[47] Interestingly, in view of the political influence of 'prescriptivists', the survey found that 'food has ceased to be the first charge on the majority of family budgets', and '*All* parents made some provision for "extras" for the children in the form of pocket money and/or provision of sweets, comics, etc.'[48]

How, then, should the minimum needs of children in 1963 be expressed? The group was clear that the subsistence items (food, clothing and fuel) alone were an insufficient guide. The fact that all families spent on miscellaneous items for children demonstrated an irresistible social pressure. But that did not mean that the cost of such expenditure should be met by the state. However, perhaps some part should be met, and the group felt that the margin in the existing scales was not large enough to do this. Citing the AB Memorandum of April 1948 about the stringency of the adult scales, the group added: 'whatever may have been thought proper when arriving at subsistence levels in the past, it is considered that such expenditure should be allowed for today', and quoted in support Adam Smith's much-cited comment about linen shirts as necessities.[49]

Thus in spite of its overall conclusions that 'the 1963 children's rates ... show no such inadequacy as would be sufficient of itself to cause hardship, although for reasons unconnected with the level of the rates some families with children may indeed be in difficulty',[50] the report clearly indicated a departure from the merely physiologically-based approach to defining minimum subsistence. Beard expressed the motive behind the departure as the desire to diminish stigma:

We did have quite a lot of discussion about pocket money, and decided that children of a certain age should have some money. I do recall that we thought it extremely important that the children of people on assistance should not feel out of place with their contemporaries at school, their friends whose families were not on assistance. They should have a reasonable amount of pocket money. It probably was the first time that had been really brought up. I don't think any of the earlier rates of assistance had got any element of it.[51]

The reference group here was not, however, average society but the peer group of the children, who might be the children of low paid workers. The conclusions of the report were thus still couched in minimum subsistence language:

The needs of children which should be met by national assistance are food and groceries which are the major need, clothing, and miscellaneous 'extras', including pocket money, each of which is relatively modest; and finally fuel and light, which are minimal.[52]

Particular aspects of the scales were, however, singled out for attention: inequities between larger and smaller families (to the latter's detriment), more logical age breaks at 8 and 13 and better provision for the young adolescent of 13 and over. While the Beard review therefore did not escape from the language of minimum subsistence, or indeed push the calculation of scale rates towards meeting the costs of children as calculated by others in national or local government[53], it did at least open the discussion to a consideration of social as well as of physiological necessities for children.

The NAB summarised the Beard report in its Memorandum 1263. It answered the question, 'do the children's rates as a whole provide an adequate standard?', by stating that the question was imponderable because the answer could not be based on costs alone. It referred back to the minimum subsistence calculations of Rowntree, Beveridge and the nutritionists, by whose standards 'the rates in general are seen to provide a satisfactory standard'.[54] The Board considered the memorandum, accepted the advice that no change was in any case called for until all the NAB scales were raised, and endorsed the suggestion that the scales for older children should then be raised by 'a substantial sum of several shillings, as an act of deliberate policy, openly defended as such'. It also made recommendations for age breaks, but was unconvinced of the arguments for discrimination between families of different size or for special clothing grants.[55]

The Board was pleased with its 'new departure' report. The chairman wrote to the MPNI, aiming to get the Treasury thinking at the official level about its implications, and to indicate that the NAB intended to carry out a further study of the adult scale rates. Sargent told the rest of the Board members about this at their next meeting. Having completed the review of the children's rates:

> the question arose of what aspect of the scale rates should next be made the subject of special study. He had discussed this with the Chairman and ... having regard particularly to the fact that in considering any particular rate an important factor must be its relativity to other rates, the best result would be obtained by proceeding straight to a comprehensive examination of the adolescent and adult rates generally. ... the new study would not be confined to an examination of the existing pattern but would also cover the question of whether there was a case for creating any new categories, representing groups considered to have needs of a special character.[56]

A decision was also taken not to mention the review 'to outsiders' – in Whitehall as well as amongst the general public – 'until the time came for action'.[57]

THE STUDY OF THE ADULT SCALE RATES CHAIRED BY ROBERT WINDSOR

The Process of Enquiry

In March 1964, Sir Donald Sargent commissioned a group of four senior officials and a secretary to study the adult scale rates. The group was chaired by Robert Windsor, the NAB's Principal Finance Officer, and it included Kenneth Stowe, the only official who had also been a member of the Beard team. In contrast to the previous study, the new terms of reference were more explicit about the need to justify the rates of benefit. They were 'to consider the scale rates above the age of 16, to examine aspects of the matter which may shed light (a) on the relationship between them and (b) so far as may be possible, on the actual level of the rates, and to make recommendations and suggestions.'[58]

The principal perceived problem at the time was of course not the level of the scales in the abstract, but the level of benefit for particular groups such as the old. Sargent, however, issued an additional memorandum to clarify that the group 'will be expected not to confine themselves to relativities between the existing categories but to consider also whether there is a case for new categories with differential rates, for example the aged and/or those living on national assistance for an extended period.'[59] We thus have here the first and only review by a British government department of the fundamental justifiability of the benefit levels being paid in the basic income maintenance system.[60]

The timing of the review was not chosen for its overt political salience, though the NAB was not isolated from the current flow of ideas. Sargent's sensitivity to the prevailing NA issues reflected the new atmosphere of enquiry and respect for facts. A 1965 briefing offering model answers to hypothetical questions refuted the suggestion that the report had been timed with the General Election of 1964 in mind by pointing out that the information was not available until later. It also included the following:

> Q: Is this survey intended to be a counter to the survey on poverty which is to be conducted by Peter Townsend and Brian Abel-Smith at the University of Essex?
> A: No. This survey was conceived before it was known that the University of Essex intended to launch such a survey.[61]

Windsor and Stowe each produced papers on their first thoughts for the group, which provide an insight into the nature of the officials' ideas about the scope of the problem of defining and measuring need. Windsor listed what he thought were the needs to be covered: food; clothing (and bedding: 'not in the current scale'[62]); heating and lighting; short-term household replacements (pots and pans); long-term household replacements (furniture); and an element for amenities. The needs of shelter (rent) were to be covered separately. In a later note, this list was extended to cover personal and household cleaning and necessary services such as window cleaning and transport. Variations of needs were to be considered, by age, climate, soil, atmosphere, sex, locality, local cost of living and duration on national assistance. The report should also address itself to how the scale rates were to be settled in future, age banding and differentials, and should include sections on the history of the scales, and their relationship to wage rates (in the past, at present, and what might be desirable in the future). There was a further problem to be considered, and that was the level of need: was it to be taken as being 'at subsistence level only', or this level plus 'a share of national prosperity', or was it to be defined by reference to external criteria such as wage rates, the levels of earnings, National Insurance scales, or family expenditure patterns? Stowe's paper addressed itself to 'Some basic questions'. These were: what was the purpose of the NA scale rates; if there were variable circumstances, should the scales vary for different classes; what criteria were relevant to judging their appropriate level; how did the current scales match up to these questions; whether anything should be done if they did not; and if so, what?

The first meeting of the group took place on 23 March 1964, and it minuted agreement on some of these issues. The purpose of the NA benefits was to provide 'maintenance', though it had never been clearly defined what this was. The original concept had been 'a minimum income required for subsistence', but after the uprating of 1959 should the scales include a built-in 'prosperity factor' – and how should it be assessed? The group agreed that the needs to be covered included food, clothing and bedding, heating and lighting, short-term household replacements, and long-term ones 'where possible'. But it was uncertain whether and how far the scales should cover 'what might be termed luxury expenditure, for example, tobacco, alcohol and entertainment, and whether they should contain a margin for inefficient spending'. The criteria for settling the scales in future were expanded to include national income per head.[63] Further, a survey was to be carried out to see how the actual expenditure of recipients differed from that prescribed for the scales, 'and whether any items of customary or necessary expenditure were omitted from the scale rates.'[64] These are all clear signs of the persistence of the prevailing minimum subsistence paradigm, within which there were now new queries about the minimum at issue. Nevertheless, we must note that in a discarded draft there was revealing evidence of an increasing openness to new ideas: 'The group was influenced by the general change in outlook which regards national assistance as designed no longer only for the relief of destitution but expects it to provide a reasonable standard which should include a margin for many of those small items of expenditure now covered by most of the discretionary additions.'[65]

Further planning for the study threw up what were described as 'policy considerations': whether meeting the need for shelter should be by provision within the scale rates, or by a separate provision for rent, or by a new formula. On the question of meeting the need for food, was this to be measured 'scientifically' (meaning prescriptively), or in terms of what people preferred to eat, or by what they could afford to eat? The same issues arose in considering the need for clothing and bedding: were these to be measured in terms of a 'scientifically' measurable requirement, or a 'reasonable' physical need, or treated as matters of habit and conventional acceptability? And the question of heating was further complicated by the costs of possible future technical developments.[66]

During the next few months, a further policy consideration arose, which came to be among the most significant. This was based on the temporal dimension of need: the implications of distinguishing the needs of the long-term recipients from those who depended on NA for only short periods: 'in so far as the long-term have no expectations, National Assistance should provide, on the grounds of *equity*, not poverty, a standard that gives enjoyment of some of our affluence.' The existing scales did not do this; the 1948 scales were 'thin (plenty of evidence)', and although they had improved since then 'to give some fat and admittedly are not now "primary" poverty lines (Note: the "theoretical" argument establishes this)', the long-term cases clearly needed more.[67] The memorandum went on to confirm that long-term cases could be identified, and proposed higher rates of benefit for all recipients of 65 and over. Here, then, is the origin of the provision for the long-term addition to Supplementary Benefit which was introduced in 1966 and lasted for 22 years.

Methods of Enquiry

The group examined the question of an appropriate level for the scales in three different ways, but before doing so, it had to define what the scales were for. The successive drafts of the report give us an insight into the officials' thinking, including those ideas which were later to be amended or even omitted. Since that thinking, rather than the bald conclusions alone, is the focus of this chapter, it is relevant to quote some of these changes at length. The first draft on file[68] dealt with the question as follows:

> The NA scale rates are the statutory answer to the question, what standard of living, in monetary terms, does the state undertake to provide for those who seek its help? Any question of standards immediately raises difficulties of definition; the whole matter

becomes confused by the use of imprecise concepts like 'need', 'sub-sistence', 'minimum requirements', 'the poverty line', 'a share of prosperity' and so on, the meaning of which depends largely upon the time, place and circumstances in which they are used and the value judgements of the user.[69]

In the final report, the notion of the state undertaking to provide help to seekers was replaced by 'a standard ... below which no one need fall'.[70] The undertaking itself – the obverse of the right to benefit – was not in fact introduced until 1966, when it formed part of the attempt to improve the tone of NA. In the belief that it would help to avoid these semantic problems, the report turned to the 1948 National Assistance Act itself, which required the NAB to assist 'persons whose resources are insufficient to meet their requirements' (National Assistance Act, 1948, Section 4). The term 'requirements' was there-fore chosen to avoid the use 'of words with overtones such as "subsist-ence" and "needs"'. Although the 1948 rates were designed to meet 'minimum requirements', the group avoided that usage because: 'Whether the standard should be minimal (however the word is defined) or something more and, if so, how much more is a question to which the answer will vary according to economic and social cir-cumstances and the temper of the times. In this study we have sought an answer which will have regard to the circumstances of Great Britain in the mid 1960s'.[71]

To answer the question, 'what are the requirements which national assistance should meet?', the report proposed three different 'lines of approach': traditional, comparative and empirical. The report described 'the traditional approach' as that 'followed by sociologists such as Booth, Rowntree and Beveridge, which holds that the lowest level of State provision has in it an element of the absolute and uses the physical and social sciences to determine what goods and services the citizen requires and how much is needed to buy them'.[72]

The report admitted that science could not answer the question of what minimum needs were in modern societies; at most, medical science might answer for nutritional needs and their cost. The rest were a matter of judgement, and even if some list were prescribed, people might not spend their money on those items; if they failed to do so, they would fall below the line unless some margin had been left for their preferences. The report therefore concluded that 'the tradi-tional approach has had to include something of the comparative approach'.[73]

The second method was a comparative study of expenditure patterns in the population at large, not just the poor, on the assumption that income and expenditure patterns give rise to perceived requirements. But the report then confused this insight about relative deprivation with the valid but conceptually distinct question of how far changes in prosperity and thus requirements should be reflected in the social security provisions.[74] If the average were rejected as a guide, it argued, that would still leave the question of where to set the minimum necessary selection of goods and services which were consumed by the population. However, the report went on to argue that this approach was constructive because recipients had lived 'as ordinary members of the community' and would have similar standards; their reference groups would be their non-claiming neighbours. In a comment which is in fact about the social security scales and not poverty lines, the report made an important and revealing statement about the symbolic as well as practical role which scales play in public consciousness:

> Thus the assistance standard could be judged as much by reference to the degree of deprivation it imposes on recipients as by the goods and services for which it provides. On this approach a national assistance allowance which provides fully – even generously – for, say, food, fuel and clothing will not be thought adequate if it means that the recipient has to give up the television, or leaves what will, in common judgement, be too large a gap in incomes between persons on national assistance and the man in employment.[75]

The third approach was an empirical study of how a sample of NA recipients was actually managing. The report rejected the risk of implying that because recipients spent a certain amount, that was what they required; it admitted that an independent measure was needed, but argued that 'finding out how people on assistance live has the merit of providing a background of realism and a point of reference against which judgements may be made with more confidence than if made in ignorance of how people manage on assistance'.[76] An earlier draft added that the method also had the advantage that 'even in isolation, a survey of recipients may bring the judgement of the Board's field staff to bear on the question whether they are going short by reference to the Board's existing standards'.[77] As we shall see, this issue of variation in staff observation of standards (and the consequent volume of unmet need) was a finding of the survey which caused serious concern to the Board.[78]

These three approaches are not conceptually in the same method-ological category; they cannot be used as a kind of triangulating survey method, although the report implies that this was the aim. The first approach could be described as the 'traditional' way of constructing a minimum budget prescriptively, and was used by B. S. Rowntree to prescribe a minimum income standard for decency in *The Human Needs of Labour* (1937; referred to as HNOL), and to rationalise asocial subsistence by Beveridge in his 1942 Report. The second approach is not a way of finding a poverty line at all, let alone a social security scale, because (as the report admitted) it does nothing except reveal conventional expenditure patterns, without prescribing what a tolerable minimum consumption of the goods and services purchased would be. That would still be left to the experts, or to convention, to prescribe. The third method exposes aspects of life on a low income without showing what higher income would be needed to make the level of living conventionally acceptable. The group realised that in the end these approaches would not answer the question posed, but asserted that 'all three taken together would provide a body of evi-dence on which a judgement could be made'.[79] In other words, the comparative and empirical methods were intended to provide reliable evidence of a kind not previously available, which could be used by civil servants designing social security scales to make them more polit-ically defensible in the new ambience of relativity. That is a sufficient and perfectly justifiable role for a civil service review. But they were confused between this justifiable aim and the search for a poverty line, something which the group was not equipped to investigate or report on. This was a conceptual and practical distinction which did not seem to be made or understood at the time. Nevertheless, it was certainly an advance of a kind that the report avoided the use of the termino-logy, which was threadbare then and outworn now, of 'subsistence', 'absolute' and 'relative' poverty. The group sought, and found, a more constructive use of terms.

The Traditional Approach

In examining how to take what it called 'The Traditional Approach', the group decided to avoid looking for 'minimum' requirements. This may seem hard to believe, as it is supposed to be inherent in the con-struction of social assistance systems that the state provides the least that is needed. But the group wanted to avoid the use of the term for fear that its taken-for-granted meaning as 'minimum needed for physical subsistence' would be confused with 'minimum level ... at which requirements should be met' by the state. 'Recent experience of public argument about the national assistance scheme supports the view that such confusion of thought is very likely', the report added pointedly.[80] Naturally the group was looking for the minimum cost of what people without sufficient resources required from the state, but this should be expressed as their:

> requirements which ... would enable them to follow the general habits of the community at large in buying the day-to-day necessities of life (food, heating and lighting, clothing and household goods) and would allow them a small margin of income so that, without going short on staple items, they might have some share in the purchasing power which is conspicuously enjoyed in Britain today. Such a standard would require no further supplementation save in quite rare circumstances and it should not be described as minimum since people can and do live on less.[81]

The report argued that the concept of minimum subsistence had no validity in social security, first, because nothing in the statute required it, but chiefly because it 'lends an appearance of objectivity to what must remain a matter of judgement'.[82] The judgement in 1934 and 1948 had been that times were hard and wages were low. Minima were perceived differently in the 1960s, and the 1959 policy change demanded more than subsistence. The group rejected Beveridge's exclusion of everything except urgent expenditure and decided that the period over which requirements were to be calculated was a year. 'Put broadly, retrenchment of the order which Beveridge appeared to have in mind does not accord with the current social and economic climate.'[83] The requirements which were examined and estimated in the traditional approach were for food, fuel, clothing, durable household goods, and miscellaneous. The basic unit was taken to be a single person living alone, for two reasons: sharing was assumed to create not greater costs but savings; and the largest separate household category of NA recipients was persons living alone (42.6 per cent in December 1964).

On the food needs, the group reviewed and rejected the estimates used up to 1949 as too low. Instead it took account of estimates published since 1950 by the BMA and Ministry of Health (for the WHO and FAO), and on information from the National Food Surveys 1950–61. An upper estimate of calorie needs corresponding to all but the needs of adult males of working age (as these were only a tiny proportion of recipients) was then taken and translated into a cash sum. Here the group rejected the prescriptive methods of pricing the calories in expert nutritionists' dietaries, or in the dietary components of the national average diet, as both methods required NA recipients to have nutritional expertise. Instead, the group chose a method recommended by the Ministry of Health's Senior Medical Officer. This took the average unit cost of each 1000 calories in the national diet as a whole (calculated from Ministry of Agriculture data on household food consumption and expenditure for households of varying composition) and multiplied accordingly. To avoid criticism, the group chose a figure 'to understate rather than overstate the cost of meeting requirements', plus a ten per cent wastage allowance. This produced a weekly cost of 39s 1.5d per person, compared with Beveridge's cost of 22s 1d and Rowntree's HNOL cost of 18s 9d for men, all at October 1964 prices. The report's estimate of needs was thus below average calorie consumption, and the proposed cost below average expenditure on food. 'Founding the requirement for food on the average daily cost of 1000 calories in the national diet does, however, have this consequence: that it is meaningless to describe it as a *minimum* requirement in money terms.' Clearly the nutrients could be bought for less, as well as for more: the figure should 'be described as a standard requirement – one could manage on less and enjoy spending more.'[84]

Estimates of the appropriate amounts to include for fuel were complicated by changes in the technology of heating. Earlier estimates had assumed coal was the principal component; this was no longer as true. Further, there was uncertainty about the sum ascribed to heating costs in the scales: was it to cover the cost of a scientifically measurable requirement, a reasonable physical need, or merely habit and convention? Throughout the period of the NAB, there had been complaints that old people had to spend more on fuel than the scales allowed, thus leaving them short of food. The winter of 1962/3 had been severe and there continued to be widespread concern about hypothermia. The group decided that it could not speak of minimum heating requirements, as these presupposed no more than what is needed to sustain life, but instead adopted the phrase 'a minimum standard of heating' as implying a judgement about what people *ought* to have.[85] That judgement followed one which had already been made by another government agency: the Central Housing Advisory Committee under the chairmanship of Sir Parker Morris, which had reported to the Ministry of Housing and Local Government in 1961 on the standards to be adopted for residential accommodation. These standards were costed and an allowance duly calculated.

Clothing provided the group with the same basic problem: the 'science' of subsistence had nothing to say about requirements, and culture was the only source of standards. The group therefore commissioned J. E. Goodwin to seek the opinions of public authorities which supplied clothing, and of the clothing trade and consumer associations. The aim was to arrive at a weekly figure for maintaining what the group assumed was an adequate wardrobe, given that there was to be no reliance on second-hand clothing or gifts. The question was: what was an adequate wardrobe, and what was the interval and cost of replacing the items in it? Goodwin's background paper set out the answers to the question which had been given in the past and concluded that:

> the provision for clothing in 1948 was not founded as a result of any widespread enquiry into need or scientific assessment of requirements. Clothes rationing obviously loomed very large then, but the assumptions made in the Board memorandum about supply of second-hand clothing, the dislike of the elderly to renew clothing suggest that the Board did not regard this matter of first importance and expected in fact that clothing needs would largely be met from sources other than the assistance grant.[86]

The issue of tone is very clear here. The paper listed earlier NAB files recording repeated proposals for the NAB or local authorities to hold stores of clothing or wartime surplus blankets for dispensing to eligible recipients. Assistance at that time was for the working class, and charitable donations of clothing and surplus blankets were good enough. Additionally, the paper shed interesting light on the NAB's own standard list of clothing needs, the B/0.40, which was used as a guide when people applied for grants. There were no records of its origin; it was meagre and had remained substantially unchanged for 17 years. It was also incomplete and often superfluous in administration (which was subject to officer discretion), although it was useful as a guide in cases of bad management.

In answer to the question about an adequate wardrobe, the paper concluded that 'It can be stated categorically that there is no recognised optimum standard, neither are there any accepted views as to what standard there ought to be for the less well off members of the community.'[87] Consequently, to frame an agreed standard it proposed that 'if a wardrobe is to be something more than a minimum scale of one garment on and one off', then:

> The clothing, in fit and condition, should enable the wearer to maintain a reasonably presentable appearance in the community. The wardrobe should contain suitable clothing for summer, winter and wet weather. It should not be so restricted in garments that a lack of comfort results, or a change of attire is impossible.[88]

The paper also considered the needs and allowances for household durables. Although the 1948 scales had excluded them, NA claimants were conventionally told that the scales included all 'normal' needs other than rent. The situation had not been clarified until 1959. In principle, the report argued, it would have been best to include a suitable amount in the scale because 'in this way people on assistance are, as near as may be, put in the same position as others in the community who meet their expenditures, both long- and short-term, regular and irregular, from their income'. But after making assumptions about stock required and replacement periods, it was hard to make allowances on a weekly basis for things which lasted ten years or more (or which were needed when coming onto assistance), and the best way to pay for them was to make grants when needed. Even then, the estimates included would still not be enough to allow long-term recipients 'to purchase labour-saving appliances which have become commonplace among the rest of the community. In this respect the allowance proposed is inadequate.'[89]

Finally, the group considered what to allow for additional miscellaneous items. It seemed an impossible task: 'There is no scientific basis on which to build as there is with food, no technical lead for arriving at an objective standard as there is with fuel, and no way of drawing up a standard pattern of requirements as there is with clothing and household linen.'[90] It was entirely a matter of judgement. Adam Smith was again brought in to justify conventional necessaries.[91] All previous estimates were considered too arbitrary for updating. Evidence of conventional consumption was therefore drawn from the two other sources used by the study, the FES data and the survey of NAB recipients' expenditure. These gave proportions of total expenditure (excluding rent) on miscellaneous items of around 27–30 per cent for single non-householders with low incomes, rising with income level to around 40 per cent for the average single person. As no usable distinction could be drawn between expenditure on essentials and non-essentials, the group decided to use, for a single person, a figure which was similar to both the personal expenses allowance paid to those receiving board and lodging scales, and to the average expenditure by single recipients. The statement of principle on which this decision was taken is particularly pertinent:

> To expect people on national assistance to spend only on an arbitrarily restricted range of goods and services is to expect them to live as a class apart. And today we believe the community at large does not wish or expect those on national assistance to live in such a way. Provision should be made to enable the individual or family to live as a member of the community; it should not be so tight that the person on assistance can spend as social custom and habits virtually dictate only by going short of food, fuel and clothes or similarly approved requirements. People on assistance should be able to make some choice among a wider range of goods than those which have been described as essentials, and it is considered that this can best be done by allowing a margin for miscellaneous expenditure. This is more realistic than extending the meaning of 'essentials' indefinitely or of calculating an allowance for specific luxuries such as entertainment, holidays or cigarettes.[92]

Living as a class apart or living as members of the community – these are by definition the criteria of social exclusion or a participation standard of living. But it is an empirical question to ask if they were accepted by the public at large, or by politicians and administrators, as the criteria on which to base a social security scale. We should need to know more about the civil service culture at the time to establish if these liberal sentiments in the report were a reflection of taken-for-granted or wished-for truths. Whichever they were, the expression of principle by civil servants was a palpable shift from the 'minimum subsistence' standard of social security to the 'participation' standard, and in that sense justifies the use of the expression, a paradigmatic shift in thinking. But thought is not practice.

The question of suitable financial provision for recipients' housing needs was also an issue affected by this principle. The precise treatment of rents by NA had always been complicated; the relevant issues here were not so much the rules as the principles by which rents were not paid in full if officials made the social judgement that the accommodation occupied was too expensive for the class of recipient. The group faced the issue squarely: the problem arose partly because of particular kinds of labour market and housing policies which were beyond its remit or the NAB's control. The complexity of the situation was such that it felt unable to recommend an element for housing costs as a standard addition in the scale rates, as had been the practice in assistance until 1944 and in Beveridge's insurance scales. It concluded that where officers had to make judgements about paying rents, the social consequences of underpayment for the recipient (removal or even eviction) should be among the first considerations.[93]

The Comparative Approach

The second, 'comparative', approach considered the actual spending patterns of non-poor people. It used the Ministry of Labour's Family Expenditure Survey data for 1956–63. Most relevant here is the table showing the proportion of expenditure on food, the Engel indicator of level of living.[94] For single householders – excluding the lowest income group (mainly retired) and those with incomes over average earnings – the table showed the food percentage of total expenditure in the two lower income categories as 22.6 per cent and 36.4 per cent, compared with 43.1 per cent spent by NA recipients. The group's proposed (traditional) budget would have allowed a food share of 40.4 per cent (of a higher total income than NA claimants received). This seemed to justify the group's observation that its scale 'does not appear over-generous'.[95]

While the group observed that its proposed 24.3 per cent for fuel seemed high when compared with other groups (18 per cent for NA recipients, down to 5.3 per cent for the group at just below average earnings), recipients tended to be more inactive and need more warmth. The group had allowed more than twice as much in cash terms for clothing (10s per week) than it found was actually spent by NA recipients in the FES, leading it to question if it had overestimated needs (though it did not comment that the NA recipients might have received Exceptional Needs Grants for clothes outside the period surveyed by the FES). The group had also allowed less for the miscellaneous expenditures than was actually spent by the recipients, again suggesting that its prescriptive approach gave incomes below empirically-derived poverty lines.

The group also considered the evidence on earnings to see if the proposals were either so generous that there might be an incentive problem, or so low that recipients recently employed would experience a drastic drop in income that 'could be held to impose an undue degree of deprivation'.[96] The surveys of recipients showed that many old people received in real terms almost as much in NA benefits as they had earned years before, but for younger people, who had benefited from the recent substantial wage increases, 'dependence on assistance more commonly means a marked drop in real income'.[97] After making adjustments for rent and deductions for income tax and NI contributions, the group's proposed level of benefit for a single person would have been about two-fifths of average male manual earnings; for a couple, the proportion would have been a bit over half. But the regional and financial spread of earnings was wide, and in some regions the proposed scale might well have come close to low earnings levels. For couples with children, the wage stop problem would loom large, and so the group reported that the proposals of the Beard report for children's scales should be examined further. Beltram later commented that the Windsor group would have been prepared to see an extension of wage stopping if, by raising the scale rates as it proposed, more families with children would have shared the expenditure patterns of those on average incomes more closely. This implied a move away from class to individualised less-eligibility. As the report itself argued, while its proposals might lessen incentives for claimants with low earning potential and large families and/or high rents, 'this should not lead us to suggest a reduction of the standard for the vast majority of recipients'.[98]

The Empirical Surveys

The third approach used by the group was empirical investigation. Two surveys of NA claimants were carried out. The first, known as the Managers' Survey, was of a sample of 4757 recipients around the country who were interviewed by the managers of local NAB offices. Its aims were to illustrate the circumstances of recipients and their spending patterns, and provide 'an evaluation from the recipients themselves and from the Board's Managers as to how they were managing. This Survey was the first of its kind undertaken by the Board'.[99] The other survey was a sample of the case papers of 1.25 per cent of the live load of recipients in December 1964, around 24,000 people. Following a less-detailed survey in 1956, it aimed to examine the degree of regional variation in the award of discretionary additions to scale benefits.

The managers' survey was a rich source of material on the state of the poor in Britain, and the group initially recommended that the findings should be made available for academic study in a suitable form – they would indeed have welcomed inputs to the survey by academics had there been time.[100] But Sargent felt that the findings of the other survey on the variations in the exercise of discretion might be too politically sensitive for such publication. An unsigned note on file revealed his major anxiety: 'We have shown in some detail variations between Regions as regards the granting of discretionary additions. I hesitated to repeat this as regards exceptional needs because it could bring out forcibly that it all depends on the lead from the top (which was not the object of the exercise).'[101] The note then referred to one region where it had been pointed out to the Regional Controller that it had had the lowest grant-making rate in the country for several years. 'The news was not received very graciously', but ENGs rose from 4 per cent of live load in 1960 to 21 per cent in 1964, compared with the highest average of 23 per cent.[102] Major variations were revealed between offices in giving ENGs and discretionary additions to different categories of recipient. 'We formed the view that there were marked differences between officers as regards the readiness to make grants' because some assumed that the scale rates covering all 'normal' needs obviated supplementation, while others seemed willing to make discretionary payments in shillings but not pounds.[103]

Another factor in variation was the lack of knowledge of some officials about nutritional needs, leading to decisions being made in terms of social and not physiological values: 'An officer visiting a frail old lady who looks undernourished and complains of difficulty in managing may decide to grant a special addition, yet her requirements, in terms of food, may be much less than those of a young, active widow with growing children to look after.'[104] Similarly, the sums awarded for articles varied from one NAB office to another, even in the same town, suggesting officers differed over 'the standard of article considered appropriate for recipients to buy'.[105] Sir Kenneth Stowe summarised the problematic issue revealed by the managers' survey as follows:

What purported to be a fair and reasonable system applied with reasonably uniform discretion was in fact an arbitrary, personally motivated system, with wide discrepancies. If one probed into it one found things went very, very differently according to the temper of the local office manager and the local office staff, and it amply justified the criticisms that were made in support of the income guarantee case, that discretion was found not to be discretion but arbitrary judgement, highly personal arbitrary judgement. Which was the Ark of the Covenant knocked over in terms of the Poor Law and Unemployment Assistance.[106]

The survey by managers thus revealed that the administrative tone of NA was inadequate. It lacked the accepted criteria of good tone for benefits for 'members of the community', including consistency and predictability. The growth in the number of discretionary allowances, which had been a cause for concern throughout the 1950s, had been ascribed in 1959 not to the inadequacy of 'the general standard of the scale rates but indicates the increasing skill and assiduity with which, from increasing experience, the Board's staff recognise and provide for the endless variations of human need which must be taken into account in a scheme of nationwide assistance according to need'.[107]

Its survey led the group to doubt the validity of this claim. It exposed the differences among claimants between those who depended on discretionary additions to increase their scale benefits, and the one-fifth who had disregarded income (which therefore increased their spending power above that given by the scale rate). The latter were considerably more likely to report that they were managing well than those without, both on their own assessments (70 to 51 per cent) and the managers' (82 to 52 per cent). Even the observation that long-term recipients coped by adjusting to low incomes was qualified by 'this probably meant no more than that they had come to accept a restricted way of life', and tended 'to dissociate themselves from the habits of life of the community because they felt unable to keep up with the general standard of living'. A crucial difference in managing was 'the unexpected extent to which help in cash or kind from friends or relatives was found to have helped recipients to balance their budgets'.[108]

By contrast, the survey found that the consequence of discretionary arbitrariness was that claimants were deprived. The managers were therefore required to carry out an assessment of the needs of each surveyed recipient for clothing, bedding and household equipment, and award extra grants as appropriate. These interviews were longer and more intensive than ordinary officers' visits and they exposed much unmet need; 'it is not usual to invite a recipient of assistance to ask for something', but on the other hand managers did not give unjustified grants. Almost half (2113) of all those surveyed received grants as a result of the managers' interviews, over half (1226) being for clothing. If grants had been made on the same basis to all recipients in 1964, over 870,000 grants would have been made instead of the 345,000 actually made by lower officials. The group concluded that staff used discretion in a highly variable manner to support inadequate benefits. It expressed the hope that if scales were raised to the level it proposed, the need for grants should become genuinely exceptional.[109]

Conclusions of the Study Group

The evidence which it collected from its various surveys and special reports convinced the group that 'we could not regard as satisfactory the standard of living provided by the scale rates in operation in 1964'.[110] The existing benefit level was too low for the approach to a new participation standard of income, which it had tentatively indicated as its criterion. The chief difference in levels of needs was between short- and long-term dependence on assistance. The old should get more, not because they were old but because they would by definition be long-term recipients. Others should also get more, but because it was not possible to predict the duration of dependence in advance, this should be after two or three years. Dependence on discretionary additions and grants should thereby be diminished.

Although the comparative and empirical approaches illuminated its thinking about the inadequacies of the existing level of benefits, the group had no independent criteria to help it decide on the level of income needed for such minimal participation. New empirical approaches to measuring poverty were only just being developed by sociologists such as Townsend. The prescriptive approach to adequacy was still customary and the only issue was whether to move from quasi-subsistence to relativistic components of needs. In that context, any evaluation of the importance of the group's recommendations must show them to be a distinct advance on previous, limited studies. We cannot know how the group's proposals for an increase of 22 per cent in the benefit level for a single householder (from 76s per week in March 1965 to 92s 6d) might have compared with empirical poverty measures, but the group made it clear that this relationship was not their concern. The question was the level of benefits, and here other considerations applied: 'Although the assistance rates cannot be considered in isolation, the fact remains that they stand apart from other forms of social security provision in that they have a different job to do: they set a standard which, at the lowest, cannot provide less than the basic requirements for food, fuel, etc.'[111] An earlier draft had put it more bluntly: 'they still retain – and always will retain – an element of the absolute in them'.[112] In other words, the residual level of state income maintenance had to reflect adequacy for a politically feasible minimum living standard, and this might differ from the popular view of the income needed for a minimum participatory level of living.

Although it was not part of its remit, the group made two further important recommendations. One was on the criteria to be used in future for raising of the levels of the scale rates. The other was on further monitoring of the adequacy of benefit levels.

Existing scales had always been based on a prescriptive subsistence construction, uprated by nothing more than some version of a cost of living index with some slight augmentation in 1959. There was no agreed means by which their calculation could be moved to a relativistic basis. The group considered various possibilities: different cost of living indices, general or low income; movements in the average incomes of wage earners; movements in weekly wage rates; or an index of net income per head (subject to much discussion on what to include or exclude, and what population – total or earners alone – to divide by). It concluded that the scales should not be tied to price indexes, not least because 'the criteria for adjusting the scale rates should not, in our view, be concerned only with the maintenance of their real value'. Finding the 'right relationship between assistance standards and the growth of national prosperity, but without making the cost to the Exchequer of an increase in assistance rates itself contribute to inflation, raises, of course, political issues of great difficulty and complexity'. However, in spite of any problems raised in relation to low earnings, the 'material reference points' of the living standards of the community as a whole 'ought to be kept in mind in the regular evaluation of the rates'. These were indicators such as average earnings or net personal incomes (though the group did not feel it proper to recommend any single national index).[113]

The politics of social security, which necessarily acted as a constant beacon to the group, did not however blind it to the issue of how to monitor the effectiveness of the basic social security provision. To be aware of 'the current difficulties of all the variety of persons receiving assistance':

> is of the very essence of the proper administration of assistance, and therefore we *recommend* that there should be instituted a small scale continuous survey into the circumstances, patterns of expenditure, and difficulties of recipients, something on the same lines as

the Managers' Survey. This, we feel, would be of great value in that it would, at any given time, give indications of whether the shoe was pinching and, if so, where. This information, necessarily to some extent in the form of subjective judgements but considered in conjunction with the statistical evidence on the movement in prices, should give firm pointers both to the timing and to the amounts of any proposed increases in the assistance scale rates.

It is nevertheless necessary that there should be from time to time (perhaps every three or four years) a full review of the scale rates taking account of any improvements in general prosperity measured by the available data and indices. Such a review should, in our judgement, include also a full survey of the actual living conditions of recipients on national assistance so as to reflect in any new standard the changing patterns – and problems – of the recipients' way of life.[114]

The Windsor Report on the Adult Scale Rates was, within the parameters set in conceptual and practical terms, a pioneering model of a departmental review on this topic, and according to Sir Kenneth Stowe it remains unique. Although the term 'adequacy' implies a poverty measure and the group were not searching for this in sociological terms, officials made a serious effort to relate the recommended NA standard to methodologically defensible measures of conventional standards of needs and social deprivations. They also proposed to build regular surveys of deprivation into the administration of a politically credible social security system.

REACTIONS TO THE WINDSOR REPORT

The Windsor Report was dated August 1965, but the files noted that the study group finally reported in October, and it was not published, nor was any publicity given to it, other than obliquely in the NAB's 1965 Annual Report.[115] The Board considered the report at its meeting on 22 September and the chairman wrote to the Minister (Margaret Herbison) on 8 October about its implications for policy.[116]

The chief issue which repeatedly emerged was that the large number and regular use of discretionary additions and grants showed that the NA benefits were deficient in both level and tone. During the Board's meeting, Sargent recalled that both major political parties had made proposals for schemes which would have better tone by 'conferring an entitlement to a clearly defined minimum income', but that the current scale rates now looked not like 'a norm, as they were intended to be, but ... a minimum, inadequate in themselves for most people's requirements'. Public opinion, which had welcomed more additions, now saw a detailed test of means as oppressively inconsistent with pensioners' rights, and the scheme was expensive to administer and glaringly inconsistent. Regional staff wanted changes, too, but as the substantially higher benefit rates recommended by the report were 'pretty clearly unattainable at the present time', the question was whether the Board wanted to move away from a system with a very large number of small discretionary additions, to one concentrating better on genuinely exceptional needs.[117]

We should note that the Board's long discussion revealed a conventional misapprehension: if scales were raised and additions subsumed, those who had received most of them would benefit least, and as they 'could be said to be those in greatest need', this was unjust. The first statement was true, but the conclusion that the greatest need was among those who had received the most additions (as opposed to those found by Cole in 1959–60 who for various reasons had not received additions, or even any NA at all) was even then arguably unsupportable.[118] The Board's conclusion was, however, that the problem was inherent in any change from the current system, and (as an ironical minute put it) 'the only alternative appeared to be to retain the existing system, with additions for example of about 1s 6d a week for a cup of Horlicks at night, for all time, however high the level of the scale rates may rise in real terms'. Avoidance of major change by attempts to improve the quality of administration of discretion might be vitiated 'having regard to the factor of personal judgement and the different outlooks and temperaments of different officers, Managers, and Regional Controllers'.[119]

The Board members were also concerned that increases in the scales might increase the number of wage stop cases. Sargent reminded them that most recipients were old people; few recipients were unemployed, and few of those wage-stopped; and

the country ought [not] to be indifferent to the problem represented by the very much larger number of people who were working and bringing up families with incomes substantially less than those provided by the present levels of assistance. He had had a good deal of discussion with this obvious question [sic] with other Government Departments concerned; and an interdepartmental committee had been set up, on which the NAB were represented, and was already at an advanced stage in its consideration of this problem.

The view taken by the Board, after discussion of these and other points, was that the objective set out in the Report of the Study Group was right, that the aim should be to have a substantially higher scale-rate level and to get away from the present system under which three-quarters of the old people had the scale rate supplemented by discretionary additions, many of them for relatively trifling needs represented by very small sums.[120]

The record of the meeting reported Sargent's view that there was general public and political support for the proposal to pay a higher rate to pensioners, though the report had recommended this for all long-term recipients (including pensioners simply as prospective long-term recipients). However, the Regional Controllers opposed a differential scale for a variety of reasons 'which were not very easy to summarise'. The minutes then recorded Sargent's personal statement to the Board:

First he did not believe it was possible to justify in national assistance, a scheme necessarily related to needs, a higher rate for the old as such. Secondly he believed there was a justifiable case for giving more to people who had to live on national assistance for a long-term [sic], and this would of course include the old. But thirdly he felt that there would be real difficulty in convincing public opinion that it was right to draw a line at this point, he felt also that there was difficulty about introducing a relatively small differential, based on no clear criterion, the justification for which might in any case largely disappear with the rising real value of the scale rates. And fourthly he felt it wrong to take no account of the almost unanimous view of the Regional Controllers, and of the repercussions on the National Insurance scheme. On balance he felt, nevertheless, that it was possible to justify a differential, provided the criterion was long-term receipt of national assistance, and accordingly if Ministerial policy favoured it he would be disposed to recommend the Board not to oppose it: but he would himself hesitate to advise the Board to sponsor the proposal and press it on Ministers.[121]

The Board took Sargent's delicately-phrased advice: it did not favour the differential rate as such but 'did not rule out the possibility of a higher rate for long-term recipients of national assistance coupled with a move in these cases away from the present system of giving very large numbers of very small discretionary additions'.[122]

The Windsor Report was soon put into context by the 1965 findings of the MPNI survey of *The Financial Circumstances of Retirement Pensioners*. Like the managers' survey, it disclosed widespread discrepancies and variations in the use of discretion, and the Board therefore considered proposals to reduce it. Officials advised against any implication that the scales were inadequate, and recommended that 'the scale rates have been regarded since 1948, and should continue to be regarded as adequate for all normal requirements as to food, fuel, clothing and miscellaneous household goods, with a small margin for personal expenditure' because the levels of benefit were higher in real terms than ever before. There was a private admission that the Windsor Report's standards would not be met, 'but it is only realistic to accept' that the existing levels of benefit would have to be treated as adequate for everything except large abnormal expenses. The officials distinguished between those expenses which would remain even if the Windsor standards were met, and those which would be subsumed by proper levels of benefit, but only in terms of level not type of expenditure: food, fuel, laundry and other domestic expenses appeared in both lists. The Board agreed that 'it would not be right ... to attempt to give the staff, or a portion of the public, a financial breakdown of the amount assumed to be available in the scales for particular items or categories of expenditure' such as food, fuel and so on (to admit publicly that the scale was in fact based on calculated components was against policy).[123]

Some Board members expressed anxiety that NA would lose its 'casework' character of being individually 'tailor-made' to the needs of each recipient. Officials had to point out that the original aim of assistance had been to provide only for average needs, with individual supplementation for abnormal additions. While administration would become easier with larger benefits and less discretion, money would not be saved because so much unmet need had been exposed. The Permanent Secretary of the MPNI, Sir Clifford Jarrett, voiced his reservations to the Minister, Margaret Herbison. It was impossible, he argued, to have both a fine examination of needs and avoid a heavy administrative load; the latter was possible only if one 'deliberately ignored needs but granted rights, in the true legal sense, to a given level of resources'. The Labour Government's income guarantee proposals, which were just being examined by officials, had similar problems (as Donnison has shown[124]). Strategically, at a time of restricted public expenditure, he concluded:

Will it seem right, so relatively early in a fresh period of Labour administration, to commit ourselves to giving priority in the use of scarce finance to the improvement (not a large improvement at that) of a means-tested scheme for which a good many members of the Labour Party have in the past expressed a good deal of distaste?[125]

CONCLUSION

This account has illustrated and illuminated thought and action among civil servants in an era of new consciousness of the problems of poverty. The officials responded to the growing awareness and concern about poverty articulated by academics and other commentators outside the policy process, and in the process they too 'rediscovered' the poverty still experienced by a section of the UK population. But at the same time they had their own battles to fight inside the policy process, both with colleagues unwilling to accept the findings of the studies of adequacy and with politicians unable to cope fully with the serious implications of these findings for income maintenance and other social policies.

The only reflection of these studies and events of which the outside world became aware was the introduction of the higher rate of Supplementary Benefit in 1966; indeed, even within the Civil Service the memory that there had ever been an in-house study of social security adequacy was lost, except to those who had taken part in it. Two decades later it was possible for other officials to write as if no study of the adequacy of income maintenance provisions was conceptually feasible, let alone practicable.[126] The reason for this apparent collective amnesia are of course beyond the scope of this chapter.

ACKNOWLEDGEMENTS

I want to express my thanks to the Department of Health and Social Security, the University of Edinburgh (and especially Adrian Sinfield and Roger Davidson), Newcastle Polytechnic, and the Leverhulme Trust, for having enabled me to carry out this research. I am also greatly indebted to the following former DHSS officials for their help and advice: Sir Kenneth Stowe, Allan Beard, Geoffrey Beltram, Strachan Heppell and Leonard Nicholson. I am grateful to Rodney Lowe for his editorial advice on this chapter.

Notes

1. Note that this is a different question from the much more widely discussed issues at that time: how many people had incomes close to or below the NA scales: see B. Abel-Smith and P. Townsend, *The Poor and the Poorest* (London: G. Bell & Sons, 1965), and how many had low levels of living because they failed to claim benefits to which they were entitled (see P. Townsend and D. Wedderburn, *The Aged in the Welfare State* (London: Bell, 1965). For a general discussion of the issues of the adequacy of Assistance benefits in this period, see J. Veit-Wilson, 'Condemned to Deprivation? Beveridge's Responsibility for the Invisibility of Poverty', Chap. 7 in J. Hills, J. Ditch and H. Glennerster (eds), *Beveridge and Social Security: An International Retrospective* (Oxford: Clarendon Press, 1994).

2. Until now, the existence of this review has been known to very few beyond the handful of civil servants who worked on it. DHSS allowed me to study it in its archives in 1988 as part of a wider research project on the history of concepts of poverty and need in the UK's Assistance scales, 1934–66. Archive files still unaccessioned by the Public Records Office are given in their departmental form (such as POF which are NAB and SBC private office files).

3. J. Veit-Wilson, 'Muddle or mendacity? The Beveridge Committee and the Poverty Line', *Journal of Social Policy*, 21(3), 269–301, 1992.

4. The group reported on many aspects of the administration of NA, such as the exercise of discretion, the disregarded resources as components of income, questions of housing and rent, the needs of single persons living alone, equivalences, the time dimension in need, and yardsticks for future use in raising scales. This chapter focuses solely on their ideas of need and minimal adequacy.

5. The term 'tone' is a term for the social acceptability of the mode of administration of benefits, just as the cash level is evaluated in terms of adequacy for a specified level of living. See J. Veit-Wilson, 'Consensual Approaches to Poverty Lines and Social Security', *Journal of Social Policy*, 16(2), 207, 1987.

6. National Assistance Board, *Improvements in National Assistance*, Cmnd 782 (London: HMSO, 1959).

7. Geoffrey Beltram, recorded interview 3 December 1987.

8. Allan Beard, recorded interview 11 March 1988.

9. Public Record Office: AST12/2. UAB Memorandum 14, *A 'Scientific Basis' for the Assessment of Needs*, 30 August 1934, para 33.

10. Sir Kenneth Stowe, recorded interview 23 February 1988. The succeeding quotation is also taken from this interview. The wage stop was an administrative device to implement less-eligibility: to stop the benefits for a family being paid above the level of the wages which the claimant was assumed to be able to earn.

11. Stowe, recorded interview, 23 February 1988.

12. National Assistance Board, *Annual Report 1965*, Cmnd 3042 (London: HMSO, 1966), p. xi.

13. Professor of Social Administration, London School of Economics, 1950–73; Member from 1966 and Deputy Chairman of the Supplementary Benefits Commission 1968–73.

14. Beltram, recorded interview 3 December 1987. 'The Titmice' was a facetious title for the original group of Titmuss's colleagues at LSE who shared his approach to social policy, people such as Professor Brian Abel-Smith (Senior Adviser to the Secretary of State for Social Services 1968–70), Professor David Donnison (Deputy Chairman, later Chairman of the Supplementary Benefits Commission 1973–80), Professor Peter Townsend, and Tony Lynes (Adviser to the Minister of Pensions and National Insurance, 1965–6). See D. Donnison, *The Politics of Poverty* (Oxford: Martin Robertson, 1982), pp. 16–18.

15. Beltram, recorded interview 3 December 1987. For a statement of traditional views that perhaps the scale rates were too high, see correspondence with regional NAB officials about the wage stop. PRO:AST7/1627, Hope Wallace to regional managers, 26 July 1960.

16. Stowe, recorded interview 23 February 1988.

17. PRO:AST7/1627. NAB: Note for the Minister, 11 November 1960.

18. T. Lynes, *National Assistance and National Prosperity* (Welwyn: Codicote Press, 1962); P. Townsend, 'The Meaning of Poverty', *British Journal of Sociology,* 18(3), 210–227, 1962; Abel-Smith and Townsend, *The Poor.*

19. PRO:AST7/1627. Undated and apparently unsent, circa January 1960.

20. *The Guardian,* 24 November 1960, filed in PRO:AST7/1627. Townsend and Lynes were using 'subsistence' in the then customary Beveridge sense of Rowntree's asocial 'primary poverty', and not in what we might today call the relative approach to minimum subsistence such as is implied by Rowntree's Human Needs of Labour poverty line. They complained that average earnings would have risen by 9 per cent between 1959 and April 1961, while the scale for a couple had risen by only 5.9 per cent. The officials advised the Minister to leave aside whether the 1959 pledge really meant that scales should rise in step with earnings, and said that 9 per cent was only a guess (though it 'may not prove to be far wrong'); the real comparison was with April 1948 – by April 1960 male earnings stood 110 per cent higher and the couples' scale 125 per cent higher. PRO:AST7/1627, Note for the Minister, 24 November 1960.

21. Twelve thousand out of 131,000 unemployed NA recipients at the end of 1961. Memorandum by the Chairman, 29 November 1962, PRO:SBC/POF53.

22. Sargent (NAB) to Bowyer (MPNI), 25 February 1963, PRO:SBC/POF32.

23. Ibid. PRO:SBC/POF32. The numbers on the wage stop made it conspicuous, and the problem was not merely the unemployed; the NAB staff disliked paying the families of the imprisoned and even the sick more than they would have received from wages.

24. PRO:AST12/76. Minutes of the 240th meeting of the NAB, 23 November 1966, para 19.

25. Notes on research studies, PRO:SBC/POF25.

26. PRO:AST12/75, Minutes of the 208th meeting of the NAB, 26 February 1964.

27. Stowe, recorded interview 23 February 1988.
28. Beard, recorded interview 11 March 1988.
29. Beltram, recorded interview, 3 December 1987.
30. PRO:AST7/1627, NAB Briefing Notes on the Debate on the Regulations, Scale Rates – the Ordinary Scales: the Children's Rates. 1 December 1960.
31. PRO:AST7/1958, Minutes of the 196th meeting of the NAB, 18 December 1962, para 10, and NAB Memorandum 1263 para 1. See also AST12/75, Minutes of the 208th meeting of the NAB, 26 February 1964.
32. Hence the citation of it as the Beard Report (BR). PRO:AST7/1958–66.
33. BR para 5. Such a larger study was carried out in 1966 by the MPNI with the NAB; see Ministry of Social Security, *Circumstances of Families* (London: HMSO, 1967).
34. BR para 5.
35. Beard to Sargent, 13 December 1963, PRO:AST7/1958.
36. BR para 62.
37. There was nothing new about the paradigm of poverty with which the group worked. What it advanced in its conclusions, as a result of its enquiries, was the scope of the category of conventional necessities which should be included in the minimum that the state made available to children. PRO:SRA12/B, DHSS Economic Advisers' Office, *A Synopsis of Research Relevant to Determining the Adequacy of Supplementary Benefit Scale Rates,* para 2(a), 16 September 1975.
38. BR appendix 1 para 5. The reference to the Children's Minimum Committee (of Labour MPs) was mistaken since the standards came from the Children's Minimum Council, an offshoot of the Family Endowment Society and driven by many of the same people (Eleanor Rathbone, Eva Hubback and Marjorie Green), with all-party support including prominent Conservative MPs (J. Macnicol, *The Movement for Family Allowances 1918–45* (London: Heinemann, 1980), p. 62.
39. BR para 11(2).
40. PRO:AST12/53. Assistance Board Memorandum 499, 'National Assistance: the adult scale rates', 15 April 1948, paras 7,9,11. See also Veit-Wilson, 'Condemned' pp. 109–10.
41. BR para 13(2).
42. PRO:AST12/52. Assistance Board Memorandum 436, 'Note on Standards of Allowances', 2 November 1945. AB Memorandum 499, q.v.
43. BR para 10; BR para 15(1), emphasis in original.
44. BR para 15(2–5).
45. Trude (Gertrude) Schulz was in fact neither PhD nor MD; the title appears to have been ascribed to her by people referring to her scientific work and assuming her credentials.
46. BR para 17(1–7).
47. BR para 20 and 21 (1–5).
48. Prescriptivists are those who, believing in freedom of choice, like to pre-scribe how poor people should choose to spend their money. BR para 21 (7 and 9). It is a possible indication that among some low income

people the urgency of hunger had been superseded by the ability to make choices about the priorities of expenditure, in which social needs ranked higher than minimal food costs, and in that case it is an indicator of the rising standard of relative poverty.

49. BR para 29.
50. BR para 72.
51. Beard, recorded interview 11 March 1988. 'To abolish the wage stop would have been quite out of keeping with the thinking at that time, even Sargent's thinking', Beard added, and the comment about families in difficulty above (BR para 21(12)) referred to such things as low rates of uptake of welfare foods, free school meals and necessitous clothing grants.
52. BR para 31.
53. PRO:AST12/85. NAB Memorandum 1340, 18 November 1965. The copy of the Beard Report on file was not complete (omitting the section on 'The adequacy of the 1963 scale rates', paras 52–61), so I could not check if the group had included this estimate. But it did consider local authorities' reports of their costs of maintaining children and the Weaver Report on Educational Maintenance Allowances.
54. PRO:AST7/1958. NAB Memorandum 1263, 'Children's Scale Rates, The Adequacy of the Scales', para 70, 14 February 1964.
55. PRO:AST12/75. Minutes of the 209th meeting of the NAB, 26 February 1964, paras 10–18.
56. PRO:AST12/75, Minutes of the 210th meeting of the NAB, 26 March 1964, para 5.
57. Ibid., para 4.
58. PRO:AST7/1992. Sargent to Windsor, 13 March 1964. See also WR vol. 1 para 6.
59. PRO:AST7/1992. Sargent to Hope Wallace, n.d.; WR vol. 1 para 7.
60. See Sir Kenneth Stowe's remarks about there never having been a scientific study of adequacy, quoted above. He was Permanent Secretary of DHSS, 1981–7. Stowe, recorded interview 23 February 1988.
61. PRO:AST7/2016, (undated) Briefing Notes and 'Questions about the Managerial Survey of National Assistance Cases'.
62. PRO:AST7/1992. This paragraph is based on: Note on chart, 28 April 1964; 'First thoughts', RW 15 March 1964; 'Areas of enquiry', 7 April 1964; 'Some basic questions', K. R. Stowe, 23 March 1964.
63. A criterion similar to that adopted by Lynes for his study of NA and national prosperity (see Lynes, *National Assistance*); it and other criteria are discussed in WR vol. 2 app 6 paras 10–11.
64. PRO:AST7/1992. Minutes of the first meeting, 23 March 1964.
65. PRO:AST7/1988. 'Bluebeard 2' draft for chapter 9 para 2 (Bluebeard was the appositely-chosen code name apparently used for drafts of the report).
66. PRO:AST7/1992. Chart, Policy Considerations, 28 April 1964.
67. PRO:AST7/1992. Memorandum: 'Adult Scale Rates – a Hypothesis for the Study Group Report', 18 September 1964, (emphasis in original). The 'theoretical' argument was the traditional budget approach to needs, WR vol. 1 chapter 4 and vol. 2 app 2.

68. The first draft on file is of course not necessarily the first draft made; there may have been earlier rough versions which were not filed. I shall refer to draft order numbers as they are filed.
69. PRO:AST7/1994, First draft, para 11.
70. The quotations in this paragraph are from WR vol. 1 paragraphs 9–10.
71. WR vol. 1 para 11.
72. WR vol. 1 para 12. Leaving aside whether any of these people could be described as sociologists, it is arguable that neither Booth nor Rowntree would have accepted this confusion between their definitions of poverty and state minimum income maintenance systems; see J. Veit-Wilson, 'Paradigms of Poverty: A Rehabilitation of B. S. Rowntree', *Journal of Social Policy*, 15(1), 69–99, 1986.
73. WR vol. 1 para 13.
74. It exhibited the common confusion between the scientific finding of the poverty line and the political setting of the social security scales; for clarification, see for instance J. Veit-Wilson, *Setting Adequacy Standards: How governments define minimum incomes* (Bristol: The Policy Press, 1998).
75. WR vol. 1 para 15.
76. WR vol. 1 para 16.
77. PRO:AST7/1994. Draft para 18; the method was then called 'pragmatic' rather than 'empirical'.
78. PRO:AST12/85; addendum to NAB Minutes of the 227th meeting, 22 September 1965, AST12/76. NAB Memorandum 1333, para 3: 'Further, as the Report had shown, it was exceedingly difficulty (sic) to administer a nation-wide scheme which professed to deal with special needs in such fine detail without producing rather glaring inconsistencies... the results it produced were open to damaging criticism.'
79. WR vol. 1 para 17.
80. WR vol. 1 para 32.
81. WR vol. 1 para 33.
82. WR vol. 1 para 31. See also PRO:AST7/1995. 3rd draft, para 28, refers to the rates in 1948 having been designed 'to meet *minimum* requirements – a qualification which does not appear in the statute' (emphasis in original).
83. WR vol. 1 para 34; vol. 2 appendix 2, paras 2–5.
84. These quotations and details of food needs are from WR vol. 2 app 2 part (2) Food (emphasis in original).
85. WR vol. 2 app 2 para (3)28.
86. PRO:AST7/2008. J. E. Goodwin, 'Report on Clothing, Footwear and Household Goods', 22 December 1964, para 10. The telegraphic style is in the original. It reported an estimate of the Council of Clothing Trade Associations that 'before 1939 probably less than 50 per cent of the industrial population was adequately clothed'.
87. Goodwin op. cit. para 81.
88. Goodwin op. cit. paras 82–3; WR vol. 2 app 2 para (4)12.
89. WR vol. 2 app 2 para (5)10; see also Goodwin op. cit. paras 73–5.
90. WR vol. 2 app 2 para (6)1.

91. WR vol. 2 app 2 para (6)2. However, an early draft (PRO:AST7/2010) which also quoted Alfred Marshall's *Principles of Economics* (1890) (See N. Aronson, 'The Making of the US Bureau of Labor Statistics Family Budget Series: relativism and the rhetoric of subsistence', unpublished paper presented to the American Sociological Association Meetings, San Antonio, 1984) added Smith's exclusion of expenditure on beer and tobacco from the social necessities because 'Nature does not render these necessary for the support of life; and custom nowhere renders it indecent to live without them'.
92. WR vol. 2 app 2 para (6)27. The data in the preceding paragraph are all from this section (6).
93. WR vol. 1 paras 138–148; WR vol. 2 app 3, 'The Problem of Rent and the Bearing of Housing on Requirements'.
94. WR vol. 1 table 5 p. 18. See discussion of the meaning of Engel proportions at this time in Veit-Wilson, 'Muddle'.
95. WR vol. 1 para 50(1). Beltram commented that the group did not have a prior view on the correct proportions of expenditure on different items; it simply used the FES data as the basis for making a judgement on the relationship between conventional and low income expenditure patterns and its own proposals, recognising that the stated income of households was not the same as their recorded expenditures in the FES. Beltram, personal communication, 15 December 1987.
96. WR vol. 1 para 51.
97. WR vol. 1 paras 63–5.
98. Beltram, personal communication, 15 December 1987; WR vol. 1 para 60.
99. WR vol. 1 para 61.
100. PRO:AST7/1997. 1st draft of WR vol. 3 (app 8) chapter 3.
101. PRO:AST7/1992, Sargent to Stowe, 24 August 1965. PRO:AST7/2012, Note on file, undated and unsigned.
102. WR vol. 2 app 4 para 50.
103. WR vol. 2 appendix 4, Adjusting the Scale Rates by Discretion, especially paras 25–51. PRO:AST7/1998, Draft of WR vol. 1, chapter on discretion, para 115.
104. WR vol. 2 app 4 para 19.
105. WR vol. 2 app 4 para 49.
106. Stowe, recorded interview, 23 February 1988. The income guarantee scheme was a Labour Party policy proposal but was never implemented because of its cost and the administrative complications of trying to coordinate the tax and benefits system.
107. Briefing for Minister, April 1959, quoted in WR vol. 2 app 4 para 12.
108. WR vol. 1 para 97.
109. WR vol. 2 app 4 paras 51 and 53.
110. WR vol. 1 para 235.
111. WR vol. 1 para 227.
112. PRO:AST7/2003, Draft of WR vol. 1, Chapter 12.
113. WR vol. 1 para 231.
114. WR vol. 1 paras 230–1; emphasis in original.
115. Notes on studies, An Examination of the Adult Scale Rates, Final Report October 1965, PRO:SBC/POF25. NAB *Annual Report 1965*, p. xii.

116. PRO:AST12/76, Minutes of the 227th meeting of the NAB, 22 September 1965, para 16; discussion of the Windsor Report is in an addendum as NAB Memorandum 1333 of same date, *Adult Scale Rates*, PRO:AST12/85. Memorandum by the Chairman of the NAB to the Minister of Pensions and National Insurance, *Possible Modifications of the National Assistance Scheme, Part 1: Financial Assistance*, 8 October 1965, PRO:BN72/115.

117. NAB Memorandum 1333, section 3, Discretionary Additions. PRO:AST12/85.

118. D. Cole with J. Utting, *The Economic Circumstances of Old People*, (Welwyn: Codicote Press, 1962).

119. NAB Memorandum 1333, op. cit. Beard recalled from his experience and study of local visiting by officers that variation also came from 'the local ethos: what need is here? People in this locality don't normally have a dressing grown, for example, they can use their mac, whereas in the south of England, yes, they'd all have a dressing gown.' Recorded interview, 11 March 1988.

120. NAB Memorandum 1333, op. cit.

121. NAB Memorandum 1333, op. cit.

122. NAB Memorandum 1333, op. cit.

123. Minutes of the 231st meeting of the NAB, 26 January 1966, paras 7–11, PRO:AST12/76.

124. Donnison, *Politics*.

125. Jarrett to Minister, 21 October 1965, PRO:BN72/115.

126. For instance in Department of Health and Social Security, *Reform of Social Security* (London: HMSO, 1985), p. 12, or Department of Social Security, 'Benefit Levels and a Minimum Income', in: House of Commons Social Services Committee, *Minimum Income: Memoranda laid before the Committee*, HoC Paper 579 (London: HMSO, 1989), pp. 3–5.

8 Jack Jones, the Social Contract and Social Policy 1970–4

Helen Fawcett

INTRODUCTION

Between 1970 and 1974 social policy had an importance in the strategy of the Labour Party which was unprecedented in the post 1945–51 period, becoming an integral part of the negotiations with the trade union movement over incomes policy. In response to the industrial strife under the Conservatives, both wings of the labour movement sought an accommodation which could be presented to the electorate as a means of achieving industrial peace and economic prosperity. To achieve this, they engaged in a process of political exchange in order to secure wage restraint, the Labour Party offering firm commitments in areas vital to the concerns of the trade union movement. Thus a number of social welfare policies formed the basis of the social wage component of a 'social contract' – the social wage representing policies which were of value to the standard of living of both workers and their families beyond the pay packet.

This chapter focuses on the trade union movement's campaign for improved state pensions which was their main priority in social welfare during this period. Their intervention elevated this issue to the top of the Labour Party's social policy agenda and made it an explicit part of the process of political exchange between the party and the unions. Once pensions policy had entered this important arena, the Labour leadership acted far more decisively than it had done in the past. In any examination of the development of the Labour Party's strategy towards state superannuation it is vital to consider how the structure of the labour movement generates new policies as well as how the Party addresses the problem of implementation when it comes to power. The period discussed in this chapter is unique in that it represents a time of unprecedented trade union activism in the field of social policy. However, an examination of the case demonstrates a number of institutional difficulties which obstruct policy innovation even when all other factors appear to facilitate it.

Whilst the intervention of the trade union movement was positive in many ways, it was not grafted harmoniously onto existing commitments and strategies. Indeed, it tended to neutralise other important sources of policy formulation, and nearly caused one of the Party's most long-standing commitments – state superannuation – to abort. It has frequently been suggested that the lack of a highly centralised trade movement is responsible for the lack of radicalism of the Labour Party. However, this period indicates that the institutional deficit in Labour Party policy-making was an additional source of confusion.

During the period of Opposition 1970–4, Labour Party policy-making took place at two different levels. Although in constitutional terms the National Executive Committee was responsible for devising Labour's programme which would be the basis for the next election manifesto, a second tier of policy-making came into existence. This tier was the TUC/Labour Party Liaison committee. In the aftermath of the Labour Government's performance during 1964–70, relations between the Labour Party and the trade union movement were severely strained. The Government had come into conflict with the trade union movement because of their incomes policies and their proposals for the reform of industrial relations (*In Place of Strife*). However, aside from the Government's attack on issues which were at the heart of trade union self-interest, there was severe disillusion with the Government's entire record and its failure to meet many of its supporters' expectations. This coincided with a generational change in the leadership of the trade union movement. Trade unionists such as Jack Jones and Hugh Scanlon were to play a leading role on the General Council of the TUC, and they were concerned to establish ways of guaranteeing the behaviour of the next Labour Government, not only in the field of trade union concerns, but in general policy areas as well.

The TUC was to have a crucial impact on Labour Party policy-making towards the welfare state, and most particularly in the field of pensions which was the social policy issue of greatest concern to them in this period. However, there were problems associated with their intervention. Whilst the TUC was able to commit the Labour Party to its own priorities in pensions policy, there were no institutional mechanisms which allowed a liaison between the Party's pensions experts and the TUC's leaders. While Jack Jones was heavily committed to an increase in the flat-rate pension, he was not as concerned with the state superannuation scheme. This meant that it was possible to jettison certain features of the State Earnings Related Pension Scheme (SERPS) package, simply because they had not been ratified by the Liaison Committee, although they had been approved by the General Council's representatives on the TUC's Social Insurance and Industrial Welfare Committee (SIIWC). However, the trade union movement's interest in pensions policy as a whole was probably responsible for the implementation of the SERPS legislation because the Labour Cabinet decided to treat most of the proposals as part of the social wage component of the Social Contract although it had never been part of the negotiations.

The pressure to improve Britain's pension arrangements emanated from the failure to implement any reform of the Beveridge system which had created a dual system of provision in which half the nation's pensioners contributed to private occupational schemes and the rest were dependent on the flat-rate pension established after the war. The Labour Party had adopted radical new plans for state superannuation in 1957, when Richard Crossman, Brian Abel-Smith and Richard Titmuss developed *National Superannuation: Labour's Plan for Security in Old Age*. These proposals would have established a system in which wage earners paid a percentage of their salary in contributions and, in return, received a pension which was related to their earnings in working life. However, when the Party came to office in 1964 there were a series of delays in implementing the scheme. As a result, the size of private sector coverage grew, but Britain lagged far behind the rest of Europe because the absence of a state superannuation scheme meant those covered by the state scheme were receiving a very low flat-rate pension.

THE TRADE UNION MOVEMENT AND THE DEVELOPMENT OF PENSIONS POLICY 1970–4

The Labour movement's attitude towards pension policy in the period 1970–4 provides the main evidence of the changing character of the TUC and trade union demands. The well-established assumption that British trade unionism was characterised by the dominance of self-interested, industrial rather than political unionism, is challenged by the Transport & General Workers Union's campaign for improved pensions, the support this received from the TUC, and the role that pensions policy was to play in the Social Contract.[1]

The trade union movement pursued its strategy towards pension policy in two different spheres. First of all, they included pensions policy as part of the social wage component of the Social Contract which they negotiated with the Labour Party before it returned to office in 1974. Secondly, they used their pressure group status to campaign independently of the Labour Party and were able to use the Labour Party as a platform in the campaign. This meant winning Labour Party support for trade union goals at annual Party conference. It also resulted in the Labour Party being committed to policies which were not necessarily compatible with their existing positions or future preferences, but because of the magnitude of the trade union movement's influence within the Party during this period, the NEC felt unwilling or unable to question the trade unions' priorities or to resist the way in which trade union objectives pre-empted the overall policy debate.

THE DEVELOPMENT OF THE SOCIAL CONTRACT

The development of the Social Contract was crucial to the trade union movement's ability to influence pension policy because it involved the Labour Party and the trade union movement in a process of political exchange: in return for wage restraint the Labour Party undertook to guarantee the implementation of certain policies when it was returned to office. The Labour Party's initial incentive to engage in such a process came from the need to repair the damage which had been done to their relations with the trade unions during the earlier Wilson Government.

Moreover, as relations between the trade unions and the Heath Government deteriorated because of the pay freeze, the party hoped that it would be possible to win the coming election on the guarantee of industrial peace and an effective prices and incomes policy. The Labour leadership fully accepted the importance of reaching agreement with the trade union movement because it was seen as crucial to the outcome of the next election. With the Social Contract agreed, Wilson felt that he would be able to argue that Labour, in contrast to the Conservatives, could guarantee harmonious industrial relations.[2] Although the Labour Party clearly had strong incentives to repair the damage and forge better relations with the trade unions, the process of reconciliation was also aided by the conflict between the trade unions and the Heath Government, which provided the TUC with the incentive to renegotiate its relationship with the Party:

It sought to take advantage of union strength in order to cement a substantive agreement with the Party about how the next Labour Government would behave. The TUC wanted to win agreements that both forestalled further conflict and provided guarantees that union interests would be promoted by favourable policies during the next Labour Government. Each battle with the Tory Government furthered this strategy, so that gradually the TUC won a comprehensive series of policy commitments.[3]

These circumstances were extremely important to the development of pensions policy because one of the leading initiators of this reconciliation and architect of the Liaison Committee and the Social Contract was Jack Jones, the leader of T&GWU and the TUC's leading campaigner on pensions. In fact it was the frustration of working with the Labour Party on the pensions campaign which convinced him that a closer and more effective relationship with the Party was needed. Commenting on his attempt to win the Party's co-operation in the early stages of the TUC's pension campaign, Jones said: 'I had to work hard for that result, and the experience convinced me that some other body was needed to bring the unions and Labour closer together.'[4]

This was one source of inspiration behind the establishment of a new and powerful executive body, the TUC/Labour Party Liaison Committee, whose membership consisted of representatives of the National Executive Committee and the General Council of the TUC. The first meeting of the Liaison Committee took place in December 1970 on an informal basis. The first two official meetings took place in 1971 to agree a campaign strategy for opposing the Industrial Relations Act, both at the parliamentary level and through the TUC's public campaign. As Robert Taylor comments the unions and the party were able to establish a renewed cohesion through their common opposition to the Industrial Relations Act and in 1971 decided to place the Committee on a more permanent basis.[5] By June 1971 the trade unions secured their most pressing demand: Labour Party agreement to repeal the Act when it returned to power. This opened the way for closer collaboration on a wide range of policy issues, and by 1972 the Liaison Committee had acquired official status, and was meeting on a regular monthly basis. The committee set up working groups on a number of policy areas. Their work mirrored the issues which were under discussion between the unions and the Heath Government: the future of the Industrial Relations Act; the conciliation and arbitration service; and prices and incomes policy. In the first two years of its operation, the Liaison Committee laid the foundations of the Social Contract. In July 1972 it issued its first policy document *Industrial Relations*[6] which was to be followed by *Economic Policy and the Cost of Living*[7] in February 1973. The importance of these two documents is demonstrated by the minority Labour Government's achievement in implementing most of the committee's initial proposals in its first nine months of office. Its ability to influence policy during Labour's term of opposition, and to have these policies carried through when the Party returned to office, indicates the unprecedented influence which the TUC exercised over the course of British politics:

'Economic Policy and the Cost of Living' was virtually a shopping list of proposals for the next Labour Government. It proposed the control of basic food prices by food subsidies, subsidised public transport, public ownership of land for building purposes, the redistribution of income and wealth, and the phasing out of charges in the social services.[8]

But the most specific undertaking was the 'immediate' commitment to increase the basic pension to £10 per week for a single person and £16 per week for a married couple, which shows the importance the TUC attached to pensions in its list of priorities. It is important to note that during this period, and certainly for the first year of Labour's term of office, the influence of the trade union movement was at its peak. The Labour Party was certainly the junior partner in this process of exchange and was prepared to accept the TUC's terms in order to reach agreement. Labour's commitment to good relations with the trade union movement was made explicit in the *Economic Policy and the Cost of Living*: 'The first task of a new Labour Government would be to conclude with the TUC a wide-ranging agreement on the policies to be pursued in all aspects of economic life and to discuss with them the order of priorities for their fulfilment.'[9]

The development of the Social Contract was of crucial importance to the future of pensions policy. Because of the priority accorded it by the TUC and the trade union movement it was top of the list of the social policy proposals[10] and key elements were implemented within days of the party returning to power in 1974 despite the administrative problems involved.[11] The Labour cabinet was well aware of the TUC's campaign against the pension policy of the Heath Government[12] and its successful moves to win formal Labour Party support for its proposals at Labour Party Annual Conference, and hence was eager to satisfy the TUC's demands in this area, especially because of Jack Jones's personal commitment to the issue. However, the Liaison Committee agreement was confined to an increase in the basic pension to £10/£16 per week. State superannuation was not discussed in this forum. Despite this, SERPS was included as part of a 'social wage' package when the party returned to power, but certain important elements of the Opposition plans were dropped.

We can see a serious flaw in the way in which Labour Party policy-making was operating in this period. While it was clearly highly advantageous for pension policy to be part of this process of political exchange, it is clear that the Labour leadership were far more enthusiastic to fulfil the trade union movement's priorities than to present a comprehensive and rational policy across the whole area of social security. The TUC was pressing for a flat-rate increase at the Liaison Committee while the NEC's sub-committees were considering superannuation. While there were representatives of the Social Insurance and Industrial Welfare committee included in this process there were no formal joint meetings to secure TUC agreement until the end of 1973 and the beginning of 1974. In practical terms it was probably not so important that the TUC was pre-empting pension policy by committing the Party to a huge increase in the flat-rate pension, although it is certainly true that the Labour Party had to reorientate its thinking on superannuation around this commitment. But it is important to note that powerful sections of the TUC were at least ambivalent, if not openly hostile to earnings-related superannuation.[13] This was obvious to the Labour leadership and could be a contributory factor in the key decision, taken as soon as Labour assumed office, to reorientate the pension policy agreed outside the Liaison Committee in the months before the February 1974 election.

THE UNIONS, THE NEC AND LABOUR'S PENSION PLANS

Prior to the 1970s, the trade union movement had tended to react to initiatives from the policy-formulating committees of the National Executive Committee. This reversal of previous roles had two consequences: first of all, the weight of trade union pressure and the increase in trade union involvement gave pensions policy an enhanced status and priority in the Party's programme; secondly, for the first time during a period of Opposition, policy was generated from two distinct and independent spheres: that of the trade union movement working through the Liaison Committee, and that of the Social Policy Advisory Committee working through the NEC structure. Trade union activism greatly increased the possibility of securing policy adoption and implementation because the trade union commitment to this particular area made it the leading element in any package of measures which would ultimately comprise the 'social wage' component of the Social Contract. However, the importance of the TUC and the trade union movement in the structure of policy-making meant that policy was being made in parallel forums and hence the role of the NEC's Social Policy Advisory Committee was prone to being overshadowed or ignored. The key point was that the leading role of the trade union movement made the Social Policy Advisory Committee reactive; they were no longer the sole policy initiators as they had been during the 1950s. In fact the situation bore a closer resemblance to that of 1964–70 when the Committee was reacting to the initiatives of Government ministers.

From the point of view of the Party leadership, not only did the Liaison Committee have the advantage of being simpler to deal with in purely organisational terms, but the seniority of its membership and the central importance of its remit in electoral terms (the construction of an agreed basis for the economic policy of a future Labour Government) meant that it eclipsed the NEC sub-committees and became the Party's most important decision-making forum in this area of policy. The Party leadership was content with such an arrangement for political reasons. The NEC had become a considerable irritant: the increased strength of the left's representation on the NEC, and the impact of the election defeat both contributed to making it a more activist body, highly critical of the leadership's record in government. There is no doubt the leadership welcomed the opportunity to circumvent an arena where their political strategy was constantly under criticism. However, the beneficial effects of trade union involvement were offset by the concomitant decline of influence in some of the NEC's sub-committees and the continuation of their inability to play their full advisory role. Trade union involvement in pension policy was not an unambiguous bonus for the development of Labour's pension policy because there were no organisational mechanisms to link it to Party policy formation, and thereby allow all those interested in the question to provide a united front, or to discuss inconsistencies in approach.

In these circumstances, pensions policy was vulnerable. The executive nature of the Liaison committee meant that its function was to evaluate the merits of competing objectives rather than the details of policy once they were agreed in principle. Furthermore, the rigour of the discussion was contingent on the degree of expertise available, and, for their part, the post-1970 Labour Party leadership lacked social policy expertise.

THE NEC AND PENSIONS POLICY

Since 1957 when Conference accepted the landmark document, *National Superannuation: Labour's Policy for Security in Old Age*, the Party had been committed to a state superannuation scheme based on the principle of earnings-related benefits and contributions and had relinquished its support for the Beveridge model of social security which was based on a system of flat-rate contributions which provided for a universal flat-rate basic state pension. For its time the scheme had been a remarkable innovation in policy-making, offering 'half-pay on retirement', redistributing resources, and solving the critical problem of financing the system of income maintenance designed by Beveridge. However, the Labour Government of 1964–70 had failed to implement these proposals. At a late stage, Richard Crossman, one of the architects of the plan, brought forward a White Paper[14] which set out a fully earnings-related system eradicating a flat-tier of provision, but which had lost many of the radical features of the original proposals. The Crossman scheme was close to becoming legislation, but the 1970 general election was called just before it could complete its passage through parliament.

The Social Policy Advisory Committee was dominated by those who had been intimately connected with the design of the 1957 proposals in *National Superannuation*, and it remained firmly committed to the principle of earnings-related benefits and contributions, despite any criticisms which they made of the 1969 Crossman proposals. Their priority was now the implementation of a state scheme at any cost. However, the committee was confronted by a new trade union activism which was focused on achieving a substantial increase in flat-rate benefits. This reflected a degree of disillusion with state superannuation, despite the fact it remained TUC policy, and was defended by the representatives of the SIIWC on the Social Policy Advisory Committee. The General Council of the TUC accepted Labour's revised proposals in the bilateral negotiations of 1973–4, but they were never endorsed by the TUC/Labour Party Liaison Committee. In theory, this should have made no difference, but in practice it left the proposals vulnerable. In 1974 the key mechanism which was to link the flat-rate increase to the state superannuation scheme was lost. Within days of coming to power the Government implemented the flat-rate increase completely independently of the state superannuation scheme, making nonsense of the plan to link the two. It will be argued here that such a decision was possible because SERPS was developed outside the Liaison Committee and hence the details of the policy were not seen as integral parts of the Social Contract.

'EVERYBODY EQUAL ON THE PARK BENCH'

Although the Social Policy Advisory Committee was already discussing the future of National Superannuation, a sense of urgency was added by Jack Jones's criticisms of past policy at the 1972 Labour Party Conference. Jones was persuaded to allow the committee's discussions to take their course and to withdraw his motion opposing a superannuation scheme based on the principles of the Crossman scheme. Nevertheless, the fact that the motion was brought before Conference by such an influential figure and was well received, indicates the extent to which the members of the Social Policy Advisory Committee were unrepresentative of the general sentiment of the Party's membership. Many Party members did not feel the same degree of commitment to superannuation as the Party's experts who had been developing the policy over a fifteen-year period. The fact that it had not been introduced meant that the basic flat-rate pension was extremely low.[15] The solution to this problem was felt to be a substantial increase in the basic pension, rather than the introduction of a complicated superannuation scheme which would take twenty years to mature. The supporters of state superannuation faced a challenge within the committee from two influential members who represented different power bases within the Labour Party itself. The main actors were Bill Simpson – the chair of the Home Policy Committee of the NEC – and Judith Hart, a former minister for Social Security in the Wilson government, member of the Tribune group, and a representative on the NEC. They both supported the abandonment of the Party's superannuation policy in favour of a flat-rate state pension, and attacked the notion of earnings-related provision as perpetuating the inequalities of the labour market arguing: 'we should all be equal on the park bench in the eyes of the socialist state'.[16]

The Social Policy Advisory Committee were first confronted by the problem at the 1972 Labour Party Conference when Jones moved a motion on pensions and the elderly which set out the demand for a pension increase which would raise the level of the basic pension to £10 per week for a single person and £16 for a married couple. It was also this motion which included a frontal attack on Labour's past policy:

> One of the prime difficulties about many of our past proposals is that they were incomprehensible. I do not think even the people who drew them up really understood them. Much of this was because the idea that pensions always had to be based on the contributory principle since this was supposed to establish the right to a pension. I believe we have to up-date our attitude on this, because so far all the contributory principle has established is the right to an abysmally low pension.[17]

It is unclear how far Jones was speaking on behalf of the trade union movement on this point. Although existing TUC policy favoured the contributory principle, TUC support had never been as great or as dogmatic as has been suggested by some commentators.[18] Jones had not received ratification of this position from the whole TUC. Nevertheless, his influential position in the TUC pensions campaign meant that it was possible his views would have commanded a great deal of trade union support, especially when we consider the possibility that their existing policy might have been out-of-date and unrepresentative of trade union opinion by 1972.

Jones's speech was effectively sweeping away the whole set of assumptions on which past policy had been based; in effect, he was calling for pensions to be partially funded from taxation revenue. Although this was already the case, in the sense that the Exchequer made a contribution to the National Insurance pension, Jones was clearly referring to some kind of radical fiscal redistribution and was attempting to move away from the notion of contributory pensions. This type of demand had not been made by such an influential figure since Nye Bevan's call for the similar measure in 1955.

Jones's motion placed the NEC in a difficult position because it was binding them to a superannuation scheme which would have to be constructed around the notion of funding from taxation. In her reply on behalf of the NEC,[19] Castle asked for more time for the NEC to complete its detailed policy discussions and to produce a blueprint for a national superannuation scheme. Arguing that an adequate superannuation scheme would provide the answer to the scandal of poverty in old age, Castle launched a defence of the Crossman scheme. She took the view that had the 1969 proposals come into operation, millions of pensioners would have been lifted above the poverty line. Her major criticism of the Crossman proposals was not their complexity, but that their implementation would have been protracted.

Thus, by the autumn of 1972, the Social Policy Advisory Committee of the National Executive Committee was committed to re-opening the question of superannuation.[20] By February 1973 the £10/£16 pension was already in the Social Contract and any superannuation scheme would have to take account of the continuation of a high flat-rate pension.[21] This was clearly a severe constraint on the committee's freedom of action. The Crossman proposals would have to be revised because they were based on the elimination of the flat-rate pension.

Nevertheless, the Social Policy Advisory Committee was able to retain the commitment to earnings-related superannuation. First of all, while opinion within the trade union movement had been swinging against superannuation, there had not been a motion to Congress to overturn past policy. The TUC was, therefore, still formally committed to national superannuation. Hence, it was possible for Peter Jacques, the TUC representative on the committee, to continue to argue in favour of superannuation, although such an important question could not be officially decided without the approval of the General Council of the TUC. Secondly, those opposing superannuation lacked sufficient social policy advice to devise convincing alternative proposals and since they lacked support from the TUC representatives were in a weak position during the discussions. Thirdly, and perhaps most important, the committee was able to present compromise proposals which would retain the flat-rate pension at the level demanded by the TUC and would also introduce a second tier of earnings-related pension. These proposals were probably the most conclusive factor because they accommodated the TUC's wishes completely, and therefore the TUC had no compelling reason to obstruct the superannuation scheme which was, in any case, of secondary importance to them.

Members of the committee responded to the challenge by developing a technique which accommodated the need to offer a better deal to existing pensioners with their objective of retaining the commitment to state superannuation. Even before the intervention of Jack

Jones, the committee was considering the Crossman scheme's failure to offer any tangible benefits to existing pensioners who would not have the opportunity to be contributors to the scheme. The twenty-year build-up period also meant that those retiring in the first few years of the scheme would derive little advantage from it. Hence, the committee advanced a proposal for a special credit to be given to existing pensioners and those nearing retirement:

> All those retiring between 1977 and 1997 could be assumed to have contributed to the new scheme since 1967 on half the national average. The build up period would thus be cut, in effect from 20 to 10 years, but without giving unfavourable treatment to the higher paid (all would benefit from the 10 year 'bonus'). Existing pensioners would have their pension recalculated as if they had just reached retirement after 10 years of the new scheme.[22]

Tony Lynes, a social policy adviser to the committee since the 1960s, envisaged a gradual transition to earnings-related pensions which were based on the individuals' actual earnings during working life. In this way he believed that the inequalities between older and younger pensioners would be much smaller than those which would have existed under the Crossman scheme. He argued that the practical effect of crediting in existing pensioners would be the same as increasing the flat-rate pension £12 per week for single pensioners and £18 for a married couple. The tactical importance of these conclusions was immense. Lynes was arguing that the continuation of an earnings-related pensions scheme (with the adaptations he proposed) would give an immediate increase to existing pensioners which was higher than the proposed increase in the flat-rate pension which was currently party policy (i.e. £10/£16 per week). Hence, he was providing a powerful defence of earnings-related pensions on the grounds that they could provide greater immediate improvements to the poorest pensioners; a case which would substantially undermine the arguments which were being employed by the proponents of the flat-rate system of benefits. In Lynes' words:

> Existing pensioners would be brought in from the outset, as if they had contributed to the scheme throughout their working lives on earnings of half the national average... Most workers would no longer have to look to occupational schemes for a substantial proportion of their retirement income. The gross inequalities produced

by the uneven growth and inadequate safeguards of occupational pension rights would thus be greatly reduced.[24]

However, the Research Department produced a paper with proposals which were at variance with those outlined by Lynes. The authors noted that the debate between the supporters of earnings-related pensions and the supporters of flat-rate pensions was 'apparently irreconcilable'.[25] On the one hand the advocates of flat-rate pensions argued that earnings-related pensions perpetuated inequality, on the other, the defenders of earnings-related pensions were prepared to accept this inequality because they felt that flat-rate pensions were unable to provide an adequate level of support.

The Research Department suggested a way out of this dilemma by advocating that both forms of provision should be available. They proposed that there should be a universal flat-rate tier set at the level of £10/£16 per week. This would be supplemented by a second earnings-related tier to cushion those who had enjoyed a relatively high income during working life. The authors argued that the advantage of this proposal was its considerable potential for redistribution and the provision of an adequate flat-rate element which would help to float pensioners off supplementary benefit.[26]

When the complete set of papers was presented to the Social Policy Advisory Committee in January 1973 the debate which took place was predictably little more than a rehearsal of entrenched positions. It is certainly true that the pressure generated by the Hart and Simpson papers and the Jones attack were strong enough to galvanise the committee into a radical re-think of the Crossman scheme so that it would be shielded from the main attacks of the supporters of flat rate pensions. The committee was aware that earnings-related contributions and benefits were regarded with hostility by some and apathy by others; outside their ranks, however, they were certainly not regarded with enthusiasm. This, coupled with forceful TUC moves in favour of the flat-rate, and indeed hints from Jack Jones that the TUC might escalate their attack on previous policy to include the Crossman scheme, meant that the committee had a great deal to fear on two fronts. First of all, it was possible that the committee's parent body – the Home Policy Sub-committee – might dissent from the recommendations and would report to the NEC in favour of a revision of policy recommending a flat-rate pension scheme. Secondly, the outcome of any such move would be influenced heavily by the attitude of the trade union movement, both from within and outside the Party's own policy-formulating structures. The campaign for better pensions had received overwhelming support from the TUC and the Labour Party Conference. However, that campaign emphasised an increase in the flat-rate pension and was not particularly concerned with superannuation. It was the commitment to an increase in the flat-rate pension which had been incorporated into the Social Contract. Thus, all the evidence suggested that the trade unions were far more interested in the basic pension than in superannuation. This was noted in a paper which the committee received prior to the discussion of the Hart and Simpson proposals:

> It has been explained above that on paper at least the Labour Party and the TUC seem to be in agreement on what have been identified as three of the four main principles behind national superannuation proposals put forward by the Party.
>
> The full picture is however slightly more complex than this for at this years Annual Conference of the Labour Party the leader of the single largest trade union, Jack Jones of the T&GWU made two points of relevance to this paper; first of all, he attacked previous pension proposals on the grounds of their incomprehensibility but, of course, to conform to the four principles outlined above, the Crossman Plan had to be a complicated document; secondly, and perhaps most important, he attacked the nature of the contributory principle... It would seem therefore that the TUC may not be as firmly committed as its published material suggests.[27]

Moreover, the magnitude of trade union influence over policy was indicated by the flat-rate increase being effectively imposed on the Social Policy Advisory Committee, with the committee being obliged to adapt existing policy around this commitment. The committee's members were aware of the cost that such provision would involve and the way in which it set the agenda for future policy making. More importantly, they seem to have exercised little influence in the campaign and had been unable to link the flat-rate campaign with an overall pensions package.

In fact it was their ability to present an adaptation of the Crossman scheme which was compatible with the central trade union objective of an increased flat-rate pension which was the key to their success in defeating the moves towards the flat-rate. The TUC was still committed to an earnings-related pension scheme on the lines set out in the 1969 Crossman proposals. There were significant tactical flaws in the

Hart/Simpson attempt to move away from earnings-related pensions. Their proposals were easily demolished because they had not had sufficient expert advice on the complexities of devising a pensions scheme, and they did not have the support of the other trade union representatives on the committee.[28] The trade union movement had not moved onto rigorous discussion of earnings-related pensions and there had been no moves at the SIIWC to revise the policy. In this sense the Hart/Simpson proposals were premature because, until the TUC altered its view, there would be no guarantee of concerted trade union support on the policy-formulating committees of the Party, particularly when the earnings-related supporters had a well-considered scheme which had been adapted to counter the most compelling criticisms levelled by the supporters of flat-rate pensions. Nevertheless the evidence that the committee was aware of trade union power was overwhelming, and is indicated by the extent to which the committee accommodated the TUC's demand for large increases in the flat-rate pension, irrespective of the consequence this might have for national superannuation.

When Castle reported to the Home Policy subcommittee she was able to do so on the basis of the scheme proposed by Lynes, namely:

i) existing pensioners and those within ten years of retirement should be credited with enough contributions to assure them a retirement pension on the lines of conference decision...

ii) earnings related contributions should be payable on incomes to well above the one and a half times average national earnings in order to create a Social Security fund out of which (with the addition of Exchequer contributions) additional social security provision, such as special benefits for the disabled could be put in payment.[29]

The case for the revised policy was incorporated into *Labour's Programme*[30] in which the Labour Party agreed to safeguard the contributory principle and also to safeguard pensioners' living standards against increases in inflation by relating pensions to average earnings. Finally, the programme described the Party's new plan by which existing pensioners could be made full members of the new pension scheme by crediting them with notional contributions which would be sufficient to qualify them for an immediate increase of £10/£16 in line with the Party's new policy. In the event, however, this attempt to situate the flat-rate increase within the new pension scheme was to prove unsuccessful: the flat rate pension was increased as soon as Labour took office before the legislation for SERPS was completed and the notion of crediting-in was lost.

When this two-tier scheme was approved by the Party the bilateral discussions with the TUC began in earnest. In October 1973 the SIIWC considered a document on the future of pensions policy[31] and concluded that a flat-rate pension scheme would exacerbate the retirement income difficulties of those who were not covered by an occupational pension scheme. They decided to continue their support for a wholly earnings-related scheme with partial contracting out for those in occupational schemes.

Their discussions with the Labour Party show that they did not have any substantive objections to the scheme proposed by the Labour Party, then being advocated by Brian O'Malley. However, the most interesting feature of the discussions is the imprecision surrounding the notion of crediting-in: 'The meeting had reached broad agreement that future pensions provision should be wholly earnings-related, and that existing pensioners should be credited into a future scheme at the £10 and £16 levels or the equivalent amounts.'[32]

It is unclear from this statement whether it was envisaged that the Party would be able to meet its commitment to an 'immediate' increase in the flat-rate pension and then credit in the pensions at some future date when the superannuation scheme was to be introduced, or whether the increase in the flat-rate pension and the introduction of the earnings-related scheme were to take place simultaneously. It is clear that the Labour Party felt that superannuation could be introduced after the increase in the flat-rate:

> Brian O'Malley pointed out two important features of his scheme. One was that it combined the basic features of a flat-rate and an earnings-related scheme. The other was that the £10/£16 pension (or whatever levels are considered appropriate) can be implemented separately, speedily, and within the current financial terms of the 1973 Social Security Act.[33]

Indeed a matter of days before the election of February 1974 when the TUC and the Labour Party held its last joint meeting it was emphasised that the £10/£16 flat-rate pension should be paid 'immediately'[34] to all existing and future pensioners. It is easy to see how it was possible for the flat-rate pension to be detached from the superannuation scheme. It seems clear that neither the TUC nor the Labour Party negotiators saw any danger introducing the two elements of the scheme at different stages.

The Labour Party might have been tempted to emphasise the feasibility of this proposal to convince the TUC that there would be no delay in introducing the flat-rate increase. However, once the main commitment was fulfilled the superannuation scheme became vulnerable because it was not one of the TUC's main priorities, and in the economic climate of 1974–5, crediting-in was seen by the Party's leadership as being too costly, especially in light of the expense of introducing the £10/£16 pensions.

By 1974 the Party had an agreed package of measures which represented a comprehensive policy for both flat-rate pensions and a state earnings-related pensions scheme. However, the elements of the package which would be given the highest priority by the Party leadership were those which were the trade union movement's particular priorities. These features of policy would be dangerous to disregard and far more likely to be implemented; hence SERPS was detached from the flat-rate pension increase when the Party came to power in 1974. The agreement to increase the basic flat-rate pension within the context of the new earnings-related pension scheme was extremely fragile because the main component was based on the flat-rate increase: the attempt to link it to the earnings-related scheme was something of an afterthought which did not command the same degree of commitment. Consequently, the exclusion of an explicit manifesto reference to crediting-in meant that its implementation was not guaranteed.

Nevertheless, the Labour Government's decision to increase the basic flat-rate pension as soon as they assumed office, and to ignore the Party's policy of crediting-in existing pensioners so that they would be part of the new superannuation scheme, needs to be explained because, in the two years prior to the Labour Party assuming office, the crediting-in arrangements had been studied and adopted by the party as an intrinsic part of their pensions policy. It might be the case that the decision to launch the flat-rate increase independently of the new earnings-related policy is further evidence not only of the systematic lack of liaison between the various bodies responsible for Labour Party policy formation, but also of the relative lack of status given to policy proposals which were essentially the creation of the Party's policy formulating bodies (NEC) as opposed to those which had been originally proposed by the trade union movement.

LABOUR IN POWER 1974–9

When the Labour Party published its election manifesto in February 1974, it became clear that the Party leadership intended to direct its efforts towards winning the co-operation of the TUC in a process of political exchange within the Social Contract. The primacy of trade union concerns was evident from the unequivocal commitments given to increase the basic flat-rate pension for existing pensioners and thereafter ensure its continuing revaluation:

> immediate help to existing pensioners, widows and the sick and the unemployed by increasing pensions and other benefits to £10 for a single person and £16 for the married couple, within the first parliamentary session. Thereafter these figures will be increased annually in proportion to increases in national average earnings.[35]

However the manifesto's commitment to an earnings-related pension scheme seemed to exclude the possibility that existing pensioners would be credited-in. Moreover, it was not clear how the earnings-related pension would be revalued once it was in payment.[36]

Labour came to power at the February 1974 general election. However, it did not win an overall majority in parliament, and formed a minority government as the largest single party. Thus government strategy was directed towards winning a second election which was held in October of the same year. Barbara Castle became the Secretary of State at the DHSS and Brian O'Malley joined her as Minister of State. In line with the priorities set out in the manifesto, Castle increased the flat-rate pension. On 10 April 1974 the pension rates were increased by 29 per cent so that a single person's pension rose from £7.75 to £10 per week and a married couple's rose from £12.50 to £16 per week.[37] The legislation also stipulated that benefit rates would be reviewed on an annual basis and would be increased in line with either rises in national average earnings or prices, whichever was the higher.

The government's determination to enact the legislation in the first parliamentary session was apparent from the way it overrode the administrative difficulties involved in up-rating benefit so swiftly. The benefit rates were not due to rise until the autumn and it was a considerable operation to prepare seven million pension books for the new rates at a time when there was also a great deal of industrial action from the public sector unions.[38] Moreover, as Castle reported to the

TUC's Social Insurance and Industrial Welfare Committee, at least one third of existing pensioners were receiving varying amounts of supplementary benefit, which increased the administrative difficulties involved.[39]

Castle reported that the total cost of the up-rating was likely to be in the region of £860m in 1974–5 and £1200m in a full year from the date of implementation, with the employers and the Exchequer bearing 86 per cent of the total cost. The employer's contribution was increased by 44p a week and the employee's contribution fell by 9p. The balance of the funding came from the graduated scheme which was to be wound up in 1975. The graduated contribution rose from 5 per cent to 5.5 per cent.[40]

In May, Castle announced that the Government would abandon the Joseph pension scheme and would implement only Parts I and IV of the 1973 Act which provided for the change to earnings-related contributions and the establishment of administrative machinery. The contribution levels which would come into force in 1975 were set at 5.5 per cent for the employee and 8.5 per cent for the employers up to an earnings ceiling of £69. However, the decision to abandon the Reserve scheme was condemned by the Conservative opposition and Labour only escaped censure by two votes in the parliamentary debate. This increased the pressure to publish Labour's plans before the autumn election and not to face an election campaign having discarded the Conservative proposals without putting anything in their place.

THE SECOND TIER

The Government's White Paper *Better Pensions*[41] set out the terms of earnings-related second tier of state provision. The aim was to replace 25 per cent of average earnings between the base level and the earnings ceiling. The base level was established as being earnings at or above the first flat-rate tier of provision (or £10/£16 per week at 1974 figures) and the ceiling was set at seven times that amount (i.e. £70 in 1974 figures). Thus all pensioners would receive a pound for pound replacement up to £10/£16 and above that level their pension would be related to a proportion of their earnings. The new earnings-related scheme would begin in 1978 and would have a twenty-year build up period so that a full earnings-related second tier would be payable in 1998.

The second-tier earnings-related pension was to be based on the contributions which had been paid during the employee's twenty best years (i.e. when their income was at its highest level). This avoided the problem of a system which would discriminate against manual workers whose earning power declined as they grew older. The formula on which the pension was calculated was based on $\frac{1}{80}$ th or 1.25 per cent of average earnings for each of the best twenty years until a pension of 25 per cent of the employee's average earnings was reached. Each year's contributions were, of course, revalued in line with increases in national average earnings.

Although the basic flat-rate tier was to be revalued annually in line with either the increase in national average earnings or inflation (whichever was higher), the earnings-related second tier was only to be increased in line with the rate of inflation. This decision ran counter to the hopes expressed by the Party's planners in opposition,[42] but no explicit commitment had been made to it in the 1974 manifesto. However, the scheme overcame a major flaw in the Crossman proposals which had not given concrete undertakings on either revaluation or inflation proofing.

The White Paper proposed that the scheme should be financed from a contribution of 16.5 per cent of employee earnings and suggested that this should be divided so that the employer paid 10 per cent and the employee 6 per cent. These figures were based on the assumption that 8m people would be contracted-out of the scheme by their employers. For those who were in occupational schemes which had contracted out a contribution rebate of 6.5 per cent of the employee's earnings was proposed. However, when the Social Security (Pensions) Act became law, the rebate was increased to 7 per cent of the contribution.

EXISTING PENSIONERS AND THE FAILURE TO ACHIEVE CREDITING-IN

The White Paper did not contain any reference to crediting-in; instead it stated that the position of existing pensioners would be reviewed in light of the development of the economy.[43] This represented a failure for the Social Policy Advisory Committee which had insisted that existing pensioners should be credited into the new scheme. The TUC's Social Insurance and Industrial Welfare Committee also were unhappy about this omission. When they first discussed the White

Paper they agreed that it conformed to the broad principles of TUC policy, but they wanted to see further commitments given to future and existing pensioners.[44] Throughout the early part of 1975 they reiterated their concern until they met with the ministers and pressed them to use the provisions of the Bill to credit-in existing pensioners.[45] Castle was impervious to the committee's objections and turned down the request saying that this was a matter of how to use the financial resources available in light of the economic situation. The commitment to review the situation at the time of the launch in 1978 must have satisfied the TUC because they did not take the matter to the Liaison Committee in order to bring further pressure on the Party leadership.

Although the new £10/£16 pensions had not lessened the pensioner's dependence on supplementary benefit the case for crediting-in was fatally weakened by its exclusion from the manifesto. The Chancellor of the Exchequer is reported to have overruled it because the Party had not given any formal commitment to it being included in the legislative programme.[46] It was also possible for him to argue that the increase in the flat-rate had greatly improved the position of existing pensioners and that the Government could not afford any policy advances other than those to which they were committed. The Cabinet is said to have recorded that the feasibility of crediting-in would be re-examined when SERPS was launched. Since the launch took place in the aftermath of the IMF crisis when the Chancellor was seeking reductions rather than increases in public expenditure it was highly unlikely that crediting-in was regarded as feasible.

CONCLUSION

The history of pensions policy-making during the 1970s, and the final implementation of a Labour Party superannuation scheme, give us important insights into the role of Opposition planning and the trade union movement in influencing the Labour Party's attainment of its social welfare policies.

The trade union movement's intervention clearly shows that the most important factor ensuring the implementation of the Party's pension policy was the influence of the trade union movement and the Party leadership's desire to comply with the trade union's policy preferences. Indeed, if SERPS had not been perceived as being part of the Social Contract its future might once again have been in doubt.

Moreover, the public references to crediting-in during the launch of SERPS, and the assurances that the decision had only been delayed until the launch of the schemes, were made in deference to the TUC's support for this aspect of policy.

In opposition, the Social Policy Advisory Committee has to be given credit for holding the line against the attempts to discard a national superannuation scheme in favour of a flat-rate national scheme. They confined their efforts to two aspects of policy development: the revaluation of the pension once it was in payment, and ways in which existing pensioners could share in the earnings-related scheme when it was launched. They were partially successful in improving the Crossman scheme in that SERPS was to be guaranteed against inflation; however, they did not achieve the goal of an earnings-related pension which rose in line with increases in national average earnings. On the second question of existing pensioners they failed, and consequently some pensioners now have an income based on the flat-rate pension whilst others receive the flat-rate pension plus some proportion of the earnings-related tier until a fully earnings-related second tier pension becomes payable. The loss of the crediting-in proposals is partially attributable to the economic conditions of the day. However, even if economic and political conditions had been more favourable the policy implementation would still have been at risk because it was not securely positioned in the manifesto or the Social Contract. Crediting-in might still have been regarded as a luxury once the flat-rate pension had been increased to £10/£16 per week and would have been vulnerable to the argument that the Government was not formally committed to legislate upon it. This highlights the importance of a clearly agreed programme in opposition and raises the crucial question of the confusion that the intervention of the trade union movement brought to the policy formulating structures. Whilst the Party successfully implemented the flat-rate increase with a commitment to revalue it, and went on to implement a national superannuation scheme, it is possible to see some deficiencies caused by the structural confusion in policy-formulation which existed during the early 1970s.

Although the TUC played a pivotal role in the period 1970–4, their impact on policy-making was not entirely beneficial. Their interest in the area meant that pensions was given a higher priority in the Labour Party's programme, and meant that the pension issues which were of particular concern to the TUC were likely to be adopted and implemented by the Party's leadership. The importance which was attached to the TUC meant that the Social Policy Advisory

Committee's influence over policy was reduced. There was no institutional mechanism which allowed the TUC and the Social Policy Advisory Committee to liaise and co-operate during the early stages of policy development. Hence policy was made in separate and independent forums. However, the crucial point is that these bodies did not wield equal influence with the leadership of the Party. The Party leadership was far more concerned to satisfy TUC interests than to heed the concerns of the Social Policy Advisory Committee. Even though the superannuation scheme which incorporated the increase in the flat-rate pension was accepted as Party policy and was agreed by the General Council of the TUC, it was still quite obvious that the TUC's main priority was the increase in the flat-rate pension. With hindsight we can see that the Social Policy Advisory Committee made a serious tactical mistake in thinking that the compromise programme could be implemented even if its component elements were enacted at different times. Nevertheless, since the compromise deal was Party policy and had been agreed by the TUC it should have been implemented in full. The fact that it was not indicates that the TUC/Labour Party Liaison committee had superseded the NEC as the most influential policy-making arena. Moreover, the fact that SERPS was not discussed by the Liaison Committee and was not fully incorporated into the Social Contract is the most powerful explanation of why the crediting-in proposals were dropped.

Notes

1. A. Warde, *Consensus and Beyond: the development of Labour Party strategy* (Manchester: Manchester University Press, 1982), p. 200.
2. Ibid. p. 113.
3. G. Dorfman, *Government versus Trade Unionism in British Politics since 1968* (London: Macmillan, 1979) p. 108.
4. J. Jones, *Union Man* (London: Collins, 1986) p. 235–6.
5. R. Taylor, *The Fifth Estate: Britain's Unions in the Modern World*, (London: Routledge & Kegan Paul, 1978) p. 130.
6. Labour Party Archives [henceforward LPA]: TUC/Labour Party Liaison Committee Joint Statement, July 1972.
7. LPA: TUC/Labour Party Liaison Committee, op. cit.
8. R. Taylor, op. cit. p. 132.
9. LPA: TUC/Labour Party Liaison Committee, *Economic Policy and the Cost of Living*, February 1973, p. 8.
10. Interview with Peter Jacques, Secretary to the Social Insurance and Industrial Welfare Committee of the TUC.
11. Interview with David Piachaud, member of Harold Wilson's Policy Unit 1974–6.

12.   'A Better Deal for the Elderly', initiated in 1970–1 to campaign for an increase in the basic pension.
13.   Interview with David Piachaud. He notes the fact that Jones gave little active support to superannuation because the majority of his T&GWU members were not sufficiently well paid to benefit from it substantially.
14.   *National Superannuation and Social Insurance: Proposals for Earnings Related Social Security* (London, HMSO, 1969).
15.   In September 1971 the single person's pension stood at £6 per week. This represented 19.5 per cent of an average male manual worker's salary. *Social Security Statistics 1982* (London, HMSO), Table 46.09, p. 251.
16.   Bill Simpson, *A New Approach to Retirement Pensions*, Labour Party Research Series, Rd. 583, p. 2.
17.   Labour Party Annual Conference Report 1972, p. 304.
18.   Cf. H. Heclo, *Modern Social Politics in Britain and Sweden* (New Haven: Yale University Press, 1974).
19.   Ibid. p. 311–314.
20.   The NEC's report which was prepared for the 1972 Conference, reaffirmed all the main principles of the Crossman scheme and mentioned that the Party was investigating the possibility of bringing existing pensioners into the scheme from the outset (cf. *Labour's Programme for Britain*, p. 49–52).
21.   In 1973 the level of expenditure on pensions was £2900m p.a. and £4100m p.a. on pensions and other benefits. The gross cost of increasing pensions to £10/£16 would be £830m p.a. and £1260m p.a. in respect of pensions and other insurance benefits, if the latter were to be raised proportionately. Cf. *The Basis for a State Superannuation Scheme*, TUC/Labour Party Joint Meeting (24/10/73) p. 7.
22.   LPA: Tony Lynes, *Possible Changes in the National Superannuation Scheme*, Labour Party Research Series, Rd. 237, Working Party on Pensions, Means-tests and Poverty.
23.   Lynes used the example of a 30-year transitional period. A man who reached pensionable age ten years after the scheme began would get an initial credit of 20 years earnings at half the national average wage plus a pension based on his actual earnings in the ten years previous to retirement, LPA: Rd 641 February 1973.
24.   Lynes, op. cit. p. 2.
25.   LPA: Labour Party Research Series Rd. 611/February 1973
26.   It was argued that such a scheme could be financed by earnings-related employee contributions with some assistance for the low paid. However, it was felt that the earnings-related pension tier could be financed by the employer possibly by means of a pay-roll tax as in Sweden which might be in the order of ten per cent of the national wages bill. The Exchequer supplement would be increased from the 18 per cent envisaged in the Crossman plan.
27.   LPA: Labour Party Research Series, Rd. 546/January 1973, *Pensions – the Labour Party and the TUC*.
28.   Interview with Peter Jacques, secretary to the SIIWC and member of SPA committee.

29. LPA: Labour Party Research Series, Rd. 578/April 1973 pp. 4–5.
30 Labour Party, *Labour's Programme*, 1973.
31. TUC Archives, Modern Records Centre, Warwick [henceforward MRC] Minutes 10/10/73, (SIIWC 2/5), refers to Brian O'Malley's paper, *The Basis of National Superannuation.*
32. MRC: Item 28, Minutes 12/12/73, TUC Social Insurance and Industrial Welfare Committee.
33. MRC: TUC Social Insurance and Industrial Welfare Committee and Labour Party Social Policy Sub-Committee Joint Meeting, Minutes, 14/11/1973 pp. 1–2.
34. MRC: SIIWC 5/4: 13/274, p. 2.
35. Labour Party Manifesto 1974: *Let's work together – Labour's Way out of the Crisis*, p. 7.
36. Ibid. pp. 7–8.
37. However, with prices rising so fast, the increase was worth something in the region of 12 per cent and was not a substitute for SERPS. (Interview with Professor David Piachaud.)
38. Interview with Prof David Piachaud.
39. MRC: SIIWC 6/12: 13/3/74. Report of a meeting with the Secretary of State 11/3/74.
40 MRC: SIIWC 10/4/74.
41. MRC: *Better Pensions Fully Protected against Inflation*, Cmnd 5713, HMSO, Sept. 1974.
42. *Labour's Programme for Britain 1972* p. 50. In this document the Party argues that protecting pensions against inflation alone is insufficient and that it was necessary 'to ensure that their standard of living rises with that of the working population.' It points out that between 1960 and 1970 average earnings rose by 93 per cent whereas prices rose by 49 per cent.
43. Cmnd 5713 op. cit. p. 2.
44. MRC: cf. SIIWC (161 XXXIII) 15/10/74: Item 5 'Better Pensions'.
45. MRC: cf. SIIWC 12/3/75 and 14/5/75.
46. Interview with Professor David Piachaud.

9 Immigration and Economics: The Politics of Race in the Postwar Period
Shamit Saggar

INTRODUCTION

Immigration of one form or another has always had, and is likely to continue to have, a significant impact upon the United Kingdom, but its social, economic and political impact has been particularly marked during the past forty or so years. This contrasted rather sharply with earlier – and indeed later – emphasis placed on the social consequences of unregulated immigration. In the late nineteenth century and early twentieth century the position of Jews was frequently discussed in terms of the perceived significance of their cultural and religious identity. Earlier, comparable 'doubts' had been expressed about the Irish influx. The hostile tone adopted by policy-makers towards migration on such social and cultural grounds remained remarkably consistent throughout the first half of the twentieth century and indeed returned in the whirlwind of Powellism a century later.

Initially, in the period between 1945 and the passage of the 1972 Commonwealth Immigrants Act, British governments and policymakers continued to approach the question of immigration in terms of an agenda led by the labour requirements of the domestic economy. Policy was largely based on a calculus of what forms of immigration would be beneficial to the economy and only then what types of immigrants would be best suited to settlement in the country.

The aims of this chapter are threefold. Firstly, it will explore the process by which a combination of public hostility towards immigrants and a defensive posture by successive governments ensured that the economic dimension of British immigration politics was driven off the policy agenda. The early stages of postwar immigration are central to this process and the analysis will concentrate on the racialised under-pinning of domestic political attitudes towards immigration and immigrants. The era up to 1962 highlights a peculiarly British approach to the cultural pluralisms of non-white immigration and, it will be argued, served to lay down the broad parameters within which immigration and its social consequences would be debated in British society.

Secondly, the nature and content of British approaches to integra-tion-type questions will be discussed. In public policy terms, integra-tion themes tended to preoccupy governing and administrative elites in the mid 1960s, when several key elements in Britain's liberal settle-ment were established. Despite several notable setbacks, remarkably few challenges have been successfully launched against the philosoph-ical values and assumptions of this era of reform. Hence the prefer-ence for the term *settlement* in describing the long term goals and orientation set in place a generation ago. The longer-run durability and unintended consequences of this liberal settlement form the main core of the second section of this chapter, which will also examine the framework of the immigration policy debate which during the 1960s culminated in a new discourse centred on cultural understandings of nation and nationhood.

The final section of the chapter will focus on the general interplay between economic and non-economic factors in the development of the politics of immigration and race. The relative neglect of economic themes within Britain's recent immigration policy debates is largely explained by the dominance afforded from about 1958 to immigra-tion's social dimension generally and the alleviation of social conflict specifically. In that sense, the reluctance to embrace explicitly an economic-centred language of immigration has had a major bearing on race relations in Britain more broadly and goes to the heart of con-temporary evaluations of the liberal settlement. This final section will also question whether a closer interplay needs to be fostered between contemporary policy regarding British economic competitiveness and British immigration control.

POST-WAR IMMIGRATION POLITICS UP TO 1962

At the end of the war, the scale of the non-white presence in Britain was generally confined to older traditional trade-related pockets of set-tlement in and around port cities.[1] The war itself had yielded a sizeable flow of refugees, clouded by thorny political questions over official responses to systematic Jewish persecution abroad and anti-semitic hostility at home.[2] However, even before the end of the war, a Royal Commission had been appointed in 1944 to examine Britain's likely postwar population requirements. Its report confirmed that postwar labour questions were lodged at the heart of the then-emerging reconstruction debate.

Reconstruction and Recovery

The Commission's 1949 Report recognised that the success of reconstruction was dependent on fresh recruitment to the labour force, not least because under-population might hamper Britain's prospects for sustained economic growth.[3] Such a worry was placed within a broader concern about Britain's economic strength and international standing, the implications of decolonisation and the likelihood of a reduced world role. However, whilst the Commission considered the immigration option to fill the population 'gap', it rejected it. In a powerfully-worded extract, the Commission's Report concluded that: 'immigration on a large scale into a fully established society like ours could only be welcome without reserve if the immigrants were of good human stock and were not prevented by their religion or race from intermarrying with the host population and becoming merged with it'.[4]

The significance of this perspective cannot be understated for three principal reasons. To begin with, the Commission's response to the subject signalled a dual line of thought. On the one hand the Commission had been given a remit to examine the broad macroeconomic implications of labour market shortages. Its frame of reference had therefore been to assess the ability of British producers to compete for global markets and, in doing so, to underpin a strategy for economic expansion. On the other hand, the prominence afforded to the social and cultural features of a strategy to absorb large numbers of immigrants suggested that in the final analysis the economic imperative was only secondary.

Secondly, the Report brought to the surface elements of a debate over non-European migrants that was to preoccupy policy-makers throughout the postwar epoch.[5] After 1949 policy-makers emphasised pragmatic opposition to 'melting pot' models of planned population growth. A 1949 report from Political and Economic Planning, a respected British policy think tank, summed up the blunt, pragmatically-worded 'truth' of it all, announcing that 'the absorption of large numbers of non-whites would be extremely difficult'.[6]

Finally, in bringing to the fore the apparently unappealing trade-off between the economic gains and cultural costs of non-European labour migration, the Report effectively served to lay the foundations of immigration debates – or rather political rows – for the following two or more decades. Whereas in the late 1940s official consideration was given to recruiting immigrants from beyond Europe, within a decade the political cutting edge of the debate had turned around to policies for its restriction.

Recruitment Followed by Reconsideration

The mood of policy-makers thus seemed clear enough: doubts were both expressed and acted upon regarding the non-economic consequences of any proposed influx. And yet, at another level, the prevailing mood was rather less clear. As early as late 1948, a Whitehall working party was set up to investigate the possibility of using colonial labour firstly to help fill the manpower gap in the home economy, and secondly to assist in reducing unemployment in the colonies.[7] Unlike the Royal Commission, this initiative directly reflected thinking within the core executive. The working party's report emphasised once again the logic of filling the void in the British economy with immigrants, both from colonial territories and through extant official schemes to recruit displaced workers from eastern and central Europe.[8] This emphasis, coupled with a response to the problem of unemployment particularly in the Caribbean, meant that supply-side factors remained firmly on the agenda of policy-makers at the heart of government. However, closer inspection of the working party's paper reveals that it strongly favoured relying on the European Volunteer Workers since their entry to, and stay in, the country could more easily be controlled. Furthermore, there was the danger of inadvertently encouraging Caribbean settlers attracted by higher real welfare payments.[9]

The working party's first report was not acted upon but in early 1950 it was reconvened. Its new remit was firstly to bear down on colonial immigration into the country and secondly to disperse and settle more effectively those who had already arrived. The climate of reconsideration was further fuelled in spring 1950 when the Labour Cabinet considered a paper on 'coloured' colonial immigration from the Colonial Secretary.[10] It was in this presentation to Cabinet that the problems of social adjustment associated with *non-white* immigrants were first considered by government as a whole. Throughout that year, despite a black colonial presence in Britain numbering only a few thousand at the most, renewed consideration was given to the question. On each occasion suggestions to restrict the numbers entering the country were put forward and endorsed in principle. But, more importantly, on each occasion it was agreed that the *imbalance* between the small numbers involved and the foreign policy repercussions of restrictions did not justify any immediate action. The potential sensitivity of the issue had therefore been recognised at high official level but its immediacy was not seen as a high priority for action.

The change of administration in 1951 appeared to have little direct impact on immigration policy. However, there is evidence to suggest that within a few years the Conservative government was beginning to encounter organised opposition to non-white immigration among its own ranks. This opposition was primarily made up of a series of anti-immigration drives encouraged by a handful of especially vocal Conservative parliamentary backbenchers. On occasion their efforts were supported by isolated Labour MPs, responding to alarm at grass-roots level. The emergence of parliamentary pressures for controls upon immigration was also fuelled by an element of split thinking on the issue within government itself and especially Whitehall. The result was unmistakable: by 1954–5 British political life was regularly and routinely punctuated by a series of *private* rows over immigration. It is worthwhile surveying these developments more closely in order to establish the context within which politicians eventually moved to a new regime of statutory controls in the early 1960s.

The Rising Political Saliency of Immigration

The general themes of immigration and race relations steadily climbed the political agenda after the mid-1950s. The retreat from Empire was almost complete in the Indian subcontinent and attention was refocusing on political Africa and the Caribbean colonies. Cabinet-level discussions during the mid-1950s showed that policy towards Empire and Commonwealth was rarely far from debates over immigration policy. In one notable episode the Commonwealth Secretary counselled Cabinet against pursuing a policy that might discriminate against would-be immigrants from the subcontinent and thus sour relations with Britain's new Commonwealth partners.[11]

In 1954 Churchill has been as quoted as having claimed that 'immig-ration is the most important subject facing the country'.[12] His motiva-tion appeared to be a deep suspicion about the creation of a society characterised by the pluralisms of race, culture, and religion; and, sur-prisingly perhaps, he was prepared to put these views openly to others in his government. However, the difficulty lay not so much in gathering support to oppose further immigration, but rather in getting ministerial colleagues to take the issue seriously. Within government itself there remained a curious aversion to tackling the question in terms other than its immediate labour markets implications. The pressure to recog-nise the social dimension of the issue instead came principally from parliamentary backbenchers led by Cyril Osborne (MP for Louth) and Norman Pannell (MP for Liverpool Kirkdale). These parliamentary voices were chiefly Conservative. Parliamentary written and verbal questions probing ministers on immigration and immigrants increased and either implicitly or explicitly argued in favour of new official con-trols, partly in order to stem a possible oversupply of labour, but more often on the grounds of 'combating' disease and criminality.

The sharp hostility of parliamentary critics led the Government to re-examine its strategy. A Cabinet Committee was set up on the issue of legislation to control immigration in November 1955.[13] It did nothing to end divisions within the Cabinet where, once again, opposi-tion to controls was voiced both on grounds of principle (a breach of commitments not to discriminate), as well as practicality (an ability to enforce controls without alienating Commonwealth partners). The statement meant that Cabinet was unable to agree any plan of action and thus maintain any hope of putting the issue on hold once more.

The new Prime Minister, Eden, however responded to the impasse by setting up a special ministerial committee, which reported in June 1956 and drew out a number of important features hitherto over-looked. First, the report noted that, despite fairly sharp rises in non-white immigration, the immigrants themselves continued to be successfully absorbed into regular employment and were making a very valuable contribution in Britain's growing economy. Second, the imme-diate housing shortages were not insurmountable in the longer run. Finally, and crucially, the report countered the received wisdom that immigration was stoking up public resentment. Rather, it claimed, there was little evidence of anti-immigrant intolerance, let alone the risk of US-style 'racial conflict'. Bearing all these arguments in mind, the committee nonetheless accepted that the possibility existed for deterioration in the situation, not least as a result of a slowdown in the economy. It opposed the introduction of controls but at the same time agreed that such controls should not be ruled out in future.[14]

The Racialisation of British Politics, 1958–62

The disturbances in Notting Hill in west London and Nottingham in the late summer of 1958 served to reshape dramatically the political context in which the immigration issue was debated.[15] The whole question of non-white immigration was suddenly and rudely placed near the top of the political agenda. The sense of simmering resentment that Osborne, Pannell and others had tried to bring to wider public attention was now displayed openly. That said, it is important to remember that political responses to the question continued to be varied, ranging from tough anti-immigration rhetoric to renewed interest in fostering inter-community understanding. But, in the end, the underlying opposition to the laissez-faire system of immigration control was reinforced.[16] Building on this increasingly hostile climate, Osborne reported to his parliamentary colleagues in November 1958 that the compelling logic of race should not be overlooked in the emerging round of calls for immigration controls: 'It is time someone spoke out for the white man in this country', he declared.[17]

Between 1958 and 1962 the immigration question became increasingly coherent in British politics.[18] Prior to 1958 it had failed to reach the heart of the political agenda but thereafter it could be argued that it never left the agenda in one form or another. It was in this sense at a *pre*-party political stage: that is, parties increasingly accepted the need to respond to the issue whilst avoiding firm or irreversible policy commitments that would force them to fight for political advantage. It was in other words an issue characterised by ever greater popular resonance, though not one that had any great bearing upon party competition. Such an important and bewildering paradox continued for much of following two decades. The shying away from open party competition on the issue (or issues)[19] has had many repercussions, not least in terms of assessments of the impact of race upon British politics and political culture.[20]

The political debate after 1958 centred on two distinct themes. To begin with, there was acceptance across both major parties that a hasty response might jeopardise good Commonwealth relations. Indeed, domestic immigration policy and overseas Commonwealth policy were seen as inextricably linked. The earlier Suez episode and its consequences for British Commonwealth policy had demonstrated the need to move ahead with caution.[21] The government's determination on this point was articulated by a junior minister in 1958: 'This country is proud to be the centre of an inter-racial Commonwealth which is the greatest assortment of peoples of all races, creeds and colours the world has ever seen. As a result we have always allowed any of the people in what was the Empire and is now the Commonwealth to come to this country and go as they please.'[22]

In other words there appeared to be a principle at stake within the issue. This principle held that the ideal of a post colonial Commonwealth represented a unique and credible British contribution to world affairs. As an ideal, its supporters held that it stood a strong chance of influencing world events by concentrating attention upon a united yet varied community of nations. Of course much of this political idealism went unsupported in international politics, not least of all by the British government itself.[23]

The upshot of this caution was that the question was largely tackled in terms of broad nationality and citizenship themes, rather than in terms of the immediate social consequences of immigration. As a result the ensuing debate centred on the proposal to amend – perhaps repeal – the terms of the 1948 Nationality Act. The Act was widely perceived to have been responsible – however unintentionally – for creating the open door to non-white immigration. The object implicit behind its amendment was that this would indirectly curb non-white immigration into the country and the task of its proponents was twofold: to draw a distinction between the various components of Commonwealth immigration, and then to establish a restriction around non-white sending countries.

The second principal theme of the post-1958 debate was the concern expressed by many politicians that introducing immigration controls would affect domestic race relations. On one hand, some politicians emphasised the notion of better community relations being fostered by a tight regime of immigration control. On the other hand, the argument was advanced by critics of formal controls that the Government would run the risk of effectively blaming immigrants themselves for the sudden wave of anti-immigrant sentiment. To target immigration control at this stage, it was argued, was tantamount to penalising the victims of prejudice at home. In the end, the debate was built on the crude premise that there were too many black immigrants in the country and that they were the root cause of tensions and friction over housing, education, employment, etc. A suitable response to this state of affairs was advanced in simple, rationalist terms: the policy solution of restricting numbers. It is significant that a similar logic underscored later attempts to mediate black-white relations in public service distribution by trying to place limits on the black presence in schools, housing estates and elsewhere.[24]

Closing the Immigration Door

A subtle though crucial tension therefore ran through the newly-ignited immigration question. The policy debate was clearly moving towards controls of some form but even those who enthusiastically backed this option had to recognise that British immigration law could not be altered without regard to the reaction to such change overseas. Nevertheless there was cross-party agreement that easing race rela-tions could only be achieved within a framework that regulated the flow of immigrants into the country. Such regulation was called for partly to help offset the 'fears' of those concerned about further immigration, and partly in order to bring immigrant numbers back into balance within the short to medium term labour requirements of the economy. The downturn in the economy during 1958 played a key part in this discussion. To that end, whilst the emphasis within policy discussions was evidently shifting towards the *social dimension* of immigration, the earlier, rather more central, *economic dimension* of policy had not been abandoned – even as the Government moved to bring in fresh controls.

The development of policy at this time has sometimes been described as the foundations of the 'numbers game' equating immig-rant concentrations with social problems. Such an equation, suggest Miles and Phizacklea,[25] has been permanently carved onto the map of British political discourse. 'For years the white people have been tol-erant' complained a Labour MP in 1958, '[and] now their tempers are up.' It was precisely this type of complaint (and warning) that govern-ment and opposition were now playing to. This development did much to ensure the *legitimation* of negative, unwelcoming and threatening positions towards immigration that future administrations would openly espouse. It would also ensure that, as the immigration question moved through the 1960s and beyond, the economic dimension would give way to a rather different agenda of nationhood and cultural poli-tics. The post-1962 framework for immigration policy debate was thus trapped within a set of normative assumptions that not only gave the political initiative to conservative, 'Little-Englander' voices, but also effectively buried the chances of reconstructing an economic-centred approach to policy. It was this feature of the framework that has had such a lasting impact upon British political culture, and more specifically, upon British instinctive responses to immigration and ethno-cultural pluralism.

INTEGRATION EQUATIONS AFTER 1962

Prior to 1962 therefore a number of labour market and foreign policy factors were initially at the heart of domestic reconsideration over immigration policy and the Osborne-Pannell-type arguments to cut off immigration were pushed to the fringes of the debate. After the Macmillan administration's decision to introduce fresh legislation, however, there was much broader acceptance of the sort of racial and cultural arguments of immigration hardliners. The 1962 legislation had created a key distinction between New and Old Commonwealth sources of immigration, thus demonstrating that the postwar Commonwealth ideal was one that was divisible. Additionally, it regulated the flow of immigrants from the colonies and ex-colonies; unrestricted entry was compromised by a simple system of vouchers comprising three basic categories and issued, in theory, on the basis of labour market conditions.[26] However, the legislation never worked particularly well in terms of its underlying labour market objective, leading one authoritative commentator to claim that: 'It would appear that New Commonwealth immigration particularly was more closely related to labour market conditions at origin than in the UK during the 1960s and 1970s'.[27] Whilst the Government may have believed that bringing in controls would serve to undermine the hardliners' case, it was only able to do so by acknowledging the legitimacy of racially-based claims about the nature of the immigrants and the consequences of their settlement. Culture and race thus emerged as central components of the post-1962 agenda.

Building a Policy Framework

The 1962 legislation was significant for another reason, namely the formal establishment of the first policy machinery for the promotion of integration. The Commonwealth Immigrants Advisory Council (CIAC) was established to find out more about grassroots race relations. Armed with the requisite evidence, it was to concentrate upon coming up with technocratic solutions, usually requiring the intervention of central or local government and accompanying funding mechanisms. Its first three reports were devoted to this kind of task in the areas of housing, education and the problems of school-leavers.[28] Its was generally well-received and helped to map out the need for a policy environment in which race and ethnicity themes that impinged upon local public service delivery could be routinely discussed, if not managed.

The local context was fast emerging as a central feature of government strategy. The rapid influx of immigrants that took place between 1960–2 (roughly paralleling the expectation of formal controls) had a major impact at local level. A number of local authorities, already experiencing difficulties with the conflicting demands of hosts and newcomers, found the rise in numbers overwhelming. This in turn served to create something of a crisis in their management of local race-related conflicts. The problem was further compounded by the complaint that no adequate mechanism existed through which their anxieties and views could be heard and channelled into fresh policy. CIAC started to fill this void but its success merely revealed the case for greater and more substantial longer term planning in this field. Part of this need was eventually met in 1964 by the in-coming Labour administration's strategy which comprised firstly a fact-finding reappraisal by Maurice Foley, the notional 'minister for race relations', and secondly the provisions of the first Race Relations Act.

The core thinking behind the establishment of CIAC was that it would combine with the control aspects of the 1962 legislation to remove race from the political agenda. In Katznelson's words: 'Macmillan's government were convinced that immigration controls and the appointment of an advisory council would adequately de-politicise race and provide for harmonious race relations'.[29] In the event, the hope was short-lived for two reasons. One was the additional pressure created by fresh immigration not adequately regulated by the 1962 Act. The other was the fact that grassroots tensions over race had entered the world of local politics and were unlikely to be defused by measures taken at such a distant and seemingly intangible level.

The Liberal Settlement

The period from 1962 represents something of a high-water mark in liberal-inclined thinking and practice in domestic race relations. CIAC and the adoption of statutory controls in 1962 had effectively signalled the broad parameters within which official strategy might operate. At first, the resort to legal controls upon Commonwealth immigrants was opposed by the Labour Opposition. The impact of such controls on the Commonwealth and abandonment of principle were prime factors cited by Labour leaders and especially Gaitskell in his unambiguous condemnation of the Act. However, much was to change, starting with the change of leadership in early 1963 and continuing through the salutary experience of the loss of Patrick Gordon Walker in Smethwick in 1964.[30] By the time Labour assumed office in 1964, party thinking had shifted greatly on the issue, confirming the new leader's claim that 'we do not contest the need for control'.[31] Labour in office thus represented a key opportunity to *relay* the foundations of a consensus that had been implicit since 1962. The opportunity could only be taken once Labour had agreed and implemented a policy to renew the 1962 controls, a move it took with little hesitation. Beyond that, Labour turned to consolidate its strategy by setting out a fresh integration policy, to be built on the twin pillars of anti-discrimination laws and expanded support for local government and voluntary bodies. The main outcome of this was the first Race Relations Act passed in spring 1965 which prohibited racial discrimination in public places (though notably excluded the housing and employment markets) and brought in a system of civil law to curb cases of proven discrimination.[32]

In an early initiative following the first Race Relations Act, the Labour administration also published in August 1965 an important White Paper, *Immigration from the Commonwealth*,[33] which proposed another advisory body, the National Committee for Commonwealth Immigrants (NCCI).[34] The new liberal strategy was fully set out, stating explicitly the tough control context within which integration measures were to be pursued. The limitation/integration equation allowed Labour – and its many supporters across the political spectrum – to concentrate the debate upon means rather than ends. This focus meant that subsidiary questions such as the desirability of, and value attached to, a multiracial society and the irreversibility of black immigration were shunted off the mainstream policy agenda. Efforts were given over to fleshing out the mechanics of integration policies and to laying the basis for a long term framework for discussion and resolution of ethnic pluralism themes. It was this latter goal that has proven so central to the long run endurance of liberal values in British race relations. The features of this framework are therefore worth examining more fully.

First, the conceptual basis of Labour's strategy – and the underlying emergence of a value-based settlement – was the acknowledgement of the reality of a multiracial society. This meant more than the sum total of Labour's 1960s reforms, comprising *inter alia*, two Race Relations Acts, new funding for local authorities, and various promotional activities. The ultimate aim of politicians such as Roy Jenkins, Home Secretary from 1965 to 1967, was to gain acceptance of and harness the fact that non-white immigration was a permanent phenomenon.[35] Enthusiasts for this goal may have hoped that it would involve a clear political lead by government – and mainstream political parties more generally – to rebut lurking fears over the future character of Britain. But in practice clarification of the concept of a multicultural society has been one of the greatest failures of British social policy.[36]

Second, while there may have been difficulties in pinning down the meaning and essential character of Britain as a multiracial society, governments since 1965 have been committed to racial harmony as a 'public good'. One commentator, Banton, has suggested that the greatest achievement of the cross-party strategy was to underwrite the notion of harmony as one in which all members of a civilised liberal democracy held a stake. Such a goal certainly underscored much of the promotional activities, both at central and local levels, that came out of the 1965 and 1968 Race Relations Acts. Jenkins himself summarised his ideal value system as one which combined the goal of 'ethnic pluralism and cultural diversity, in an atmosphere of mutual tolerance'.[37] Definitional problems have persisted, however, rather dogging public policy attempts to secure agreement over policy instruments and assessment of outcomes. Moreover, however laudable their vision may have been, critics have argued that mature liberal democracies merely define harmony as the absence of *overt* social conflict. Thus, the argument goes, they have ignored underlying racial inequality because, so long as it has only infrequently been associated with overt conflict, they have concluded that racial harmony has both existed and been improving over the past thirty years. That said, there can be little doubt that British politics and political culture in the past thirty years has been united around the goal of securing harmony. Whatever the inadequacies in the distinction between the goals of equality and harmony, it has not fundamentally undermined the viability of a political consensus centred on harmony as a 'public good'.

Third, the British approach of reliance upon the voluntary sector has given the strong impression of public bodies seeking to keep the issue of grassroots race relations at arms length.[38] Voluntary effort clearly has been central in managing race relations at local level and, in general, much of these activities have taken place with fairly modest levels of official government support or regimentation. However, critics have complained that local voluntarism has often been a sham (at best) and an ineffective conspiracy (at worst). Radical voices in particular have claimed that these bodies have had the unenviable job of insulating mainstream politics, institutions and parties from racial conflicts. Local political systems have thus generally managed to avoid handling race as an issue, though many have worried about the motives underpinning such avoidance. Irrespective of these charges, however, it is hard to see how British race politics could develop without the continuing presence of locally-based voluntary bodies performing a range of roles ascribed to them by supporters and critics alike.

Fourth, and related to the previous characterisation, British race relations have developed on the broad cross-party understanding that 'race' be kept out of party competition. The depoliticising of race has at times been a tough condition for parties to abide by. Indeed, its effective suspension, if not demise, has been witnessed on at least one occasion since the mid 1960s.[39] Despite this fairly limited counter evidence, it is important to remember that consensus over depoliticisation has generally been observed as a vital ground-rule. The foundations of this agreement were set by the 1965 Act and White Paper which thus represent a key watershed: the parliamentary and press debates reveal the full extent of inter-party agreement sometimes bordering on flattery. Additionally, a number of related factors tended to solidify the consensus: an attempt by central political institutions to deflect the issue to sub-central level,[40] plus a willingness to place bodies such as NCCI (and the Community Relations Commission later on) in a frontline role to manage the issue and absorb its venom wherever and whenever possible.

The long term impact of depoliticisation is difficult to assess. The distinction offered by Banton between 'race radicals' and 'race liberals' is valuable.[41] Accordingly, the underlying objectives of these respective camps are isolated, with the former tending to emphasise the futility of separating race from politics and the latter insisting that race remains too volatile to permit parties the luxury of competing for votes. To be sure, radicals have also gone rather further, making the compelling point that the tackling of race-related forms of discrimination and social exclusion are matters that are fundamentally about power relationships. By denying this, so the argument goes, liberals have run the risk of exacerbating sensitivities over race. The issue for radicals, is in effect, a political one, and attempts to drive if off the political agenda are doomed to failure. In contrast, liberals have tried to avoid confronting the claim that 'discrimination equals power', and instead have adopted a strategy which enthusiasts would think of as the 'art of the possible'. In these terms, the areas of education and promotional activities have been prioritised so that grassroots inter-community understanding takes place without the distractions of party competition stoking the embers of racial conflict.

Whatever the interpretation of its value, the consensus to keep race out of the politics of party competition continues to be a central feature of British society a generation after its inception. The race issue may not be dead in modern British politics as a result, but it is fairly certain that its quasi-permanent, dormant status is perceived to be a key operational ground-rule of electoral competition.

Limitation and Integration: The Politics of Culture and Nationhood

If British approaches to immigration and its consequences have tended to be preoccupied with harmony, the question may then be raised as to why these concerns were only legitimate within a climate of tough restrictions on immigration. Equally, just how tight and self-fulfilling has been the consensus to keep immigrants out? Many commentators have raised this point, wondering whether current and future discussions over British immigration policy within an increasingly European context will forever be hostages to the 1960s' legacy.[42] Limitations of space prohibit a full examination of European-centred influences on domestic political debates.[43] However, it is worth reviewing briefly the recent trajectory of immigration concerns and the prospects for a less socially- and culturally-driven policy debate.

In what sense can government seek to foster a more positive and enlightened approach to fresh immigration in the future? The response must begin with the prevailing political settlement. As has been argued, the evolution almost thirty years ago of a liberal-inspired framework for public policy towards ethnic pluralism is central in this respect. Speaking in the mid-1960s, Roy Hattersley, then a junior minister at the Home Office, set out the basis of the framework. His government's strategy amounted to the following: 'Integration without control is impossible but control without integration is indefensible', a slogan sometimes known as the Hattersley equation.[44] Hattersley's linkage of the two areas of policy responsibility confirmed publicly and explicitly that official policy reflected a dualism, whereby politicians were unable to tackle one area of policy without re-examining the other.[45] Moreover, on the plus side, as this paper has shown, this linkage served to hold together a much wider bipartisan settlement in values and assumptions towards race and immigration.[46] In the generation since, with the notable exception of the period between 1976–81, both parties have made considerable efforts to keep to the terms of this consensus. Their determination to do so itself reflects the relatively high value attached to the immigrant and immigrant-descended community by politicians of both major parties. Such politicians have not only recognised the danger of losing votes over the fear of further immigration but have, to all intents and purposes, internalised the logic of closing and keeping locked the door to immigrants.

It is not so surprising then to learn that surveys of public attitudes towards ethnic minorities reveal that not only do large numbers accept that governments discriminate against such minorities, but that they are right to do so at the point of entry into the country. Data put forward a generation ago by Butler and Stokes in the British Election Study shows there was a very strong link between the anti-immigrant hostility of both the public and government alike.[47] There is no particular reason to think that this link has been eroded or been checked by political parties in the years since. Public attitudes in this regard appear to follow closely leads given by policy-makers and political elites. The matter of the causal relationship underpinning public opinion and government posture is however a more complex matter. Whilst much has been made of the 'race card' and its alleged deployment in electoral competition, the evidence remains unclear. There is little doubt that governments and party leaderships have been only too aware of the electoral unpopularity of being seen as 'soft' on immigration. The problem lies in detecting the point at which this general law of 'keeping your distance' from the immigration issue has become a deliberate foundation of political strategy to court anti-immigrant public sentiment.[48] It should be stressed that developing a test to draw out this distinction requires more than casual, isolated examples of tough talk by parties, since the question of wider public saliency must first be demonstrated.

Since the heyday of the liberal consensus in the 1960s governments have continued to highlight the importance of retaining tight restrictions over immigration and have argued that restraint is a precondition of good race relations. Domestic policy towards immigrants and their offspring has in turn stressed the value of curbs upon discrimination against ethnic minorities whilst tolerating, even nurturing, a modicum of cultural diversity. However, against this general emphasis to try to balance rights and obligations, critics on the right in particular have contested the ability of elected governments to preserve national unity.[49] Powell of course has been the most celebrated critic of the liberal settlement, but others have argued in favour of an assimilationist model of absorbing immigrants and their cultural legacies into a dominant British cultural tradition. However, to accept that immigrants and their cultural identities constitute some form of threat to British nationhood would perhaps be to exaggerate their influence in British society. Moreover, the argument overstates the extent to which national integrity itself is founded on cultural homogeneity.[50]

THE ECONOMIC IMPERATIVE AND IMMIGRATION POLITICS

This chapter has argued that the broad context within which government has managed immigration policies has altered dramatically in the postwar period. Several commentators have suggested that this context needs to be viewed as part of a wider ideological construction of norms, values and assumptions in modern society regarding the role of the immigrant or newcomer. Indeed, it would be myopic to view the postwar experience, involving chiefly immigration from South Asia and the Caribbean, as in some way distinct or unique in its shaping of popular ideas about the outsider in British society. The experience of Jewish migration and settlement in particular shows the remarkable influence this presence had on the development of traditions of immigrant politics, most notably of course in east London, 'home' of successive waves of migrant groups, and the parallel story of internal migration from ghetto to suburb.[51]

In this final section of the chapter, attention will be turned to the possibilities of the future policy debate being influenced to a greater degree by economic factors. If governments – or at least governing elites – are to challenge existing popular prejudice about immigration and immigrants, they will need to put forward positive arguments demonstrating that immigration can yield benefits for British economic prosperity. Indeed, it can be argued that such a positive campaign can only be achieved through tackling the ideological framework within which immigration and immigrants have increasingly become associated with a variety of social problems and tensions.[52]

Such a strategy would not only be extremely bold and ambitious but would also require government-led reappraisal of the social and cultural consequences of mass non-white immigration. Any such strategy or reappraisal must in the first instance recognise the nature of the existing political and ideological framework for immigration policy, a framework which is deeply committed to keeping immigrants at arm's length and which fails to see their potential contribution to British society and economy. To that end, the strategy would be as much about instinctive British social attitudes towards ethnic pluralism as about the mechanics of immigration itself.[53]

Economic Competitiveness and Immigrant Resources

Perhaps the most compelling argument in favour of reappraisal – and possible redirection – of policy is the *original* rationale for postwar immigration, namely the economic contribution of immigration. In examining this general argument – as policy-makers have modestly in recent years – it may be prudent to take account of several central issues. First, it is clearly important that policy-makers are willing to see immigration policy choices as part of a wider picture concerning economic and trade policy.[54] Within this picture, the significance of immigration to more micro-level policy involving commercial competitiveness, labour and other supply side questions must be stressed.[55] In viewing the picture in compartmentalised terms, it is all too likely that policy responses will fail to appreciate the interdependence between British economic prosperity and Britain's population size and structure.

Second, immigration's impact upon the local economy cannot have gone unnoticed. To be sure, where the shape and characteristics of local immigrant settlement has comprised groups of relatively well-educated, highly-skilled immigrants bringing with them sizeable amounts of investment capital, the prognosis has been rather rosy. A number of well-documented examples of such valuable human capital exist for parts of the United States,[56] Canada and Australia. However, considerable disagreement exists over the basis of these and other familiar immigrant success stories.[57] For one thing, the rapid influx of competitive and mobile immigrant groups, it is argued, can often have the effect of breaking unionised labour and the accelerated contraction of older labour-intensive industries. According to one recently celebrated observer of these forces in Los Angeles: 'Boosters preferred to describe the LA economy in terms of emblematic immigrant success stories – Hong Kong meets Horatio Alger – and described the fundamental shift as being toward an entrepreneurial, free-market system. They were quick to insist that ... out of these sweatshops and light industrial plants would develop a new, immigrant middle class.'[58] It is apparent that the rhetoric of so-called 'boosterism' has been a powerful influence upon immigration debates, especially at a local, sub-national level.[59] The evidence is far from uniform but there can be little doubt that examples of such positive results have been sufficient to keep the rhetorical vision going. Indeed, improvements in the economy of some previously depressed urban areas where there has been an association with an immigrant presence has sometimes been stark. Writing of Asian-American influences on the urban economy, Rose has indeed suggested that former pariahs have come to be accepted as paragons and have been singled out as examples of 'model minorities' in US society.[60] Similar work on the entrepreneurial role of the immigrant has been carried out in Britain where the South Asian presence in self-employment has yielded some notable, though perhaps over-reported, success stories.[61]

Third, whilst the superficial political appeal of turning earlier pariahs into tomorrow's paragons may be too great to resist, a few cautionary notes may be in order.[62] The association of immigrants with market-driven enterprise is itself likely to conceal a variety of additional influences and processes at work. To begin with, the link with entrepreneurial commercial activity may mask an underlying difficulty in gaining successful employment. If this is the case, immigrant enterprise should be seen more in terms of the shortcomings of the existing labour market than as an end in itself. Furthermore, the association with self-employment in itself does not demonstrate success or sufficient return on investment. The evidence regarding the success rates of such economic enterprises continues to be mixed. Lastly, it is important to note that many immigrant enterprises in fact serve the immigrant communities themselves and are therefore built largely on an ethnic market; a treasure-trove of empirical research has shown that the ability to translate and recreate these undoubted skills beyond the niche remains a rather larger and harder task.[63]

Finally, as the rather more selective and sophisticated immigration policies of Australia[64] and, to a lesser extent, Canada,[65] have shown, the recruitment of highly skilled, adaptable and mobile workers should be seen as central to the economic competitiveness of mature industrial democracies. Insofar as Britain is firmly locked into tighter and more sophisticated forms of competition for its trade, then Britain is unlikely to be able to escape the competition for resources including human capital. As this chapter has suggested, what is less clear, however, is whether Britain will opt to retain its own tradition of culturally and socially-derived hostility towards immigration. If policy-makers are determined to overcome the hostages to fortune of this framework, then it is likely that immigration can develop into an important and dynamic element of the political debate to arrest and reverse British relative economic decline.

CONCLUSION

This chapter has argued that the 'racialisation' of British politics in the postwar period has prompted a number of evaluative questions concerning, for instance, the achievements of Britain's liberal settlement and the early abandonment of an economic-driven immigration debate. The debate prior to 1962 contrasts fairly sharply with the debate since. In particular, the economic rationale for early postwar immigration was eclipsed by a new and powerful agenda dominated by social and cultural fears. The chapter has focused on the causes behind the economic dimension being driven off the policy agenda, highlighting the extent to which further discussions over immigration have been couched in narrow and defensive terms. The chapter has additionally examined the nature of British integration policy efforts and their associated dilemmas. Finally, the chapter has explored the continuing interplay between economic and non-economic factors in shaping British politics and policy toward immigration and ethnic pluralism. It has argued that the present climate and future prospects for both are overwhelmingly hostages to the agenda-setting developments in British immigration policy management surrounding the 1962 Act. Serious political attempts to prise open the door of immigration in the future must therefore resurrect the basic economic case for immigration. The economic imperative remains as critical as ever.

Notes

1. M. Sherwood, *Many Struggles: West Indian Workers and Service Personnel in Britain 1939–45* (London: Karim Press, 1984). Further estimates of these settlements are to be found in M. Banton, *The Coloured Quarter* (London: Jonathan Cape, 1955).
2. J. Walvin, *Passage to Britain* (Harmondsworth: Penguin, 1984). See also M. Berghahn, *German–Jewish Refugees in England* (London: Macmillan, 1984). A fuller discussion of the impact of anti-semitism on government thinking at this time is provided by T. Kushner, *The Persistence of Prejudice* (Manchester: Manchester University Press, 1989).
3. *Report of the Royal Commission on Population*, Cmnd 7695, HMSO, 1949.
4. Ibid., p. 124.
5. See S. Saggar, *Race and Politics in Britain* (Hemel Hempstead: Harvester Wheatsheaf, 1992), pp. 16–23.
6. Political and Economic Planning, *Population Policy in Great Britain* (London: PEP, 1948).
7. Quoted in Z. Layton-Henry, *The Politics of Immigration* (Oxford: Basil Blackwell, 1992), pp. 28–9.
8. For further details of the European Volunteer Workers programme (and especially the recruitment of Polish workers) see A. Cairncross, *Years of Recovery, British Economic Policy 1945–51* (London: Methuen, 1985).
9. Public Record Office [henceforward PRO]: LAB26/22/7503, unpublished report of the working party on the employment in the UK of surplus colonial labour, 1948.
10. PRO: CAB129/40, CP(SO) 113 'Coloured people from the British colonial territories' by the Secretary of State for the Colonies, May 1950.
11. PRO: CAB129/77, CP(SS) 113, 'Colonial immigrants' by the Secretary of State for Commonwealth Relations, September 1955.
12. Quoted in Layton-Henry, *The Politics of Immigration* (Oxford: Blackwell, 1992), p. 31.
13. PRO: CAB129/78, CP (SS) 180, 'Colonial Immigrants', note by the Prime Minister, November 1955. See also CAB129/78, CP(SS)166.
14. PRO: CAB129/81, CP(S6) 145, 'Colonial immigrants', Report by the Committee of Ministers, June 1956.
15. E. Pilkington, *Beyond the Mother Country: West Indians and the Notting Hill white riots* (London: I. B. Tauris, 1988).
16. For instance, a *Daily Express* poll published in late 1958 showed a colossal four in five respondents in favour of introducing controls; see Layton-Henry, *Politics of Immigration*, p. 73.
17. Quoted in P. Foot, *Race and Immigration in British Politics* (London: Penguin, 1965), p. 129.
18. I. Katznelson, *Black Men, White Cities: race relations and migration in the United States 1900–30 and Britain 1948–68* (London: Oxford University Press/Institute of Race Relations, 1970). Katznelson in fact goes on to argue that the framework within which *limited* competitive party advantage was sought on the issue did not emerge until after the 1962 legislation

and even then appeared to give way after the 1964 election to a new era of cross-party consensus.

19. For a discussion of the changing character of 'race issues', particularly in the context of trends in ethnic minority political engagement, see S. Saggar, 'The transformation of the "race" issue and black political participation', *New Community*, 20, 27–41, 1993.

20. M. Banton, 'The beginning and the end of the racial issue in British politics', *Policy and Politics,* 15.1, 39–47.

21. D. Childs, *Britain Since 1945: A Political History* (London: Routledge, 1986, 2nd edn), p. 89.

22. *House of Commons Debates* 5th Ser., Vol. 596, Col. 1552.

23. N. Deakin, 'The politics of the Commonwealth Immigrants Bill', *Political Quarterly*, Vol. 391, pp. 24–45, 1968.

24. For detailed case studies of policy attempts to place upper limits on the 'immigrant presence' in state schools and in public housing respectively, see S. Saggar, *Race and Public Policy* (Aldershot: Avebury, 1991), pp. 81–111, and H. Flett, *The Politics of Dispersal in Birmingham* (Birmingham: SSRC Research Unit on Ethnic Relations, 1981).

25. R. Miles and A. Phizacklea, *White Man's Country: racism in British politics* (London: Pluto Press, 1984, 1st edn).

26. A. Dummet, 'British migration policy in the twentieth century', in D. Lowe (ed.), *Immigration and Integration: Britain and Australia* (London: Sir Robert Menzies Centre for Australian Studies, 1995).

27. J. Salt, 'Foreign labour migration and the UK', in Lowe (ed.), *Immigration and Integration*.

28. Cmnd 2119, HMSO, London, 1963, Cmnd 2266, HMSO, London, 1964. Cmnd 2458, HMSO, London, 1964.

29. Katznelson, *White Men, Black Cities*, p. 146.

30. N. Deakin, *Colour and the British Electorate* (London: Pall Mall, 1965).

31. Harold Wilson in *House of Commons Debates* 5th ser. Vol. 702, Col. 1254.

32. K. Hindell, 'The genesis of the Race Relations Bill', *Political Quarterly*, Vol. 36, pp. 390–406, 1965.

33. Cmnd 2739.

34. NCCI's principal job was to incorporate the views of local voluntary organisations and groups into an effective national network to support and advise government. For a discussion of their sometimes ambiguous role, see P. Calvocoressi, 'The official structure of conciliation', *Political Quarterly*, 39, 46–53.

35. Roy Jenkins went on to hold the Home Secretaryship for a second time between 1974–6, at which time he played a pivotal role in arguing for a third Race Relations Act.

36. K. Young, 'Racial disadvantage', in G. Jones et al. (eds), *Between Centre and Locality* (London: Gower, 1985).

37. R. Jenkins, transcript of speech to the National Committee for Commonwealth Immigrants, London, 23 May 1966.

38. For instance, the overwhelming pressures placed on the community relations movement have frequently fuelled frustrations and antagonisms, not least in local political arenas involving local authorities as

ad hoc 'paymasters'. See A. Messina, 'Mediating race relations: British community relations councils revisited', *Ethnic and Racial Studies*, 10, 186–202, 1987.

39. The Conservative attempt to shift dramatically rightward on the non-white immigration issue between 1976–9 has been extensively described and debated among commentators. See for example Z. Layton-Henry, 'Race, electoral strategy and the major parties', *Parliamentary Affairs,* 31.3, 1978; and W. L. Miller, 'What was the profit in following the crowd?: Aspects of Conservative and Labour strategy since 1970', *British Journal of Political Science*, 10, 1980. Additionally, a related claim has been made about the indirect benefit accrued to the Conservative Opposition as a result of the 1968 Powell row in the run-up to the 1970 General Election. See for example D. Studlar, 'Policy voting in Britain: the coloured immigration issue in the 1964, 1966 and 1970 General Elections', *American Political Science Review*, 72, 1978.

40. J. Bulpitt, 'The anatomy of the Centre's race statecraft in England', *Environment and Planning C*, 3, 129–47, 1985.

41. Banton, 'The beginning and the end of the race issue'.

42. For a recent illustration of this point, see for example several contributions in S. Spencer (ed.), *Strangers and Citizens* (London: Institute for Public Policy Research, 1994).

43. For a discussion of British objectives for future EU policy on immigration, see A. Dummett, 'Immigration – On United Kingdom Objectives for Future European Community Policy', unpublished paper presented to a seminar on *The Economic and Social Impact of Migration*, Institute of Public Policy Research/Friedrich Ebert Foundation, March 1993.

44. Quoted in Saggar, *Race and Politics*, p. 90.

45. See Miles and Phizacklea, *White Man's Country*, p. 57.

46. See S. Saggar, 'The politics of "race policy" in Britain', *Critical Social Policy*, Vol. 37, pp. 32–51, 1993.

47. See D. Butler and D. Stokes, *Political Change in Britain* (London: Macmillan, 1974, 2nd edn), p. 306.

48. For both sides of this debate, especially in relation to the closely-fought 1992 General Election campaign, see: S. Saggar, 'Can political parties play the "race card" in general elections? The 1992 poll revisited', *New Community*, Vol. 19, pp. 693–99, 1993, and M. Billig and P. Golding, 'Did the race card tip the balance?', *New Community*, Vol. 19, pp. 161–3, 1993.

49. A full discussion of these arguments is to be found in G. Seidel, 'Culture, nation and "race" in the British and French New Right', in R. Levitas (ed.), *The Ideology of the New Right* (Oxford: Polity Press, 1986).

50. B. Parekh, 'The "New Right" and the politics of nationhood', in The Runnymede Trust, *The New Right: Image and Reality* (London: The Runnymede Trust, 1986).

51. See T. Kushner, 'Jew and non-Jew in the East End of London: towards an anthology of "everyday" relations', in G. Alderman and C. Holmes (eds), *Outsiders and Outcasts: essays in honour of W. J. Fishman* (London: Duckworth, 1993).

52. For a fuller discussion of the political dilemmas thrown up by recent immigration into the United States, as well as the development of an

increasingly illiberal immigration climate in the US following reform in the mid 1960s, see the collection of essays edited by N. Glazer (ed.), *Clamour at the Gates: the new American immigration* (San Francisco: Institute of Contemporary Studies, 1985).

53. Aspects of the tensions within mass public attitudes are touched upon in K. Young, 'Class, race and opportunity', in R. Jowell et al. (eds), *British Social Attitudes* (Aldershot: Gower, 1992).

54. S. Spencer, 'The future of British immigration policy', seminar presentation, Department of Politics, Queen Mary and Westfield College, University of London, 17 January 1996.

55. An example of this kind of analysis applied to the hypothetical prospect of significant immigration to Britain from Hong Kong can be seen in Hong Kong/UK Economy Research Group, 'The Corry Report', *The South China Sunday Morning Post*, July 1989.

56. R. Takaki (ed.), *From Different Shores: perspectives on race and ethnicity in America* (New York: Oxford University Press, 1987).

57. A strong counter-critique of the familiar 'model minority' thesis is put forward by C. Henry, 'Understanding the underclass: the role of culture and economic progress', in J. Jennings (ed.), *Race, Politics and Economic Development* (New York: Verso, 1992), esp. pp. 76–8.

58. D. Rieff, *Los Angeles: Capital of the Third World* (London: Jonathan Cape, 1991), p. 211.

59. S. Saggar, 'Resourcing urban regeneration: the US experience', presentation given to a conference on *Making Cities Work*, St Catharine's Foundation at Cumberland Lodge, Windsor, May 1995.

60. See P. Rose, 'Asian Americans: from pariahs to paragons' in Glazer (ed.), *Clamour at the Gates*, chapter 9.

61. See V. Robinson, 'Roots to mobility: the social mobility of Britain's black population, 1971–87', *Ethnic and Racial Studies*, 13.2: 274–86, 1991.

62. See S. Saggar, *Entrepreneurial Minorities and Urban Economic Development* (New York: Commonwealth Fund of New York, 1994).

63. H. Alrich et al., 'Business development and self-segregation: Asian enterprise in three British cities', in C. Peach et al (eds), *Ethnic Segregation in Cities* (Athens Georgia: University of Georgia Press, 1981).

64. J. Jupp, *Immigration* (Sydney: Sydney University Press, 1991).

65. J. Atkinson, 'Policy perspectives: Canada', in Lowe (ed.), *Immigration and Integration*.

10 The Welfare State: from Beveridge to Borrie

Chris Pierson

INTRODUCTION

The (partial) implementation of William Beveridge's wartime report on *Social Insurance and Allied Services* was for long seen as one of the main pillars upon which the postwar order in Britain had been built. Almost as frequently, this postwar regime has been described as social democratic, in intention and consequence, if not always in name. Fifty years on, the confidence that surrounded both the formation of the postwar welfare state and the more general political ambitions of social democrats has largely evaporated. Since the mid-1970s, and more particularly since the arrival of Mrs Thatcher's first administration in 1979, opinion has seemingly moved decisively against the welfare state or at least against that form of it which social democrats had traditionally recommended. In this chapter, I consider whether the social democratic political agenda is truly exhausted or whether, under the radically changed social and economic circumstances of the 1990s, it is still possible to generate a social policy programme consonant with the ambitions of social democrats. I do so in the context of a detailed assessment of the main principles underlying the Borrie Commissions's Report on *Social Justice*.[1]

In December, 1992, the late John Smith, leader of the British Labour Party, established a Commission on Social Justice under the auspices of the Institute for Public Policy Research (IPPR) and the chairmanship of Sir Gordon Borrie. It was the task of the Commission to consider how the aspiration to social justice within the welfare state (broadly conceived) might be reconciled with the imperatives of a modern social and economic order. The 400-page Report of the Commission was published in the autumn of 1994. In an age when traditional social democratic conceptions of social justice, and its articulation through the welfare state, have come under increasing challenge, the Report presented the case for an updated institutional order which is equal to the aspirations of social justice.

The Commission's final report was quite unusual, especially in the British context, for the prominence it gave to a single key political idea: social justice. It is unusual to find any contemporary political party claiming to re-orient its policy (albeit at one step removed) around a core political ideal. This may be doubly so in the British Labour Party which has been variously described by its friends as 'practical-minded', 'bookless' and 'rampantly opportunistic'. The principal ambition here, however, is not to focus upon the Commission's conception of social justice (which proves to be rather conventional and has a fairly modest place in its final report) but rather to consider the relationship between this core conception of social justice and the quite detailed policy recommendations that are said to follow from it. I consider first if there is such an association, second, why this association (or lack of it) is as it is, and (rather tentatively) third, what this suggests about the ideological and programmatic coherence of contemporary social democracy. I begin with a brief discussion of the Commission's own treatment of social justice.

'SOCIAL JUSTICE IN A CHANGING WORLD'

The Commission makes clear from the outset that its ambition is not to proceed *deductively* from a justifiable normative conception of social justice to the economic and social institutions through which this could be realised. Its primary task is a *meliorist* one – 'to find compelling ways of making our society *more* just' – and it aims to promote this by seeking the broadest possible consensus about social and economic reform. It is, therefore, acutely mindful of the need to generate a conception of social justice that runs with the grain of popular sentiment, seeking some sort of 'reflective equilibrium' between its own initial ambitions for social justice and what it supposes to be the limits of public opinion. Its discussion proceeds from a recognition that people's ideas about social justice, whilst strongly held, are *complex* and *indeterminate*. Social justice is not monological but involves, at various times and in varying proportions, notions of *equality, need, entitlement, merit* and *desert*. Whilst the claims of equality and need enjoy priority in the Commission's elaboration of social justice, popular sentiments about entitlement, merit and desert have to be respected if a programme of reform is to command public support.[2]

In the final report (p. 18), social justice is rendered in terms of 'a hierarchy of four ideas':

1   that the foundation of a free society is the equal worth of all citizens, expressed most basically in political and civil liberties, equal rights before the law and so on;

2   that everyone is entitled, as a right of citizenship, to be able to meet their basic needs for income, shelter and other necessities... the ability to meet basic needs is the foundation of a substantive commitment to the equal worth of all citizens;

3   that self-respect and equal citizenship demand ... opportunities and life chances ['That is why we are concerned with the primary distribution of opportunity, as well as its redistribution'];

4   *to achieve the first three conditions of social justice,* we must recognise that although not all inequalities are unjust ... unjust inequalities should be reduced and where possible eliminated.

We turn now to the programmatic recommendations that make up the bulk of the Commission's Report.

THE STATE OF THE NATION

The first substantive chapter of the Report puts on record what is, in its terms, the growth of social injustice in Britain over the past fifteen years. It is a distressing catalogue of growing inequality and impoverishment, of sustained joblessness, of continuing class inequalities in morbidity and mortality and of inadequate investment in education. It charts a depressing record of rising homelessness, crime and generalised social insecurity. Even if we take the Commission's own aspirations to social justice to be rather modest, they are countermanded by a seemingly relentless widening of 'the justice gap' in the period since the election of the first Thatcher government.[3] It is the sheer scale of these problems and the depth of dereliction into which social protection has fallen that underpins the Commission's aspiration to seek the broadest possible support for a strategy of 'national renewal' that goes well beyond the traditional left. The terms for any such renewal are set by the scale of the accumulated defeats of the last fifteen years.

This broad strategy is reinforced by the Report's further identification of 'three great revolutions' which make a return to the *status quo ante* 1979 both impossible and undesirable. These three revolutions are:

1   **the economic revolution**: 'a global revolution of finance, competition, skill and technology in which the United Kingdom is being left behind';
2   **the social revolution**: 'a revolution of women's life-chances, of family structures and of demography';
3   **the political revolution**: involving 'a challenge to the UK's old assumptions of parliamentary sovereignty and to its growing centralisation of government power; it involves a fundamental reorientation of the relationship between those who govern and those who are governed' (pp. 64–89).

The Report presents three rather stylised alternative responses to this set of challenges. These are the strategies respectively of the *Deregulators*, the *Levellers* and the *Investors*. The *Deregulators* who currently run the show would respond to the present crisis with more of the same: further deregulation of labour markets, further reductions in public services, further erosion of society's intermediary institutions, all delivered through an increasingly centralised state. The *Levellers*, upon the Commission's account, are concerned with the protection of the most vulnerable and the redistribution of wealth, but see this process in a context of continuing comparative economic decline. 'They believe that we should try to achieve social justice through the benefits system, rather than through a new combination of active welfare state, reformed labour market, and strong community' (p. 96). Unsurprisingly, all the best lines and the sunniest virtues are saved for the Commission's preferred option – *Investor's Britain*:

> The Investors believe we can combine the ethics of community with the dynamics of a market economy. [They believe] that the extension of economic opportunity is not only the source of economic prosperity but also the basis of social justice. The competitive requirement for constant innovation and higher quality demands opportunities for every individual. ... to contribute to national economic renewal; this in turn demands strong social institutions, strong families and strong communities, which enable people and companies to grow, adapt and succeed... Investment in people is the top priority. Investors see security, not fear, as the basis for renewal. (pp. 95, 4)

The call for a virtuous marriage between efficient production and just distribution (of both wealth and opportunities) is developed in the central policy chapters of the Commission's Report. This aspiration is especially clear in the priority given to education: 'Lifelong learning is at the heart of our vision of a better country' (p. 120). The primary emphasis is upon the production of wealth through developing a highly-skilled and adaptable workforce. Maximising the skills and earning capacity of individuals optimises both individual *and* social welfare.

The full import of the commitment to investment in learning becomes clear in the Commission's subsequent discussion of employment. Work, they argue, 'is the heart of wealth and welfare' and 'paid work remains the best pathway out of poverty, as well as the only way in which most people can hope to achieve a decent standard of living' (p. 151). Consequently, the Commission insists that 'Government must accept its responsibility to secure full employment' and it identifies three strategies for maximising employment:

1   **Increasing the demand for labour,** above all through internationally co-ordinated macroeconomic action to stimulate economic growth.
2   **Fair and efficient distribution of unemployment and employment.** This would involve a Jobs, Education and Training strategy (JET) combining incentives and opportunities for new employees and employers 'to get the long-term unemployed and lone mothers back to work'. It would also involve a re-allocation of opportunities and responsibilities between men and women in the performance of paid and unpaid work.
3   **Rewarding employment.** Normally, paid work should guarantee an adequate income. The government should legislate for a minimum wage and minimum legal rights for workers, including the right to trade union representation.

THE 'INTELLIGENT TRAMPOLINE'

The *Social Justice* Report has been widely glossed as a blueprint for the future of the welfare state. But this is true only if we are operating with an extremely broad definition of what the welfare state is about. The *prior* (though related) concern of the Commission is with welfare generated through value added in the formal economy. In an increasingly global market economy, the only way to achieve a broadly-distributed prosperity is said to be through an economy of high added value, built upon a skilled, adaptable and innovative workforce in circumstances where government intervenes to promote the fullest possible levels of employability. The Commission insists that 'a higher social security budget is a sign of economic failure, not social success' (p. 104).

Nonetheless, the single longest chapter of the Report is devoted to quite detailed plans for the creation of an 'active' and 'intelligent' welfare state. The overall strategy is for a social security system that promotes pathways 'from welfare to work'. In what is rapidly becoming every politician's favourite cliché, the welfare state must be changed 'from a safety net cushioning economic failure into a trampoline for economic success' (p. 103). In meeting this ambition, the Report rejects widespread means-testing – 'the Deregulators' panacea' – in favour of a 'new universalism' constructed around 'a modern social insurance system'. Reflecting the fundamental changes that have taken place since the inauguration of the Beveridge system, this new social insurance system would include benefits for part-time workers and the self-employed, new provision to reflect parental responsibilities and a new Incapacity Benefit. The primary motivation in reforming means-tested benefits is to overcome the existing disincentives to taking up paid work and thus to produce the preferred transition from welfare to work. In terms of income maintenance for the elderly, the Commissioners propose maintenance of the basic pension at a modest level plus a new *pension guarantee* which would ensure that an individual's or couple's *overall* income from all pensions should reach a certain threshold, if necessary made up by the state. Rather less attention is directed to the reform of health and community care, though the Report does make clear its view that individuals may well have to make their own financial provision for long-term care in old age.

THE 'C' WORD

The penultimate chapter of the Report is devoted to the promotion of the apparently central, but still rather elusive category of 'community'. As befits the term's varied use, this section is a bit of a mixed bag of differing ideas in differing domains. A substantial part is devoted to family policy, to a proposed reform of child support, a proposed increase in child benefit (but taxed for higher earners) and a new statement of parents' responsibilities. There are proposals for government sponsorship of community self-help and self-renewal. On housing, there are proposals for a reform of housing finance, for a greater diversity of forms of tenure, proposals for greater tenant participation in housing management and a commitment to address the problem of homelessness. Proposals for 'reviving civic leadership' include measures for decentralised government, greater popular control over quangos and greater accountability of public services to their citizen-users. The Commission also echoes Blair's call for a voluntary 'Citizen's Service' amongst 18–25 year olds which would allow young people to become involved in varying 'social projects', learning new skills and developing a sense of teamwork and active citizenship.

PAYING FOR IT

Although the Report is peppered with costings of individual programmes and policies, there is no attempt to generate an overall costing for the Commission's full raft of measures. Since the design is one to be gradually implemented over a fifteen year period and since the Commission expects that much of the reform process will prove self-financing (as general economic activity is increased), it is hard to see that any global figure would have very much meaning. Correspondingly, the Commission's proposals on funding are confined to some general principles about the nature of an acceptable taxation regime. Taxes should be 'necessary, fair, acceptable, clear, and levied on a broad base'. They should 'contribute to economic performance and employment, respect individuals' independence and be easy to understand and collect'. They must also 'take account of capital, business and labour mobility across the global economy' (pp. 12–13). The Commissioners attempt to address the problems of very high rates of marginal taxation on low incomes, disincentives to employment (for both employers and employees) and an unfair structure of tax allowances. They put forward the possibility of a minimum and maximum tax bill for high earners, with no one being expected to forfeit more than 50 per cent of their earnings (pp. 389–90). They see little mileage in hypothecating taxes and whilst favouring a shift in the burden of taxation from social 'goods' (such as employment) to social 'bads' (such as pollution) come to no definitive resolution about how best this may be done.

EVALUATION: DOING SOCIAL JUSTICE

Whilst broadly (if briefly) welcomed, the Commission's Report has
faced that mixture of weary cynicism, vested interests and quack cures
which seem to greet any attempt at deep-seated welfare reform. It has
been condemned in just about equal measure for having been both too
bold and too timid, for 'targeting' resources and for failing to 'target'
them. Given this, it is worth raising at least two cheers for the
Commission's efforts. This is a serious attempt to address the scale of
the problems that confront us, to look in some detail at the sort of solutions that may be possible and to try to temper realism with a rather
old-fashioned belief that something can be done. The priority given to
investment in people and the corresponding weight for education at all
levels and ages is welcome. So is the level of detail that characterises the
Commission's recommendations for reforming the social security
system. I think its members are right to believe that, *starting from where
we are*, the best route out of poverty and the best chance for most
people of enjoying a reasonably prosperous and secure future lies in
access to paid work. Although the Report's attempt to confront the
'sixth great evil' – racial discrimination – and discrimination against the
disabled is limited, they make a sustained attempt to flesh out their
commitment to women and part-time workers with policy detail.

The Report has considerable merits as an attempt to update traditional social democratic strategy on work and welfare to meet the
changed circumstances of the 1990s. Although British social democracy
has always advocated some redistribution through the welfare state, its
principal strategy has been that social security should be achieved
through paid work and its attendant benefits. It is, however, much less
clear that the Report works as a vindication of the Commission's ambition to forge a political strategy consonant with its conception of social
justice. We have already seen that the Commission's conception of
justice is actually quite modest and that its promoters are extremely
mindful of the limits placed upon it by popular expectations. Yet it is
not clear that these rather modest ambitions are carried through in the
Report's substantive recommendations.

THE EQUAL WORTH OF ALL CITIZENS

We might begin by considering the Commission's top-ranking commitment to realise the equal worth of all citizens. This commitment is

immediately and rather conservatively glossed in terms of prevailing political and civil liberties. The sorts of *constitutional* proposals which might be thought important to securing this effective equal worth of all citizens are rather modest, (involving some devolution of governmental powers and greater accountability of the quangocracy). To be fair, the Report does contain a number of important and detailed measures designed to equalise the effective status of citizens particularly in the world of work. There are proposals to help eliminate unmerited distinctions between part-time and full-time workers and between those in waged and unwaged work. Indeed, the imperative of equalising effective citizenship for men and women is one of the Report's major strengths. But beyond a few encouraging noises about EU legislation on rights in the workplace, nothing much is said about the possibility of greater economic democracy as a means to realising a more effective equality of citizens.

This is disappointing. One could hardly expect (or wish) a centre-left programme for Britain in the 1990s to call for workers' control and a co-operative economy. (After all, the Commission has to screw up all its courage to say one or two nice things about trade unions!) It may be appropriate (though not without considerable reservations) to act as if 'globalisation' set the unbreachable parameters within which any political project can be pursued. But the consequences of this change are paradoxical: not only do they make it harder to pursue a traditional centre-left strategy, but at the same time they may also undercut the effectiveness of (still) more modest forms of social democratic accommodation.

There are still plenty of social democrats, perhaps even a growing number, who insist in the classical manner that 'ownership does not matter'. But this, (as the avid privatisers of state assets in the 1980s seemed to realise), is surely not correct. Certainly, Keynes held 'that ownership of the instruments of production' was 'not important', whilst Crosland insisted upon 'the growing irrelevance of the ownership of the means of production'.[4] But both men subscribed to this view precisely because the state was able to direct economic activity *without* bringing privately-owned economic assets under public control. Circumstances have now changed fundamentally in ways which mean that *indirect* public control of the national economy is much less effective. This is not a case for nationalisation. Indeed, nationalisation in its traditional forms is neither very desirable nor at all practicable. There is however a different and much stronger case for an element of 'social' ownership of society's productive assets.

Though there are undoubtedly difficulties in establishing what this 'social' element of ownership should look like, we are not obliged to accept the neo-liberal view that ownership is really 'all or nothing'. Fully-specified private ownership is not the norm in market economies, but rather something of a limiting case. Much of the investment upon which existing market economies rely proves not to have come from the pockets of abstaining venture capitalists, but from 'deferred wages' accumulated in large-scale pension funds and from institutions managing the aggregated resources of very large numbers of comparatively small savers.[5] Ownership already takes a plurality of forms, and the instruments of saving and debt management are so varied that we may certainly hope to be able to generate new forms of ownership which could satisfy at least some of the criteria of social property.[6] Of course, such a regime would not look much like the classical socialist model of a socialised economy. But in this classical form the wholesale socialisation of ownership was not a resounding historical success and it is, as the Commission rightly supposes, an imperative of contemporary circumstances that we should find forms of change which are gradual and incrementalist. At the same time, seeking changes to the structure and forms of ownership seems unavoidable now, in a way which it did not for Keynesian social democrats in the 1930s and beyond.

The Commission's Report aspires to see the traditional powers of interventionist governments reconstituted within the European Union and enormous weight seems to fall upon the belief that a new form of international macroeconomic co-ordination (and the sorts of social democratic politics that goes with it) can be generated at the EU level (p. 66). Certainly, there may be much to be learnt from the practice of the European Commission and, at the European and national level, it may be possible to use *regulation* as a comparatively inexpensive way of effecting a change in work and welfare opportunities. It may be true that the future is inevitably European. But, in fact, the battle between 'Keynesianism in one continent' and 'a community of deflation' is still to be properly joined. Under these circumstances, it is really quite unclear that the left or centre-left can actually prosecute even its modestly reformist agenda without raising questions of ownership and control. It is a pity, (but not altogether surprising), that these important questions tended to get lost in the set-piece battle between the party's 'modernisers' and its 'traditionalists' over re-wording the hallowed Clause Four of the party's constitution.

Similar difficulties surround the Commission's core contention that 'the extension of economic opportunity is not only the source of economic prosperity but also the basis of social justice'. Certainly, the virtuous circle of education, work and welfare and the *happy marriage of equality and efficiency* which the Report sets out are attractive ideas. In the face of the right's incessant claim that the route to economic efficiency lies through ever greater inequality and that the way to increase employment is to press for ever lower wages, these counter-claims need voicing loud and clear (and often). And yet, unhappily, we cannot be so sure that the transition to an economy which marries equality and efficiency will be so easy to achieve. The Report shares the optimistic view recently expressed by *The Economist*, that globalisation of the market economy will not leave British workers struggling to compete with the cheapest of Third World labour. Rather will the general rise in world economic activity create new employment opportunities for highly skilled, high value-added employment in the West. But can we be confident that this is really what will happen? Already the countries of the Pacific Rim are moving to equip themselves to compete in these value-added labour markets, making more substantial investment in training and education. With the best-intentioned of active governments, we cannot be confident that an under-managed global economy will necessarily secure adequate employment opportunities for all workers here (or elsewhere). Fuller employability is a desirable and realisable goal, and in the face of the newer orthodoxy that mass unemployment is 'an economic price worth paying' this is again a claim that bears some repetition. But it is at least possible that dual labour markets and the division between core and peripheral workers will prove much more intractable than the confident noises about training and re-skilling suggest.

If this is the case, what should we do when equality and efficiency do *not* coincide? And what if democratic publics are reluctant to fund the provision to overcome discrimination? Justice (even upon the Commission's modest definition) would seem to require that equality should take priority over efficiency, but can we foresee the circumstances in which a government would be willing and able to realise this commitment? These hard questions are largely defined away by the Report's confidence about what is possible. In what we might see as a classically social democratic move, the hard questions about justice – how should limited resources be (re-)distributed – are finessed by the expectation that overall economic growth will make such issues irrelevant.

MEETING BASIC NEED

Ranking second in the Commission's four propositions on justice is the belief 'that everyone is entitled, as a right of citizenship, to be able to meet their basic needs for income, shelter and other necessities'. This commitment to meeting basic need is closely connected to the first and prior proposition in so far as 'the ability to meet basic needs is the foundation of a *substantive* commitment to the equal worth of all citizens'. Of course, 'meeting basic need' is an ambition to which even a Conservative social security minister might subscribe. The grounds on which we might expect the Commission to part company with Conservative opinion would include these: what constitutes *'basic'* need, how *extensive* is to be the domain of social provision according to need (rather than according to some other distributive principle, such as merit or desert) and to what extent is such entitlement a measure of *citizenship*? It is, in fact, in describing the apparatus for the meeting of need that the social policy expertise of the Commission is at its clearest. The Report espouses reforms which entrench more generous criteria for defining basic need, (including a commitment to establish a minimum income standard), upon a broader basis (including a commitment to secure full employment) and established in terms of entitlement (rather than at the discretion of the state). It is hard not to regard these reforms, in terms of the Commission's own meliorist ambitions, as defining a regime of social protection that is more just than the current cost-led decrementalism. Being more just than current Conservative social policy is not, of course, a very exacting criterion, but not less welcome for that.

It is worth noting, however, that a more radical alternative which would unambiguously meet the terms of the Report's second proposition on social justice – instituting a Basic Income – is something which is briefly considered but (at least for the present) rejected. In essence, a Basic Income is an income, funded out of general taxation and paid unconditionally as of right to all citizens. The ambition is that it should be set at a level which guarantees to everyone an income sufficient to enable them to live adequately and to participate in society. The Report enters a number of reservations about Basic Income, some of which relate to technical issues or to its economic consequences. But the most prominent reason for rejecting it (at this stage) is the Commission's judgement about its popular unacceptability. This is probably a sound political judgement, but it does illustrate two more general points about the Commission's general enterprise.

One is that the Commission's ambitions are only very partially defined by its concern with social justice. If the Commission were concerned simply to find an institutional arrangement that satisfied its criteria for social justice, a Basic Income surely looks much stronger than the arrangements that it actually does endorse. But, of course, the Commission is also mindful of what it believes the public can be persuaded to support – and it is this consideration that leads them to rule out BI. The reason the Commission's Report cannot be wholly successful as a description of the conditions for securing social justice is that the policy instruments for its implementation must be in line with its perceptions of existing popular opinion. This concern actually infects what the Commission is willing to say originally about social justice. It may be that left-of-centre policy-makers should seek to be more *preference-shaping*. Rather than following existing public opinion, they are exhorted to seek to move the public towards proposals for reform which they hold to be just. As that great exemplar of a *preference-shaping* hegemon, Mrs Thatcher, found, just how much shaping can be done is actually a matter of very fine judgement. In the end, it is a matter of raw but rather delicate political judgement, a sensibility with which academic commentators are not usually over-endowed.

EQUALITY OF OPPORTUNITY: A RADICAL AMBITION?

Given the state of empirical public opinion, the Commission is right to stress the extent to which reform should focus upon the primary allocation of opportunities and goods rather than upon the redistribution of its products. (Though, at the same time, the Commission could have been rather bolder in what they say about taxation. There is a good case for redistributive taxation and the Commission should have made it). This concern is reflected in the Commission's third principle which insists that 'self respect and equal citizenship demand...opportunities and life chances. 'That is why we are concerned with the primary distribution of opportunity, as well as its redistribution'. Everyone knows that defining what would count as equality (and of what kind?) is contentious and difficult. The Commission insists that 'the ideal of "equality of opportunity", which has often been thought by reformers to be a rather weak aspiration, is in fact very radical, if it is taken seriously'.[7] And so it may be. But it is not clear that a concern with equality of condition (or rather a narrowing of the extent of justifiable inequality) must really look like the Commission's caricature of the grim-faced 'levellers'. In fact, much of the Commission's case for equality of opportunity is really a case against existing forms of discrimination (in education or in the labour and housing markets, for example). For the most part, it stops short of a consideration of those inequalities that arise from the unequal control of investment decisions. Characteristically, it concentrates on unequal *pay* (focusing on 'top people's' salaries) rather than wider inequalities of wealth. It uses every possible conceit, (including a quaintly eighteenth-century invocation of 'commercial society') rather than remind us that they are thinking about a capitalist society. This is surely, in part, because the Commission does not wish or is not able to address those forms of inequality which are endemic to capitalism (again, one presumes, because capitalism is perceived as a part of that given order within which any strategy for reform must operate). What we end up with is something like a recommendation for 'equal citizenship in one class'.

Again, as a political judgement, this may be correct. (Recall Fritz Scharpf's rather sombre judgement that the only way of securing full employment under the prevailing circumstances is for social democratic forces to manage a redistribution of income *from* labour *to* capital.)[8] The best that any envisageable centre-left government in Britain could aspire to is a more benign form of capitalist economy – and we might as well say so. But slipping this empirical supposition into their supposedly broader account of social justice weakens the Commission's argument considerably. In the lexical ranking of the four propositions, greater opportunities and life chances (in the final Report it is not even the greater *equality* of such opportunities and chances that is recommended) should be there to promote the prior ambition of realising the equal worth of all citizens. Existing forms of corporate power and economic decision-making are clearly a barrier to this primary principle. In fact, this reinforces the sense that if many goods, services and opportunities are to continue to be delivered through markets *and* the distribution of these goods is to be rendered more 'just', a great deal more attention has to be focused upon the ways in which power *within* these markets can be reallocated. What can be done in this direction must be a matter of political judgement (and, to some extent, expediency), but this does not mean that it should be defined out of the equation before these prudential judgements have been made.

JUSTIFIABLE INEQUALITIES?

The final principle identified by the Commission is that *'to achieve the first three conditions of social justice*, we must recognise that although not all inequalities are unjust ... unjust inequalities should be reduced and where possible eliminated'. At first reading this claim has a rather Rawlsian ring. It seems that inequalities are only justified in as much as they contribute to meeting the three *prior* principles of justice, above all, the equal worth of all citizens. But the further gloss on this fourth criterion makes it clear that something much less egalitarian than Rawls' famous difference principle is intended. Rawls supposed 'that social and economic inequalities are to be arranged so that they are to the greatest benefit of the least advantaged'. This is not the premise that underlies the Commission's position. It is not clear if the Commission favours a market economy on grounds of justice, ('generally people get their due'), or utility, ('it's not very fair, but it is very productive') or the sheer awfulness of the available alternatives, ('command economies are unworkable and authoritarian'). Probably, it is a mixture of all three. But here, once again, the Commission's judgement is powerfully shaped by what they take to be popular perceptions of what would count as a just distribution. Whatever Rawls or anyone else may say, it just is the case, so far as the Commission is concerned, that people generally accept that inequalities in the market arising from luck or natural talent or effort are deserved and to this extent the inequalities to which they give rise are just. In the end, we may want to accept that some forms of inequality are warranted (upon whatever sorts of ground). But if we take the Commission's lexical ordering of the four propositions about social justice seriously, and we accept their claim that the fourth proposition is to be accepted 'in order *to achieve the first three principles of social justice'* it is difficult to see that their own gloss on this idea can be sustained. It might just about be defendable in a labour-managed economy. It hardly seems sustainable in an economy premised on the existing distribution of capital assets and investment-shaping powers.

CONCLUSION

In the hundred years that have passed since the promulgation of the Erfurt Programme we have become used to political statements with ideological premises that are rather inconsequentially linked to the policy programme to which they are said to give rise. This is only a part of the 'problem' with the Borrie Commission's Report. Although the policy provisions do not always seem to flow from the four principles of social justice, rather more is it the case that these principles have themselves been powerfully shaped by the policy context in which the centre-left's agenda for social justice could be prosecuted. The forgers of the normative statement of what should count as social justice have seemingly had more than one eye on the sorts of measures that might be saleable to a sceptical British public and the kind of context in which they might be introduced. In passing judgement on the Commission's Report, it is worth bearing in mind just how difficult this political context has been for social democrats, including, though not being confined to, four consecutive electoral defeats for the Labour Party. Far from being timid, in these circumstances the Report represents a considerable exercise of the 'optimism of the political will'. Judgements about the overall standing of the policy programme vary enormously. Rather than enter into a discussion of these, I wish to conclude by making three observations which relate to the mixture of normative and programmatic elements in the Social Justice Report.

First, the Borrie Report proffers, under quite changed circumstances, a fairly traditional social democratic strategy. The instruments of policy may be rather different – there is less emphasis upon the state and redistribution, rather more upon the extension of opportunity and self-provisioning. But the overall ambition remains one of redressing social ills through growth (more work, more tax revenue, more welfare generated in the market economy). In some sense, the Commission's case for social justice rests upon an economic gamble that growth can be delivered. Of course, to some extent, all but the most ascetic conceptions of social justice rest upon such an assumption. But the principles outlined here make out a rather weak case for increased justice *if the economy does not grow*. By accommodating so much to the circumstances in which a social democratic programme might be pursued, the Commission's principles of social justice give little *autonomous* standing to the reallocation of opportunities and resources in hard times. Related to this is a second question about the environmental limits to such a conception of social justice. The Commission rules out of its remit (perhaps with some justification) a consideration of the international and intergenerational elements of social justice. But if we take such claims seriously, the traditional social democratic case – that growth can be a surrogate for redistribution – looks very much weaker. Perhaps we can be persuaded of their case within what is still an affluent middling-sized Western European state. But can we really accept it for an increasingly unequal global economy and society? If not we shall need rather different criteria of social justice which can confront 'hard' questions of redistribution.

Thirdly, contemporary social democracy faces a curious double-bind. The weakening of *indirect* control over investment decisions requires that the question of *direct* control be re-addressed. But the same circumstances that resurrect questions about ownership and control make feasible solutions even harder to furnish. Wholesale re-nationalisation is an unlikely and not especially attractive option but there are a number of policy instruments, some of them quite modest, which might at least afford the possibility of redistributing economic power. Perversely, some of these (including, for example, reform of pension funds) might be more 'respectable' or 'with the grain of public opinion', than attempts at more redistributive taxation.

How, finally, should we relate the Borrie Report to Beveridge? Of course, the Beveridge Report emerged from *within* the public service and was implemented (if partially) by the postwar government. Produced when in opposition, the Report of the Commission on Social Justice may become just one more 'worthy' attempt to suggest a reform agenda for Britain's ailing welfare order. In the long run, what under-mined the policy ambitions if not the institutional structures of Beveridge's plans was the poor performance of the British economy. If expectations about economic change underpinning social justice were to be disappointed, Borrie's recommendations might face a similar fate.

Notes

1. Social Justice Commission, *Social Justice: Strategies for National Renewal* (London: Vintage Books, 1994). Unless otherwise indicated, page numbers in the text hereafter refer to this source.
2. See Social Justice Commission, *The Justice Gap* (London: IPPR, 1993).
3. Social Justice Commission, *The Justice Gap*, op. cit.
4. J. M. Keynes, *The General Theory of Employment, Interest and Money* (London: Macmillan, 1973) , p. 378; Crosland, *The Future of Socialism* (London: Cape, 1964), p. 34.
5. G. Thompson, *The Political Economy of the New Right* (London: Pinter, 1990), pp. 144–5.
6. See, for example, J. Roemer, *A Case for Socialism* (Cambridge, Mass.: Harvard University Press, 1994).
7. Social Justice Commission, *The Justice Gap*, op. cit., p. 9.
8. F. Scharpf, *Crisis and Choice in European Social Democracy* (Ithaca, New York: Cornell University Press, 1991).

Index